UNIVERSAL

DICTIONARY

OF

WEIGHTS AND MEASURES,

ANCIENT AND MODERN;

REDUCED TO THE STANDARDS

OF THE

United States of America.

BY

J. H. ALEXANDER.

BALTIMORE:

PUBLISHED BY WM. MINIFIE.

1857.

JOHN D. TOY, PRINTER.

TO

ALEXANDER DALLAS BACHE,

SUPERINTENDANT OF WEIGHTS AND MEASURES

OF THE UNITED STATES,

ETC. ETC. ETC.

TOKEN

OF

FRIENDSHIP AND RESPECT.

——Ego quidem, postquam a tenellâ jam ætate iis maxime rebus operam dare cœpi quæ in publicum forent aliquando utiles, crescente dein avo, quicquid olim profuturum videri poterat, sedulò annotavi.—— Alea igitur a mè jacta est in edendis quæ tum ex propriis, tum et ex aliorum observationibus collegeram.

Eisenschmid: de Pond. et Mens.

PREFACE.

THE chief materials of the following Work have been gradually accumulated during researches which from time to time, for several years, I have occupied myself in making upon Weights and Measures. These researches have been principally in an historical aspect; and the materials themselves were collected to serve for my own use as a guide in detecting and, in the absence of other proof, of proving the migrations and commerce of different nations and at different periods.

But when they had grown to nearly their present bulk, it occurred to me that their publication in a shape somewhat like the present, might be useful; not only to those whose tastes and studies were like my own and whose investigations might thus come to be helped by my labor, but also to others who might find them of convenient reference and application in ordinary concerns of business or education.

To all these classes of persons and objects, I believe the present collection will be found to offer information more extensive, and more convenient than any existing work; while for the two latter, particularly—the young, who are to learn, and those engaged in Commerce, who are to apply—it supplies a defect which has been suffered for a long time, the absence of any book, giving to any considerable extent, much less universally, the reduction of foreign Weights and Measures to our own American Standards. It is true the elder English Cambists, before 1825, answered the purpose; because up to that time the standards of Great Britain and of the United States were substantially the same. But these older works are now out of print and no longer generally accessible; and besides, since that time, there has been more than one important addition to accuracy on this subject, so that they would need considerable corrections. Since 1825, the English capacity-standards differ systematically from our own; and the values of the gallon and bushel, for instance, given in newer Works for that country, no longer serve for this.

I believe it will be admitted, too, that the aim under which the materials for this book were collected, does not fit it the less (but rather the more) for practical utility, than if it had been set about originally for that special end. The historian who is seeking to trace the footsteps of Civilization through the dusky forest of antiquity and the tumultuous and disturbed fields of more modern times, has as much motive for fastidious accuracy as if he was calculating the premium of an actual bill of exchange; the systems, upon which Weights and Measures have been combined, and out of which their various values grow by multiplication and subdivision of the unit, are for him of interest not only as a means of deriving those values, but in their arithmetical proportions as indications of the influence of Race and the effect of national habitude; and in the terminology and the very orthography of names, too generally neglected or slurred over by the mere cambist, he looks for, and finds sometimes, a thread to guide him through the maze. In attention to these particulars, the present Work will be found, I hope, unless by accident, unexceptionable.

The student, who may be tempted by his own inclination to use it farther than as a means of reference only, may find, here and there, discrepancies between the systematic and actual value of terms. These, in some cases, have arisen and are allowed to stand; on the principle of presenting for every term its best ascertained actual value in all cases where the units of the system have not been connected with some physical constants, as, for instance, the gravitation of water or the vibrations of a pendulum. Thus, comparisons have been made sometimes of two or more members of the same system (e. g. of a half-gallon and a pint;) and the result would be a different value for the unit, (e. g. the gallon) according as one or the other determination was adopted. In such cases, the denominations actually compared, are given with their own resulting values; while that of the unit and the other members derived from it, has been generally deduced to correspond with the larger measure as being liable to the least absolute error. Where results have been given, between whose claims to confidence I could not decide, I have taken the mean; and where the difference was not great, altered the dependent measures accordingly. So that values may be found here, differing from those given generally; but, I believe nearer the truth. I would gladly, were there room, enter somewhat into the discussion of these principles and of the cases where they have been applied.

In other regards, the details of form and arrangement, etc., I believe the order is sufficiently simple and perspicuous (as it ought to be) not to need further reference or explanation. Had the circumstances allowed, I would have added a supplementary alphabetical Part, to contain various items which, although not Weights or Measures themselves, are yet susceptible of being weighed or measured, and have actually to be so in the practical concerns of life; for instance, tables of the specific gravity, cohesive force, expansion, etc., of different substances; the reduction and comparison of thermometric and hygrometric scales; the result of dynamometric experiments upon the effect of different natural agents for producing motion; the comparison of figure, weight, and size in different branches of the human race, etc. etc. Should what is now offered, meet with favor from the Public, such particulars may be added hereafter to fill up the practical scope of the Work.

I have not included Coins and Money in the present arrangement, which are themselves such valuable means for determining the Weights and Measures of antiquity especially; not because they have not formed an important part of my research, but because they have been already largely explored, the results are generally accessible, and the introduction of them here would have greatly enlarged the size and cost without proportionately increasing the value of the book. A reduction of modern Coins, especially, to the standard of the United States, in a similarly alphabetical arrangement, would no doubt be a useful manual of reference; so far as the theory of the Mints of many European States goes, this would be an inconsiderable task: but its principal value would be in shewing the actual deviations in practice from the theoretical aim—what the coins really are, not what they ought to be—and in the authenticity of such a demonstration. It is manifest that a work of this sort, is more appropriate to such a public Institution as a National Mint, which both could command, better than most private individuals, a sufficient collection of the coins in question to afford a reliable average, and would win, better than a more obscure source, confidence and reliance in the results.

Finally, if I may be allowed in connection with this Work and its appropriate applications, to allude to certain dreams of my own (as they may be; although I consider them capable, without undue effort, of a more prompt and thorough realization than seems to be ordinarily anticipated) as to the prevalence, some day, of an universal conformity of Weights and Measures, I must acknowledge, that such a result was one of the ends I had in view in the original collection of materials.   Not, that such a work was going to show more emphatically than business men feel and reflecting men know, the importance of such an universal conformity; or that a book, whose pages deal in discords, could of itself produce unison: but that the first step to any harmonious settlement, is to see clearly and at a glance where the differences lie, and what they are.   If a Millennial period for this world is ever to come as many wise have deemed and pious prayed, it must be preceded by one common language and one common system of Weights and Measures as the basis of intercourse. And the way to that is to be built, not by the violent absorption of other and diverse systems into one, but rather by a compromise into which all may blend.   When the Earth in her historical orbit shall have reached that point (as it stood ere mankind were scattered from the plain of Shinar) and not till then, may we begin to hope that her revolutions will be stilled, and that before long the Weights and Measures of fleeting Time, will be merged and lost in the infinite scales and illimitable quantities of Eternity.

BALTIMORE, 29 *August*, 1850.

DICTIONARY

OF

WEIGHTS AND MEASURES.

NAME.	LOCALITY.	CHARACTER.	VALUE.	
Aam; *for wine*	*Amsterdam*	liquid capacity	41,00041	gallons.
" *for oil*	...,,...	...,,...	37,72990	"
"	*Antwerp*	...,,...	37,56347	"
"	*Brunswic*	...,,...	39,52018	"
"	*Rotterdam*	...,,...	40,55925	"
Abas; *for pearls*	*Persia*	weight	2,88	grains.
Abŭcco	*Pegu*	...,,...	0,424107	pounds.
Accīno	*Naples*	...,,...	0,66	grains.
Acetăbulum	*Ancient Romans.*	liquid capacity	0,01782	gallons.
"	...,,...	dry capacity	0,00191	bushels.
Achăna	*Ancient Greeks.*	...,,...	1,46973	"
Achtel	*Augsburg*	liquid capacity	0,03877	gallons.
"	*Frankfort*	dry capacity	3,25626	bushels.
"	*Hanover*	length	0,1198	inches.
"	*Munich*	dry capacity	0,13125	bushels.
"	*Prussia*	solid	393,065	cub. feet.
"	*Vienna*	dry capacity	0,21814	gallons.
"	*Würtemberg*	...,,...	0,07861	"
"	...,,...	solid	14,948	cub. feet.
"	*Würzburg*	liquid capacity	2,47345	gallons.
" *for wheat*	...,,...	dry capacity	2,45443	bushels.
" *for oats*	...,,...	...,,...	3,79181	"
Achtendeel	*Dordrecht*	...,,...	0,86198	"
"	*Rotterdam*	...,,...	0,95095	"
"	*Worcum*	...,,...	1,17315	"
Achterli	*Berne*	...,,...	0,04970	"

Acre = 4840 square yards. Bushel = 2150,42 cubic inches. Cubic foot = 1728 cubic inches. Gallon = 231 cubic inches. Mile = 1760 yards. Pound = 7000 grains. Yard = 36 inches.

NAME.	LOCALITY.	CHARACTER.	VALUE.	
Acker ; *meadow*............	*Bamberg*........	superficial	1,5024	acres.
" *tillage*...............	...,,...........	.....,,..........	1,1661	"
" *wood-land*...........	...,,...........	.....,,..........	1,2857	"
"	*Erfurt*.........	.....,,..........	0,6522	"
" *tillage*...............	*Gotha*..........	.....,,..........	0,5610	"
" *wood-land*...........	..,,...........	.....,,..........	0,8373	"
"	*Hesse Cassel*....	.....,,..........	0,5897	"
"	*Leipsic*........	.....,,..........	1,3624	"
"	*Weimar*.........	.....,,..........	0,7042	"
Acre.................	*Great Britain*....	.....,,..........	1.——	"
" *old measure*.........	*Scotland*.......	.....,,..........	1,2707	"
"	*United States* ...	.....,,..........	1.——	"
Actus................	*Ancient Romans*.	length........	38,82655	yards.
" major.............	......,,.......	superficial	0,3115	acres.
" simplex...........	......,,.......	.....,,..........	0,0104	"
Adārmé...............	*Castille*........	weight	27,78	grains.
"	*Canary I*.......	....,,..........	27,70	"
Adoŭlie..............	*Bombay*........	dry capacity...	0,20833	bushels.
Ady..................	*Malabar*........	length.........	0,29047	yards.
Åtting................	*Sweden*.........	liquid capacity	4,14495	gallons.
Agastēra.............	*Cerigo*.........	......,,..........	0,30131	"
Agīto................	*Pegu*...........	weight........	0,848214	pounds.
Aguīrages	*Guinea*.........	.....,,..........	62,04	grains.
Ahm..................	*Aix-la-Chapelle*..	liquid capacity	36,08777	gallons.
"	*Hamburg*.......	......,,..........	38,14730	"
"	*Hanover*........	......,,..........	41,43950	"
"	*Leipsic*.........	......,,..........	40,07686	"
"	*Lübec*..........	......,,..........	39,57385	"
Akëna................	*Ancient Greeks*..	superficial.....	0,0023	acres.
Akey.................	*Guinea*.........	weight	20,03	grains.
Akker................	*Amsterdam*......	superficial.....	2,0318	acres.
Ako..................	*Hungary*........	liquid capacity	18,49510	gallons.
Album................	*Copenhagen*	superficial	0,0568	acres.
Alen.................	......,,..........	length........	0,68647	yards.
"	*Iceland*.........	....,,..........	0,62417	"
Almüd...............	*Turkey*.........	liquid capacity	1,38086	gallons.
Almüde	*Canary I*.......	dry capacity...	0,14807	bushels.
"	....,,..........	superficial	0,0416	acres.
"	*Lisbon*..........	liquid capacity	4,36973	gallons.
Aln	*Stockholm*.......	length........	0,64763	yards.
Alquêîre..............	*Lisbon*..........	liquid capacity	2,18475	gallons.
"	*Oporto*.........	......,,..........	3,31279	"

Acre = 4840 square yards. Bushel = 2150,42 cubic inches. Cubic foot = 1728 cubic inches.
Gallon = 231 cubic inches. Mile = 1760 yards. Pound = 7000 grains. Yard = 36 inches.

NAME.	LOCALITY.	CHARACTER.	VALUE.
Alquêīre...................	Bahia...........	dry capacity...	0,86326 bushels.
"	Lisbon..........	...........,,........	0,38367 "
"	Maranham......	...........,,........	1,28905 "
"	Rio Janeiro.....	...........,,........	1,13512 "
Ām...................	Stockholm......	liquid capacity	41,46537 gallons.
Ame	Copenhagen.....	...........,,........	39,55637 "
Ammah; sanctuary........	Ancient Hebrews.	length.........	0,57359 yards.
" talmudic...........	..........,,.......	......,,...........	0,47799 "
Amōla..............	Genoa..........	liquid capacity	0,21746 gallons.
Amphōra..............	Ancient Romans.	........,,.........	6,84100 "
Amphŏreus..............	Ancient Greeks..	..........,,........	10,26150 "
Anfŏra	Venice..........		136,94988 "
Angŭla...............	Ancient Hindoos.	length.........	1,0499 inches.
"	Calcutta	..........,,........	0,7500 "
Ankăre................	Stockholm......	liquid capacity	10,36634 gallons.
Anker................	Amsterdam......	............,,........	10,25010 "
" old measure........	Berlin............	...........,,........	12,45491 "
" new measure........	...,,...........	...........,,........	9,07319 "
"	Bremen..........	...........,,........	9,57413 "
"	Brunswic	...........,,........	9,88004 "
"	Copenhagen	...........,,........	9,88157 "
"	Hamburg........	...........,,........	9,53683 "
"	Hanover	...........,,........	10,35988 "
"	Lippe...........	...........,,........	9,81622 "
"	Lübec...........	...........,,........	9,89346 "
"	Mecklenburg....	...........,,........	9,56853 "
"	Rotterdam......	...........,,........	10,13915 "
Anna...................	Sindh..........	weight........	0,058333 pounds.
" for gold and silver...	Calcutta	...........,,........	14,04 grains.
" for pearls...........	Bombay.........	...........,,........	0,19 "
Anthal..................	Hungary........	liquid capacity	13,35235 gallons.
Arançāda..................	Spain..........	superficial......	0,9556 acres.
Archīn arisch..............	Persia..........	length........	1,06334 yards.
" schah..............	Persia..........	...........,,........	0,87377 "
Archĭne................	Russia..........	...........,,........	0,77803 "
Ardeb	Cairo..........	dry capacity...	5,16484 bushels.
"	Gondar........	.........,,.......	0,11465 "
"	Massouah......	.........,,.......	0,33333 "
Are	France..........	superficial.....	0,0247 acres.
Arepēnna.............	Ancient Gauls...	.........,,.......	0,3115 "
Ariēnzo...............	Spain..........	weight.........	27,78 grains.
Arn	Dantzic	length.........	0,62750 yards.

Acre = 4840 square yards. Bushel = 2150,42 cubic inches. Cubic foot = 1728 cubic inches.
Gallon = 231 cubic inches. Mile = 1760 yards. Pound = 7000 grains. Yard = 36 inches.

NAME.	LOCALITY.	CHARACTER.	VALUE.
Aroŭra.....................	Ancient Greeks..	superficial	0,0587 acres.
Arpent.....................	Auch...........	......,,........	3,7850 "
"	Bayonne........	......,,........	1,0345 "
" legal...............	France..........	......,,........	1,2620 "
" ordinary...........	...,,...........	......,,........	1,0457 "
" of Paris...........	...,,..........	......,,........	0,8449 "
"	Geneva.........	......,,........	1,2766 "
"	Strasburg.......	......,,........	0,4967 "
" small..............	Toulouse........	......,,........	1,4054 "
" large...............	...,,..........	......,,........	2,8108 "
"	Tours..........	......,,........	1,6289 "
"	Troyes.........	......,,........	1,0425 "
Arrätel..................	Portugal........	weight.........	1,011860 pounds.
Arrŏba..................	Alicant........	...,,........	27,434619 "
" for vermillion.......	...,,.........	...,,........	24,386328 "
"	Aragon..........	...,,........	27,434619 "
"	Barcelona.......	...,,........	21,820500 "
"	Balearic I.......	...,,.....;....	22,875 "
"	Galicia.........	...,,........	31,753031 "
"	Portugal, etc....	...,,........	32,515104 "
"	Spain, etc.......	...,,........	25,402425 "
"	Valencia........	...,,........	27,434619 "
" for flour...........	...,,.........	...,,........	24,386328 "
" for oil.............	...,,..........	...,,........	22,862183 "
" for wine...........	Alicant........	liquid capacity	3,03805 gallons.
" for oil.............	...,,.........	......,,........	3,64037 "
"	Aragon.........	......,,........	3,57961 "
" for wine...........	Barcelona.......	......,,........	2,72368 "
"	Canary I........	......,,........	4,25 "
"	Havana.........	......,,........	4,1 "
"	Malaga.........	......,,........	4,18722 "
" for wine...........	Spain, generally..	......,,........	4,26304 "
" for oil.............	...,,..........	......,,........	3,31853 "
"	Valencia........	......,,........	3,57961 "
"	Valparaiso......	......,,........	9,90667 "
Arrobēta ; for oil...........	Aragon.........	......,,........	2,38553 "
Artaba.................	Ancient Arabs...	weight.........	145,5 pounds.
"	Anc't Egyptians.	dry capacity...	1,10230 bushels.
"	Ancient Persians	....,,........	1,56159 "
As...................	Ancient Romans.	weight.........	0,721897 pounds.
As or Aas..............	Amsterdam......	...,,.	0,74 grains.
As or Ass............. ...	Baden.........	....,,.........	0,77 "

Acre = 4840 square yards.   Bushel = 2150,42 cubic inches   Cubic foot = 1728 cubic inches.
Gallon = 231 cubic inches.   Mile = 1760 yards.   Pound = 7000 grains.   Yard = 36 inches.

NAME.	LOCALITY.	CHARACTER.	VALUE.	
As *or* Ass	*Cologne*	weight	0,90	grains.
As *or* Es	*Copenhagen*	....,,	0,89	"
As *or* Ass	*Stockholm*	....,,	0,74	"
"	*Zurich*	....,,	0,83	"
Asnée ; *for wine*	*Lyons*	liquid capacity	21,65099	gallons.
"	...,,	dry capacity	5,83660	bushels.
"	*Maçon*	....,,	7,26767	"
Asparẽz ; *great*	*Anc't Armenians*	itinerary	0,1918	miles.
" *small*	....,,	....,,	0,1342	"
Atōmo	*Milan*	length	0,0134	inches.
"	*Parma*	....,,	9,0124	"
"	*Turin*	....,,	0,0117	"
Aulos *or* Stadium	*Ancient Greeks*	itinerary	0,1149	miles.
Aune ; *old measure*	*Avignon*	length	1,27644	yards.
" *old measure*	*Burgundy,*	....,,	0,88397	"
" *of Brabant*	*Brussels*	....,,	0,76106	"
" *old measure*	*Cambray*	....,,	0,78353	"
" *old measure*	*France*	....,,	1,29972	"
" *usual, till 1837*	...,,	....,,	1,31236	"
" *usual*	*French W. Indies*	....,,	1,30264	"
" *retail*	*Geneva*	....,,	1,25081	"
" *wholesale*	...,,	....,,	1,29972	"
" *before 1823*	*Lausanne*	....,,	1,17678	"
" *since 1823*	....,,	....,,	1,31236	"
" *old measure*	*Lorraine*	....,,	0,69939	"
" *of Paris*	...,,	....,,	1,29972	"
"	*Lucerne*	....,,	0,68647	"
" *old measure*	*Lyons*	....,,	1,22855	"
" *usual*	...,,	....,,	1,31236	"
"	*Mechlin*	....,,	0,75350	"
" *old measure*	*Morlaix*	....,,	1,47333	"
" *old measure*	*Picardy*	....,,	0,87492	"
" *old measure*	*Rennes*	....,,	1,51386	"
"	*Rochelle*	....,,	1,29972	"
" *old measure*	*S. Malo*	....,,	1,47333	"
" *old measure*	*S. Omer*	....,,	0,78894	"
Ayminãte	*Perpignan*	superficial	1,4641	acres.
Azũmbre	*Asturias*	liquid capacity	0,59704	gallons.
"	*Castille*	..... ,,	0,50986	"
"	*Valencia*	.....,,	0,77827	"

Acre = 4840 square yards. Bushel = 2150,42 cubic inches. Cubic foot = 1728 cubic inches. Gallon = 231 cubic inches. Mile = 1760 yards. Pound = 7000 grains. Yard = 36 inches.

NAME.	LOCALITY.	CHARACTER.	VALUE.	
Bachel....................	Patras..........	dry capacity...	0,84945	bushels.
Bacîle.....................	Cephalonia......	.......,,........	1,39996	"
"	Ithaca..........	.......,,........	0,99999	"
"	Zante..........	.......,,........	1,27912	"
"	Ionian Isles......	superficial.....	0,2987	acres.
Bacîno....................	Corsica.........	dry capacity...	0,35413	bushels.
Bahār,....................	Amboyna.......	weight........	597,607	pounds.
"	Bantam..........	.......,,........	396.——	"
" for pepper...........	....,,...........	.......,,........	406,777500	"
" great...............	Batavia.........	.......,,........	610,166250	"
"	Bet-el-faki.......	.......,,........	815,625	"
" Dutch...............	Ceylon..........	.......,,........	520,6752	"
" English.............	....,,............	.......,,........	500.——	"
"	Goa..	.......,,........	495.——	"
"	Jidda............	.......,,........	183,007813	"
"	Malacca.........	.......,,........	405.———	"
"	Mocha...........	.......,,........	450.———	"
Baille; for coal............	Rochelle.........	dry capacity...	2,025	bushels.
Balde; for coal............	Lisbon..........	.......,,........	12,70	"
Bale; for coffee............	Bet-el-faki......	weight........	285,5	pounds.
" for cotton; mean.....	Alabama.........	.......,,.........	500.—	"
" " "	Georgia..........	.......,,.........	375.—	"
" " " ...	Louisiana........	.......,,.........	500.—	"
" " "	Mississippi.......	.......,,.........	500.—	"
" " "	South Carolina...	.......,,.........	362,5	"
Bāmbou,..................	Bantam.........	dry capacity...	0,09223	bushels.
"	Madagascar.....	.......,,.........	0,05676	"
" of Akbar.........	Ancient Hindoos.	length.........	13,99667	yards.
"	Pegu...........	.......,,.........	4,20833	"
Barāl; for wine,...........	South of France..	liquid capacity.	6,67049	gallons.
" for oil.............	Montpellier......	.......,,.........	9,85120	"
" "	Toulouse.........	.......,,.........	13,57875	"
Barcēlla,..................	Alicant..........	dry capacity....	0,58260	bushels.
"	Balearic I........	.......,..........	0,34110	"
Barchîlla.................	Benicarlo.........	.......,,........	0,47297	"
"	Valencia.........	.......,,........	0,48526	"
Barîle....................	Ancona..........	liquid capacity.	11,34909	gallons.
" for oil.............	Cerigo..........	.......,,........	14,40298	"
"	Corsica.........	.......,,........	36,98492	"
" for wine............	Florence.........	.......,,........	12,04229	"
" for oil.............	......,,.........	.......,,........	9,63384	"
" for wine............	Genoa..........	.......,,........	19,60861	"

Acre = 4840 square yards. Bushel = 2150,42 cubic inches. Cubic foot = 1728 cubic inches.
Gallon = 231 cubic inches. Mile = 1760 yards. Pound = 7000 grains. Yard = 36 inches.

NAME.	LOCALITY.	CHARACTER.	VALUE.	
Barile; *for oil*	*Genoa*	liquid capacity.	17,08351	gallons.
"	*Ionian Isles*	.....,,....	17,99845	"
" *for wine*	*Leghorn*	.....,,....	12,04123	"
" *for brandy, rum, &c*	....,,....	.....,,....	11.——	"
"	*Malta*	.....,,....	11.——	"
"	*Modena*	.....,,....	11,00566	"
"	*Naples*	.....,,....	11,57321	"
"	*Palermo*	.....,,....	9,43644	"
"	*Patras*	.....,,....	13,53912	"
" *for wine*	*Pisa*	.....,,....	12,04229	"
" *for oil*	..,,....	.....,,....	9,63384	"
"	*Ragusa*	.....,,....	20,36151	"
" *for wine*	*Rome*	.....,,....	15,41250	"
" *for oil*	..,,....	.....,,....	15,18510	"
"	*Sardinia*	.....,,....	8,87638	"
"	*Zante*	.....,,....	17,62596	"
" *for salt*	*Cephalonia*	weight	67,244478	pounds.
" *for fish*	*Leghorn*	.....,,....	74,850821	"
Barley-corn ; *imaginary*	*England*	length	0,33	inches.
Barrel; *for lamp oil*	*Cincinnati*	liquid capacity.	43.——	gallons.
" *for wine and brandy*	*Great Britain*	.....,,....	31,5	"
" *for beer, before* 1803	....,,....	.....,,....	32,0	"
" *for ale, etc.*	....,,....	.....,,....	36,0	"
" *Barcelona wine*	*London*	.....,,....	30,0	"
" *Claret*	..,,....	.....,,....	29,0	"
" *Lisbon*	..,,....	.....,,....	35,0	"
" *Madeira*	..,,....	.....,,....	27,5	"
" *Port*	..,,....	.....,,....	34,5	"
" *Sherry*	..,,....	.....,,....	32,5	"
" *Brandy, etc.*	*United States*	.....,,....	31,5	"
" *for corn*	*Maryland*	dry capacity	5.——	bushels.
" *for fish*	..,,....	weight	220.——	pounds.
" *for flour*	..,,....	.....,,....	196.——	"
" *for lime*	..,,....	.....,,....	320.——	"
" *for salted provisions*	....,,....	liquid capacity.	31,9	gallons.
Barril; *for honey*	*Havana*	.....,,....	6.——	"
"	*Lisbon*	.....,,....	78,65514	"
" *for raisins*	*Malaga*	weight	50,6	pounds.
"	*Minorca*	liquid capacity.	8,34375	gallons.
"	*Tripoli*	.....,,....	17,11873	"
Baruay	*Madras*	weight	499,971360	pounds.
"	*Mysore*	.....,,....	485,485114	"

Acre = 4840 square yards. Bushel = 2150,42 cubic inches. Cubic foot = 1728 cubic inches.
Gallon = 231 cubic inches. Mile = 1760 yards. Pound = 7000 grains. Yard = 36 inches.

NAME.	LOCALITY.	CHARACTER.	VALUE.	
Bath...................	*Ancient Hebrews*	liquid capacity	10,26150	gallons.
Batman.................	*Aleppo*..........	weight........	16,880930	pounds.
`"`	*Constantinople*..	....,,.........	19,131937	`"`
`"`	*Shiraz*.........	....,,.........	10,123687	`".`
`"`	*Smyrna*.........	....,,.........	16,874930	`"`
`"`	*Tauris*.........	....,,.........	5,016849	`"`
Batzendingli	*Solothurn*.......	dry capacity...	0,02349	bushels.
Bau...................	*Oldenburg*......	superficial.....	0,3572	acres.
Becher................	*Basel*..........	dry capacity...	0,06059	bushels.
`"`	*Berne*..........	liquid capacity	0,05521	gallons.
`"`	*Brunswic*......	dry capacity...	0,05417	bushels.
`"`	*Carlsruhe*......	....,,.........	0,00426	`"`
`"`	*Lucerne*........	....,,.........	0,06164	`"`
`"`	*Unterwalden*....	....,,.........	0,06164	`"`
`"`	*Vienna*........	....,,.........	0,01363	`"`
`"`	*Zurich*.........	liquid capacity	0,18162	gallons.
Becherlein	*Lausanne*.......	....,,.........	0,03566	`"`
Beczka...............	*Poland*.........	....,,.........	36,07086	`"`
`"` *since* 1819......	...,,...........	....,,.........	26,41780	`"`
Bedoōr	*Malacca*	weight........	2,711850	pounds.
Beka	*Ancient Hebrews*	....,,.........	0,016043	`"`
Bēma; *aploön*..........	*Ancient Greeks*..	length	0,84286	yards.
`"` *diploön*..........	....	....,,.........	1,68572	`"`
Benda...............	*Guinea*.........	weight........	0,141356	pounds.
Benda-offa...........	....,,...........	....,,.........	0,070678	`"`
Bener; *for milk*	*Graubündten*	liquid capacity	0,70447	gallons.
Berkŏwitz............	*Narva*	weight........	412,758814	pounds.
`"`	*Riga*..........	....,,.........	368,676121	`"`
`"`	*St. Petersburg*...	....,,.........	360,676400	`"`
Berri................	*Constantinople*...	itinerary......	1,0358	miles.
Bes *or* Bessis..........	*Ancient Romans*	weight........	0,481265	pounds.
`"`	........,,......	liquid capacity	0,57008	gallons.
`"`	........,,......	dry capacity....	0,01021	bushels.
`"`	........,,......	length	7,7653	inches.
`"`	........,,......	superficial.....	0,4153	acres.
Beson...............	*Augsburg*.......	liquid capacity	2,48693	gallons.
Bhaur...............	*Surat*..........	weight........	900.——	pounds.
Bichërée.............	*Lyons*..........	superficial.....	0,3196	acres.
Bichet	*Beaune*.........	dry capacity ...	6,64045	bushels.
`"`	*Choiseul*.......	....,,.........	1,53241	`"`
`"`	*Friburg*	....,,.........	0,45311	`"`
`"`	*Geneva*........	....,,.........	1,10192	`"`

Acre = 4840 square yards. Bushel = 2150,42 cubic inches. Cubic foot = 1728 cubic inches.
Gallon = 231 cubic inches. Mile = 1760 yards. Pound = 7000 grains. Yard = 36 inches.

NAME.	LOCALITY.	CHARACTER.	VALUE.
Bichet....................	*Lorraine*	dry capacity ...	2,21348 bushels.
"	*Lyons*	........,,.........	1,13427 "
"	*Strasburg*	........,,.........	0,42567 "
"	*Tournus*	........,.........	7,09450 "
"	*Verdun*	........,,.........	5,56209 "
Bicŏngius..............	*Ancient Romans*.	liquid capacity .	1,71025 gallons.
Biggah..................	*Calcutta*.........	superficial......	0,3306 acres.
"	*Malwah*..........	........,,.........	0,4500 "
"	...,,.........	........,,.........	0,5119 "
"	...,,.........	........,,.........	0,5877 "
"	*Surat*...........	........,,.........	0,6074 "
Bigŏncia................	*Milan*..........	liquid capacity .	34,23747 gallons.
"	*Venice*	........,,.........	34,23747 "
Binh.................	*An-nam*.........	weight........	68,876 pounds.
Biŏlca................	*Bologna*.........	superficial	0,6997 acres.
"	*Ferrara*	........,,.........	1,6122 "
"	*Modena*.........	........,,.........	0,7009 "
"	*Parma*..........	........,,.........	0,7531 "
Bisăccia	*Sicily*...........	dry capacity ...	1,94418 bushels.
Bismërpund	*Copenhagen*	weight.........	13,210620 pounds.
"	*Norway*	....,, ...	13,2 "
Boccăle................	*Ancona*.........	liquid capacity .	0,47288 gallons.
"	*Bologna*	........,,.........	0,34603 "
"	*Corsica*	........,,.........	0,34237 "
"	*Ferrara*	........,,.........	0,36589 "
" *for wine*	*Florence*	........,,.........	0,30090 "
" *for oil*	....,,.........	........,,.........	0,27607 "
"	*Ionian Isles*	........,,.........	0,25018 "
"	*Leghorn*.........	........,,.........	0,30090 "
" *for oil*	....,,.........	........,,.........	0,27607 "
"	*Milan*..........	........,,.........	0,20791 "
"	*Modena*.........	........,,.........	0,37514 "
"	*Patras*.........	........,,.........	0,56413 "
" *for wine*	*Rome*	........,,.........	0,48164 "
" *for oil*	...,,.........	........,,.........	0,54233 "
"	*Turin*	........,,.........	0,20670 "
"	*Venice*.........	........,,.........	0,26735 "
Bocoy	*Havana*.........	........,,.........	36.—— "
Boisseau; *old measure*.......	*Amboise*	dry capacity ...	0,31244 bushels.
" "	*Avignon*.........	........,,.........	2,65789 "
" "	*Bordeaux*........	........,,.........	2,21491 "
" "	*Brest*	........,,.........	2,03034 "

Acre = 4840 square yards. Bushel = 2150,42 cubic inches. Cubic foot = 1728 cubic inches.
Gallon = 231 cubic inches. Mile = 1760 yards. Pound = 7000 grains. Yard = 36 inches.

NAME.	LOCALITY.	CHARACTER.	VALUE.
Boisseau, *old measure*	*Chalais*..........	dry capacity ...	0,92288 bushels.
" *from* 1812 *to* 1840..	*France*..........	.....,,........	0,35473 "
" *old measure*........	*Lyons*..........	.....,,........	1,13427 "
" "	*Montreuil*........	.....,,........	0,24610 "
" "	*Nantes*	.....,,........	0,25824 "
" *present measure*....	....,,..........	.....,,........	0,35473 "
" *old measure*........	*Paris*	.....,,........	0,36915 "
" *till* 1840..........	....,,..........	.....,,........	0,35473 "
" *for wheat, old meas.*	*Rochelle*........	.....,,........	0,95918 "
" *for salt*..........	....,,..........	.....,,........	1,41890 "
" *old measure*........	*Rouen*	.....,,........	0,64602 "
" *for oats*	*Troyes*..........	.....,,........	0,68107 "
"	*Alais*..........	superficial	0,0308 acres.
"	*Cahors*..........	.....,,........	0,0788 "
"	*Montpellier*.....	.....,,........	0,0219 "
Boissëleé..............	*Poitiers*........	.....,,........	0,1877 "
"	....,,..........	.....,,........	0,2443 "
Boll ; *for wheat*..........	*Scotland*	dry capacity....	4,08727 bushels.
" *for barley*..........	....,,..........	.....,,........	5,96258 "
Bonnier..............	*Antwerp*	superficial	3,2507 acres.
"	*Brussels, W.*	.....,,........	2,0042 "
"	....,,....*E.*	.....,,........	2,2571 "
"	*Courtray*........	.....,,........	3,5025 "
"	*Liege*	.....,,........	2,1536 "
" *woodland*..........	....,,..........	.....,,........	2,3365 "
"	*Mechlin*........	.....,,........	3,0542 "
"	*Venloo*	.....,,........	2,3585 "
Borrël..............	*Travancore*......	length	1,2110 inches.
Bosse	*Neufchâtel*.......	liquid capacity .	241,47474 gallons.
Bota ; *for wine*	*Spain*	.....,,........	127,89121 "
" *for oil*..............	....,,..........	.....,,........	127,79082 "
"	*Portugal*........	.....,,........	113,63088 "
"	*Xéres*	.....,,........	120.—— "
Botschka..............	*Russia*..........	.....,,........	129,95973 "
Botta	*Messina*........	.....,,........	108.—— "
"	*Milan*..........	.....,,........	171,18735 "
"	*Minorca*	.....,,........	133,5 "
"	*Naples*..........	.....,,........	128,87852 "
"	*Palermo*........	.....,,........	113,23728 "
"	*Rome*	.....,,,........	246,6 "
"	*Sardinia*	.....,,........	132,08900 "
"	*Venice*..........	.....,,,........	171,18735 "

Acre = 4840 square yards. Bushel = 2150,42 cubic inches. Cubic foot = 1728 cubic inches.
Gallon = 231 cubic inches. Mile = 1760 yards. Pound = 7000 grains. Yard = 36 inches.

NAME.	LOCALITY.	CHARACTER.	VALUE.	
Bottle; *for wine; mean*	*United States*	liquid capacity	0,1875	gallons.
" *for malt liquor; mean*	.....,,......	.....,,......	0,2	"
Bozïa	*Cerigo*	.....,,......	0,60021	"
Bozza	*Milan*	.....,,......	0,71328	"
"	*Padua*	.....,,......	0,26162	"
"	*Venice*	.....,,......	0,71328	"
"	*Vicenza*	.....,,......	0,25065	"
Braça	*Brazil*	.....,,......	2,37756	yards.
"	*Lisbon*	length	2,39057	"
" *marine*	*Portugal*	....,,......	1,80449	"
Braccïo	*Ancona*	....,,......	0,70370	"
"	*Basel*	....,,......	0,59505	"
"	*Bergamo*	....,,......	0,71759	"
"	*Bologna*	....,,......	0,70561	"
" *for woollens*	*Brescia*	....,,......	0,73711	"
" *for silk*	....,,......	....,,......	0,69992	"
"	*Cremona*	....,,......	0,65061	"
" *for silk*	*Ferrara*	....,,......	0,69378	"
" *for woollens*	....,,......	....,,......	0,73667	"
"	*Florence*	....,,......	0,63762	"
"	*Genoa*	....,,......	0,63564	"
" *for silk*	*Ionian Isles*	....,,......	0,70483	"
" *for woollens*	....,,......	....,,......	0,75517	"
"	*Leghorn*	....,,......	0,63825	"
"	*Lodi*	....,,......	0,49883	"
"	*Lucca*	....,,......	0,65082	"
" *old measure*	*Milan*	....,,......	0,64142	"
" *new meas. since* 1803	...,,......	....,,......	1,09363	"
"	*Modena*	....,,......	0,63170	"
"	*Naples*	....,,......	0,76411	"
" *for silk*	*Parma*	....,,......	0,64306	"
" *for woollens*	....,,......	....,,......	0,69992	"
" di legno; *surveying*	...,,......	....,,......	0,59289	"
" di panno; *woollens*	*Pisa*	....,,......	0,63825	"
"	*Placentia*	....,,......	0,73819	"
"	*Reggio*	....,,......	0,57941	"
" *merchants'*	*Rome*	....,,......	0,92742	"
" *weavers'*	...,,......	....,,......	0,69556	"
" *for linens*	*Sienna*	....,,......	0,65647	"
" *for woollens*	...,,......	....,,......	0,41297	"
" *for silk*	*Treviso*	....,,......	0,69336	"
" *for woollens*	...,,......	....,,......	0,73931	"

Acre = 4840 square yards. Bushel = 2150,42 cubic inches. Cubic foot = 1728 cubic inches.
Gallon = 231 cubic inches. Mile = 1760 yards. Pound = 7000 grains. Yard = 36 inches.

NAME.	LOCALITY.	CHARACTER.	VALUE.	
Braccio ; *for silk*	*Venice*	length	0,69850	yards.
" *for woollens*	,,	,,	0,74739	"
Braccio quadrato	*Florence*	superficial	0,0008	acres.
" "	*Parma*	,,	0,00007	"
Brande	*Neufchatel*	liquid capacity	10,06145	gallons.
Braza	*Alicant*	length	1,97947	yards.
Braza *or* Brazăda	*Canary I*	,,	1,99461	"
"	*Spain*	,,	1,82636	"
" *marine*	,,	,,	1,82636	"
" reale	*Valencia*	,,	2,23183	"
Braza cuadrăda	*Canary I*	superficial	0,0008	acres.
" "	*Spain*	,,	0,00076	"
" "	*Valencia*	,,	0,0010	"
Brazzĕtto	*Tessino*	length	0,43417	yards.
Brent ; *for plaster*	*Berne*	dry capacity	1,52078	bushels.
Brenta	*Bergamo*	liquid capacity	18,98383	gallons.
"	*Cremona*	,,	38,83417	"
"	*Milan*	,,	19,95917	"
"	*Parma*	,,	19,02082	"
"	*Placentia*	,,	20,07753	"
"	*Tessino*	,,	11,70837	"
"	*Turin*	,,	14,88220	"
"	*Verona*	,,	18,62455	"
Brente	*Aarau*	,,	17,66030	"
"	*Berne*	,,	11,03736	"
"	*Friburg*	,,	10,31615	"
"	*Solothurn*	,,	10,52868	"
Broc	*Lausanne*	,,	3,56640	"
Brochet	*Neufchatel*	,,	4,02458	"
Bucket ; *for chalk*	*England*	dry capacity	1,54660	bushels.
Bullah ; *for grain*	*Mysore*	weight	4,226400	pounds.
Buncal ; *for gold*	*Malacca*	,,	0,102457	"
" "	*Singapore*	,,	0,118857	"
" "	*Sumatra*	,,	0,105857	"
Bunder	*Holland*	superficial	2,4711	acres.
Bushel ; *imperial*	*England*	dry capacity	1,03152	bushels.
" *old m. Winchester*	,,	,,	1.——	"
" *old m. for coal ; nett*	,,	,,	1,03130	"
" " *heaped*	,,	,,	1,30900	"
" *old measure*	*Ireland*	,,	1,01190	"
" *for coal ; heaped*	,,	,,	1,26603	"
" *standard*	*United States*	,,	1.——	"

Acre = 4840 square yards.   Bushel = 2150,42 cubic inches.   Cubic foot = 1728 cubic inches.
Gallon = 231 cubic inches.   Mile = 1760 yards.   Pound = 7000 grains.   Yard = 36 inches.

NAME.	LOCALITY.	CHARACTER.	VALUE.	
Bushel; *apples, dried*	*Philadelphia*.....	weight.........	22.—	pounds.
" *barley*	*London*........	..,,..........	47.—	"
" "	*Philadelphia*.....	..,,..........	48.—	"
" "	*Ohio*...........	..,,..........	48.—	"
" *beans*...............	*London*........	..,,..........	63.—	"
" " ....·	*Philadelphia*.....	..,,..........	60.—	"
" *blue-grass seed*......	....,,,.........	..,,..........	14.—	"
" *bran*	....,,.........	..•,,......	20.—	"
" *buckwheat*	....,,,.........	..,,..........	52.—	"
" *castor-beans*	....,,.........	..,,..........	56.—	"
" *clover seed*..........	*London*........	..,,..........	68.—	"
" "	*Ohio*........	..,,..........	64.—	"
" *flax seed*............	*Philadelphia*.....	..,,,.	56.—	"
" "	*Ohio*...........	..,,..........	56.—	"
" *maize or Indian corn.*	*Philadelphia*.....	..·,,..........	56.—	"
" " "	*Ohio*...........	..,,..........	56.—	"
" *oats*...............	*London*........	..,,..........	38.—	"
" "	*Philadelphia*.....	..,,..........	24.—	"
" "	*Ohio*...........	..,,..........	32.—	"
" *onions*	*Philadelphia*.....	..,,..........	57.—	"
" *peaches, dried.*.......	....,,,.........	..,,..........	33.—	"
" *peas*	*London*...	..,,..........	64.—	"
" *potatoes*	*Philadelphia*.....	..,,..........	60.—	"
" *rape-seed*...........	*London*	..,,..........	48.—	"
" *rye*	..,,.	..,,..........	53.—	"
" "	*Philadelphia*.....	..,,..........	56.—	"
" "	*Ohio*...........	..,,..........	56.—	"
" *ground salt.*.........	*London*	..,,..........	56.—	"
" *rock salt.*............	..,,........	..,,..........	65.—	"
" *wheat*	..,,.........	..,,..........	60.—	"
" "	*Maryland*	..,,..........	60.—	"
" "	*Philadelphia*.....	..,,..........	60.—	"
" "	*Ohio*...........	..,,..........	60.—	"
Busuck; *gold and prec. stones*	*Borneo*..........	..,,..........	4,80	grains.
Bütte; *for coal; nett*........	*Frankfort*........	dry capacity ...	3,43941	bushels.
" *for lime;* "	..,,.........	..,,..........	4,02826	"
" *coal and lime*........	*Hesse Cassel*....	..,,..........	4,33162	"
" *for lime*.............	*Hesse Darmstadt.*	..,,..........	4,43406	"
Butt *of beer or porter*........	*London*	liquid capacity	131,84416	gallons.
" *mountain*.............	..,,.........	..,,..........	120.—	"
" *sherry*...............	..,,.........	..,,..........	130.—	"

Acre = 4840 square yards. Bushel = 2150,42 cubic inches. Cubic foot = 1728 cubic inches.
Gallon = 231 cubic inches. Mile = 1760 yards. Pound = 7000 grains. Yard = 36 inches.

13

NAME.	LOCALITY.	CHARACTER.	VALUE.	
Cab or Kab...............	*Ancient Hebrews*	dry capacity...	0,06124	bushels.
Caban *of rice*...............	*Manilla*.........	weight........	133.——	pounds.
" *of cocoa*............	...,,............	...,,............	83,50	"
" *of rice*..............	*Ternate*.........	...,,............	100,333333	"
Cable-length; *marine*......	*England* and *U. S.*	length.........	240.——	yards.
Cadarp....................	*Tortosa*.........	liquid capacity	0,54421	gallons.
Cadée....................	*Morocco*........	length.........	0,56497	yards.
Cado.....................	*Santa Maura*....	dry capacity...	1,73082	bushels.
Caffíso ; *for oil*...........	*Malta*..........	liquid capacity	5,49966	gallons.
" "	*Messina*........	...,,.........	3,09062	"
"	*Palermo*........	...,,.........	3,09062	"
" *for oil*...........	*Trieste*.........	...,,.........	3,15439	"
"	*Algiers*.........	dry capacity...	9,00718	bushels.
"	*Tunis*..........	...,,.........	15.——	"
Cahíz....................	*Alicant*.........	...,,.........	6,99149	"
"	*Aragon*.........	...,,.........	5,12195	"
"	*Castille*........	...,,.........	18,66137	"
"	*Valencia*........	...,,.........	5,76130	"
Cahizăda.................	...,,.........	superficial....	1,0261	acres.
Calow....................	*Cracow*.........	length........	1,1694	inches.
" *old measure*...........	*Poland*..........	...,,.........	0,9771	"
" *since 1819*...........	...,,.........	...,,.........	0,9449	"
Calvía...................	*Belluno*........	dry capacity...	0,33983	bushels.
Campo....................	*Padua*..........	superficial....	0,9541	acres.
"	*Rovigo*.........	...,,.........	1,0996	"
"	*Treviso*.........	...,,.........	1,2855	"
"	*Venice*.........	...,,.........	0,6881	"
"	*Verona*.........	...,,.........	0,7528	"
Cân......................	*An-nam*........	weight........	1,377520	pounds.
Caña	*Aragon*.........	length........	2,26568	yards.
"	*Barcelona*.......	...,,.........	1,69732	"
" *for cloth*.............	...,,.........	...,,.........	0,84866	"
"	*Majorca*........	...,,.........	1,71044	"
"	*Minorca*........	...,,.........	1,75419	"
"	*Tortosa*.........	...,,.........	1,74074	"
Canăda...................	*Bahia*..........	liquid capacity	1,87272	gallons.
"	*Lisbon*.........	...,,.........	0,36414	"
"	*Rio Janeiro*.....	...,,.........	0,36414	"
Cañădo...................	*Galicia*.........	...,,.........	10,42182	"
Canan....................	*Siam*..........	...,,.........	0,62874	"
Candăca.................	*Mysore*........	dry capacity...	11,13333	bushels.
Candil..................	*Sumatra*........	weight........	423,43	pounds.

Acre = 4840 square yards. Bushel = 2150,42 cubic inches. Cubic foot = 1728 cubic inches. Gallon = 231 cubic inches. Mile = 1760 yards. Pound = 7000 grains. Yard = 36 inches.

NAME.	LOCALITY.	CHARACTER.	VALUE.	
Candy....................	*Ahmednuggur* ...	weight.........	1577,14	pounds.
" *legal*................	*Bangalore*.......	....,,..........	483,02	"
" *ordinary*...........	....,,...........	....,,..........	500.—	"
"	*Bombay*.........	....,,..........	559,968	"
" *for grain*...........	....,,...........	dry capacity ...	25.—	bushels.
" *old measure*	*Ceylon*..........	weight.........	520,67	pounds.
" *since English rule*.....	....,,...........	....,,..........	500.—	"
"	*Madras*.........	....,,..........	499,97136	"
"	....,,...........	liquid capacity	74,46464	gallons.
"	*Malabar*	weight.........	695,54	pounds.
"	*Mysore*.........	....,,..........	485,485714	"
"	*Pondichery*.....	....,,..........	588,0386	"
"	*Seringapatam* ...	....,,..........	485,49	"
"	....,,...........	dry capacity....	11,15199	bushels.
"	*Surat*...........	weight.........	340,16	pounds.
" *for pepper*...........	*Travancore*.....	....,,..........	500,54	"
Canette; *average*...........	*Belgium*........	liquid capacity	0,26169	gallons.
Canna; *woodland*	*Carrara*........	length	0,68308	yards.
"	*Florence*	....,,..........	2,55048	"
" *archit. and surveyors'* .	....,,...........	....,,..........	3,19122	"
"	*Genoa*	....,,..........	2,45177	"
" *surveyors'*............	....,,...........	....,,..........	3,26902	"
"	*Leghorn*........	....,,..........	2,55297	"
" *for cloth*	*Lucca*	....,,..........	2,64658	"
" *for silk*	....,,...........	....,,..........	2,59408	"
"	*Malta*..........	....,,..........	2,48123	"
"	*Messina*........	....,,..........	2,31114	"
"	*Naples*.........	....,,..........	2,30686	"
"	*Palermo*........	....,,..........	2,06951	"
"	*Pisa*...........	....,,..........	3,19011	"
" *commercial*..........	*Rome*	....,,..........	2,17853	"
" *archit. and artificers'*..	....,,...........	....,,.........′..	2,44344	"
"	*Sardinia*	....,,..........	2,87078	"
Canne....................	*Aix*............	....,,..........	2,17480	"
"	*Arles*	....,,..........	2,23890	"
"	*Carcassonne*.....	....,,..........	1,95180	"
"	*Dauphiny*	....,,..........	2,21286	"
"	*Marseilles*.......	....,,..........	2,20117	"
"	*Montpellier*......	....,,..........	2,17350	"
" *of France*............	*Piedmont*.......	....,,..........	2,18727	"
"	*Toulouse*........	....,,..........	1,96417	"
Cantära; *minimum*........	*Spain; Tortosa*..	liquid capacity	1,99190	gallons.

Acre = 4840 square yards.   Bushel = 2150,42 cubic inches.   Cubic foot = 1728 cubic inches. Gallon = 231 cubic inches.   Mile = 1760 yards.   Pound = 7000 grains.   Yard = 36 inches.

NAME.	LOCALITY.	CHARACTER.	VALUE.	
Cantāra; *maximum*	*Spain; Oviedo* ..	liquid capacity .	4,87144	gallons.
" *mean of* 21	.. ,, ...	....,,........	3,37528	"
Cantarēllo................	*Sardinia*	weight........	93,21	pounds.
Cantāro..................	*Aleppo*	....,, ...	506,428	"
" *zurlo*.............	...,,..........	....,,........	154,47054	"
" *before* 1836........	*Alexandria*.....	....,,........	119,05	"
" *since* 1836........	...,,..........	....,,........	95,56	"
" *for cotton*	...,,..........	....,,........	95.—	"
" *minimum*	*Algiers*........	....,,........	120,4	"
" *maximum*..........	...,,..........	....,,........	199,87	"
" *mean of* 5.........	...,,..........	....,,........	153,752	"
" *for flax*	...,,..........	....,,........	240,8	"
"	*Balearic Isles*....	....,,........	91,73	"
"	*Cairo*..........	....,,........	95,0312	"
"	*Candia*	....,,........	116,57	"
"	*Constantinople*..	....,,........	140,30084	"
"	*Damascus*.......	....,,........	395,4800	"
"	*Florence*........	....,,........	112,3	"
" *legal since* 1836.....	...,,..........	....,,........	74,86	"
" *for wool*	...,,..........	....,,........	119,78	"
" *grosso*	*Genoa*	....,,........	115,31	"
" *sottile*...........	...,,..........	....,,........	104,83	"
"	*Greece*	....,,........	148,34	"
"	*Ionian Isles*.....	....,,........	118,8	"
"	*Leghorn,*	....,,........	112,3	"
"	...,,..........	....,,........	119,78	"
" *grosso*...........	*Malta*.........	....,,........	191,97	"
" *sottile*...........	...,,..........	....,,........	174,5047	"
" *barbaresco*.........	*Minorca*.......	....,,........	88,20	"
"	*Morea*	....,,........	123,71	"
"	*Morocco*........	....,,........	118,66	"
" *grosso*	*Naples*........	....,,........	196,450454	"
" *piccole*...........	...,,..........	....,,........	106,080	"
" *grosso*	*Palermo*.......	....,,........	192,556880	"
" *sottile*...........	...,,..........	....,,........	175,04	"
"	*Patras*.........	....,,........	116,31	"
"	*Rome*	....,,........	74,756	"
"	...,,..........	....,,........	119,6096	"
"	...,,..........	....,,........	186,89	"
"	...,,..........	....,,........	747,56	"
"	*Smyrna*........	....,,........	127,48	"
"	*Tripoli in Africa*	....,,..........	111,20954	"

Acre = 4840 square yards.   Bushel = 2150,42 cubic inches.   Cubic foot = 1728 cubic inches.   Gallon = 231 cubic inches.   Mile = 1760 yards.   Pound = 7000 grains.   Yard = 36 inches.

NAME.	LOCALITY.	CHARACTER.	VALUE.	
Cantăro....................	Tripoli in Syria..	weight.........	480,69	pounds.
"	Tunis...........	...,,..........	109,1547	"
Capĭcha...................	Persia..........	dry capacity...	0,07464	bushels.
Carăcter; apothecary........	Spain...........	weight.........	3,09	grains.
Caráffa....................	Naples..........	liquid capacity.	0,19289	gallons.
" for oil..............	Tripoli in Africa	weight.........	3,428571	pounds.
Carăra....................	Leghorn.........	...,,..........	119,78	"
Carăt; precious stones.......	France..........	...,,..........	3,18	grains.
" diamonds, etc........	London..........	...,,..........	3,17	"
" pearls.............	...,,..........	...,,..........	3,2	"
" precious stones.......	Madras.........	...,,..........	3,2	"
"	United States....	...,,..........	3,2	"
Carăto....................	Bologna.........	...,,..........	2,91	"
"	Florence.........	...,,..........	3,03	"
" precious stones........	Ragusa..........	...,,..........	3,19	"
"	Turin...........	...,,..........	3,30	"
" precious stones........	Venice..........	...,,..........	3,20	"
" peso sottile............	...,,..........	...,,..........	2,70	"
Carga....................	Alicant..........	...,,..........	282,57	pounds.
" or Carica; for oats....	Milan...........	dry capacity...	4,66879	bushels.
"	Aragon..........	weight.........	333,18	pounds.
"	Balearic Isles....	...,,..........	275,18	"
" for raisins............	Malaga..........	...,,..........	177,50	"
"	Valencia........	...,,..........	338,44	"
" mean................	Aragon..........	liquid capacity.	42,93686	gallons.
" for wine............	Barcelona.......	...,,..........	31,84934	"
" for oil..............	...,,..........	...,,..........	32,65244	"
" for wine............	Majorca.........	...,,..........	28,67124	"
" "	Minorca.........	...,,..........	33,31817	"
" "	Valencia........	...,,..........	46,69082	"
"	Barcelona.......	dry capacity...	5,11818	bushels.
"	Candia..........	...,,..........	4,32311	"
Carĭca....................	Venice..........	weight.........	266,35424	pounds.
Cariŏlla; for salt...........	Santa Maura....	...,,..........	104,13	"
Carrăta; for marble........	Carrara.........	...,,..........	2240.—	"
"	...,,..........	solid..........	12,768	cub. feet.
Carre or Carse.............	Briare..........	dry capacity...	0,40524	bushels.
Carré....................	French W. Indies	superficial......	3,1909	acres.
Carreau; for stone..........	Paris..........	solid..........	3,632	cub. feet.
Carro....................	Naples..........	dry capacity...	56,32579	bushels.
"	...,,..........	liquid capacity	257,75704	gallons.
"	Turin...........	...,,..........	148,82202	"

Acre = 4840 square yards. Bushel = 2150,42 cubic inches. Cubic foot = 1728 cubic inches.
Gallon = 231 cubic inches. Mile = 1760 yards. Pound = 7000 grains. Yard = 36 inches..

NAME.	LOCALITY.	CHARACTER.	VALUE.	
Carro.................,.....	Apulia.........	superficial	9,9707	acres.
Carte	Cahors..........	dry capacity...	0,85134	bushels.
"	Nancy..........	.....,,.........	1,36101	"
"	Montpellier.....	.....,,.........	0,36915	"
"	Alais...........	superficial.....	0,1232	acres.
Cartél ; old meas., minimum.	Belgium........	dry capacity ...	0,59026	bushels.
" " maximum.	....,,..........	.....,,.........	0,73357	"
" "	Meziéres.......	.....,,.........	0,55337	"
" "	Rocroi.........	.....,,.........	0,64702	"
" "	Sedan..........	.....,,.........	0,72080	"
Cartóccio.................	Rome..........	liquid capacity .	0,03010	gallons.
Cartonáte.................	Perpignan	superficial	0,3660	acres.
Cartónnée....	Cahors.........	.....,,.........	0,3154	"
Cassëney	Madras........	.....,,.........	1,3223	"
Castelláno ; for gold.......	South America...	weight.........	71,07	grains.
Catëna	Naples..........	length	17,19283	yards.
"	Apulia.........	....,,.........	20,05833	"
"	Rome...........	....,,.........	14,04983	"
Catty ; commercial.........	China..........	weight.........	1,333333	pounds.
" for gold and silver...	....,,.........	....,,.........	1,325350	"
"	Japan..........	....,,.........	1,308468	"
"	Java..........	....,,.........	1,355925	"
" for gold and silver...	Malacca	....,,.........	2,049143	"
" commercial...........	....,,.........	....,,.........	1,35	"
"	Siam..........	....,,.........	1,352536	"
"	Sumatra	....,,.........	2,118429	"
"	Ternate........	....,,.........	1,301688	"
Cavëzzo	Bergamo	length	2,87280	yards.
"	Cremona	....,,.........	3,15142	"
"	Florence........	....,,.........	3,82572	"
"	Mantua	....,,.........	4,22460	"
"	Milan..........	....,,.........	2,85558	"
"	Modena........	....,,.........	3,43214	"
"	Padua	....,,.........	2,34520	"
"	Reggio........	....,,.........	3,48366	"
"	Rovigo........	....,,.........	2,52120	"
"	Venice	....,,.........	2,28180	"
"	Verona........	....,,.........	2,25010	"
Cawney ; legal.............	Carnatic........	superficial	1,0047	acres.
" usual...........	....,,.........	....,,.........	1,1791	"
"	Madras	....,,.........	1,3223	"
Celëmin.................	Alicant	dry capacity ...	0,14657	bushels.

Acre = 4840 square yards.   Bushel = 2150,42 cubic inches.   Cubic foot = 1728 cubic inches.
Gallon = 231 cubic inches.   Mile = 1760 yards.   Pound = 7000 grains.   Yard = 36 inches.

NAME.	LOCALITY.	CHARACTER.	VALUE.	
Celëmin	Aragon	dry capacity	0,05335	bushels.
"	Asturias	,,	0,17768	"
"	Castille	,,	0,13326	"
"	Canary I.	,,	0,14805	"
"	Maluga	,,	0,12932	"
"	Seville	,,	0,12833	"
"	Valencia	,,	0,12004	"
"	Canary I.	superficial	0,0417	acres.
"	Spain	,,	0,1323	"
Cent; *old measure; mean.*	Belgium	,,	0,2036	"
" *for lumber*	France	solid	363,168	cub. feet.
Centass	Baden	weight	0,011024	pounds.
Centénaar	Amsterdam	,,	108,94	"
Centiäre	France	superficial	0,0002	acres.
Centïgramme	,,	weight	0,15	grains.
Centinäjo	Florence	,,	74,86	pounds.
" *since* 1803	Milan	,,	220,4737	"
Centïlitre	France	liquid capacity	0,00264	gallons.
"	,,	dry capacity	0,00028	bushels.
Centïmètre	,,	length	0,3937	inches.
Centïstère; *not used*	,,	solid	0,353	cub. feet.
Centlet	Ragusa	liquid capacity	0,24251	gallons.
Centner; *old measure*	Bohemia	weight	136,11	pounds.
"	Bremen	,,	127,490960	"
" *old measure*	Breslau	,,	119,072791	"
" *actual measure*	,,	,,	113,44	"
"	Brunsvic	,,	117,488400	"
"	Darmstadt	,,	110,23685	"
"	Copenhagen	,,	110,11	"
"	Cracow	,,	142,831680	"
"	Lübec	,,	119,699328	"
"	Norway	,,	110,11	"
"	Nürnberg	,,	112,4321	"
"	Prague	,,	136,08	"
"	Prussia	,,	113,44	"
"	Vienna	,,	123,467710	"
"	Warsaw	,,	133,302857	"
"	Zoll-Verein	,,	110,23685	"
Centumpondium	Ancient Rome	,,	72,189714	"
Centüria	,,	superficial	124,5869	acres.
Centüssis	,,	weight	72,189714	pounds.
Cequi	Smyrna	,,	1,750780	"

Acre = 4840 square yards. Bushel = 2150,42 cubic inches. Cubic foot = 1728 cubic inches.
Gallon = 231 cubic inches. Mile = 1760 yards. Pound = 7000 grains. Yard = 36 inches.

NAME.	LOCALITY.	CHARACTER.	VALUE.	
Chain ; *for surveying*	*England*	length	22.——	yards.
" "	*Scotland*	...,,...........	24,8	"
" "	*United States*	...,,...........	22.——	"
" " *square.*	....,,...........	superficial	0,1000	acres.
Chaîne "	*Belgium*........	length	21,87266	yards.
" "	*France*..........	...,,...........	21,87266	"
Chaînée ; *old measure*......	...,,..........	superficial	0,0163	acres.
Chalcos..................	*Ancient Greeks* ..	weight........	1,40	grains.
Chalder	*Scotland*	dry capacity ...	65,39627	bushels.
Chaldron ; *for coal*	*London*	weight........	3063,742	pounds.
" "	...,,..........	dry capacity ...	36.——	bushels.
" "	*Newcastle*......	weight........	5936.——	pounds.
Chalter	*Stettin*	dry capacity ...	84,22364	bushels.
Chamä	*Ancient Greeks* ..	liquid capacity	0,00238	gallons.
Char..................	*Geneva*	...,,..........	133,36623	"
Charge	*Antwerp*	weight.........	414,666	pounds.
"	*Embrun*........	superficial	1,0381	acres.
"	*France*..........	weight........	323,7657	pounds.
"	*Marseilles*.......	dry capacity ...	4,53050	bushels.
" *for charcoal*..........	*Paris*	...,,..........	5,80631	"
" *for oil*..............	*Montpellier*......	liquid capacity	39,40743	gallons.
Chattäc..................	*Calcutta*	weight........	0,116658	pounds.
"	...,,..........	dry capacity ..	0,00037	bushels.
"	...,,..........	superficial	0,0010	acres.
" *for milk*............	*Seringapatam*....	liquid capacity	0,02024	gallons.
" *for grain*............	...,,........	dry capacity...	0,00218	bushels.
Chau	*China*..........	...,,..........	0,00002	"
Chawl ; *for gold and silver* ..	*Malwah*........	weight........	0,25	grains.
Chebbo	*Venice*..........	length	1,71131	yards.
Cheki..................	*Bassora*........	weight........	1,028571	pounds.
"	*Constantinople*...	...,,...........	0,701504	"
" *for opium*	...,,..........	...,,...........	1,767857	"
"	*Smyrna*.........	...,,...........	0,708214	"
" *for opium*............	...,,..........	...,,...........	1,770526	"
Cheük..................	*China*..........	dry capacity ...	0,00022	bushels.
Cheüng..................	*Canton*	length.........	4,10069	yards.
"	*Pekin*..........	...,,...........	3,64583	"
Chevîlle.............. ...	*Havre*..........	solid........	0,009	cub. feet.
Chik ; *commercial ; mean*.....	*Canton*..........	length	14,7625	inches.
" *architects'*............	...,,..........	...,,...........	12,7093	"
" *surveyors'*	...,,..........	...,,...........	12,0588	"
" *mathematical*	*Pekin*..........	...,,...........	13,125	"

Acre = 4840 square yards.   Bushel = 2150,42 cubic inches.   Cubic foot = 1728 cubic inches.
Gallon = 231 cubic inches.   Mile = 1760 yards.   Pound = 7000 grains.   Yard = 36 inches.

NAME.	LOCALITY.	CHARACTER.	VALUE.
Chilo...................	Cerigo..........	dry capacity ...	0,99999 bushels.
Chittac...................	Ahmednuggur ...	weight........	0,123214 pounds.
"	Bengal.........	...,,...........	0,093894 "
" minimum, for metals..	Masulipatan	...,,...........	0,035156 "
" maximum...........	...,,............	...,,...........	0,125 "
Choinix...................	Ancient Greeks ..	dry capacity ...	0,03062 bushels.
Chomer.................	Ancient Hebrews.	.....,,........	11,02300 "
Chopïne	French W. Indies	liquid capacity	0,13235 gallons.
"	Namur.........	.....,,.........	0,09369 "
"	Paris...........	.....,,.........	0,12302 "
"	Strasburg	.....,,.........	0,12734 "
Choppin..................	Scotland	.....,,........	0,22382 "
Choũs	Ancient Greeks ..	.....,,.........	0,85513 "
Chu.....................	China..........	weight........	0,003472 pounds.
Chunãm.	Masulipatan.....	...,,...........	5,97 grains.
Chundoo.	Ceylon..........	dry capacity ...	0,00076 bushels.
Clam....................	Siam...........	weight........	3,53 grains.
Clima	Ancient Romans .	superficial......	0,0779 acres.
Clove ; for wool	England	weight........	7.—— pounds.
Cobre...................	China..........	length	0,39067 yards.
Coccïo..................	Sicily..........	weight........	0,85 grains.
Cochliãrion	Ancient Greeks ..	liquid capacity	0,00119 gallons.
"	.....,,.........	dry capacity ...	0,00013 bushels.
Codo....................	Spain..........	length........	0,46368 yards.
" of Ribeira.............	...,,...........	...,,...........	0,61824 "
Coffãla ; for gold and silver..	Mocha.........	weight........	48,0 grains.
Cogno...................	Florence........	liquid capacity	12,93355 gallons.
Cohi....................	Siam...........	.....,,.........	13,38476 "
Cola....................	Aleppo.........	weight........	177,2498 pounds.
Colãgah..................	Seringapatam....	dry capacity ...	0,55663 bushels.
Compas..................	Gironde........	length	1,71700 yards.
Concãde	Auch...........	superficial	0,9460 acres.
Concha..................	Ancient Greeks..	liquid capacity	0,00594 gallons.
"	.....,,.........	dry capacity ...	0,00064 bushels.
Concia..................	Venice.........	liquid capacity	17,11872 gallons.
Condorïne	Japan..........	weight........	5,72.—— grains.
Condylos.................	Ancient Greeks..	length	1,5172 inches.
Congïus	Ancient Romans .	liquid capacity	0,85513 gallons.
Conque ; for wheat and salt..	Bayonne	dry capacity....	1,22095 bushels.
Conzo	Trent..........	liquid capacity	20,60588 gallons.
"	Treviso........	.....,,.........	20,60588 "
"	Udino..........	.....,,.........	20,94931 "

Acre = 4840 square yards. Bushel = 2150,42 cubic inches. Cubic foot = 1728 cubic inches.
Gallon = 231 cubic inches. Mile = 1760 yards. Pound = 7000 grains. Yard = 36 inches.

NAME.	LOCALITY.	CHARACTER.	VALUE.	
Coom......................	*England*	dry capacity....	4.——	bushels.
Coondee; *for gold and silver*	*Sumatra*........	weight.........	1,77	grains.
Copa......................	*Spain*	liquid capacity	0,03331	gallons.
Copăng....................	*Sumatra*	weight.........	2,32	grains.
"	*Borneo*..........	....,,...........	9,60	"
Copĕllo....................	*Bergamo*........	dry capacity...	0,09790	bushels.
Copët.....................	*Lausanne*	....,,......	0,00383	"
"	*Neufchâtel*.......	....,,......	0,14410	"
Coppa.....................	*Ancona*..........	....,,........	1,01479	"
Coppo; *for oil*.............	*Lucca*..........	liquid capacity	25,95652	gallons.
"	*Milan*	....,,...........	0,02642	"
"	....,,...........	dry capacity....	0,00284	bushels.
"	*Turin*...........	....,,.....	0,08162	"
Cor......................	*Ancient Hebrews*.	....,,.........	11,02300	"
Corah; *minimum*	*Bengal*..........	length.........	1,13889	yards.
" *maximum*..........	....,,........	....,,.......	1,45556	"
Corba....................	*Bologna*	liquid capacity	20,76175	gallons.
"	....,,........	dry capacity....	2,23166	bushels.
Corbŭla..................	*Sardinia*	....,,........	0,34905	"
"	....,,........	superficial	0,2451	acres.
Cord; *for wood*............	*England*	solid	128.——	cub. feet
" "	*United States*....	....,,.........	128.——	"
Corde "	*Antwerp*	....,,.........	22,494	"
" "	*Brussels*.........	....,,.........	16,827	"
" "	*Liège*	....,,.........	126,359	"
" "	*Louvain*.........	....,,.........	54,953	"
" *eaux et forets; old meas.*	*Paris*	....,,.........	135,616	"
" *wharfs* "	....,,.......	....,,.........	172,481	"
" *surveying*	*Brittany*.........	length.........	8,52614	yards.
" "	....,,........	superficial......	0,0150	acres.
Cordèl....................	*Spain*..........	length	13,60132	yards.
Cortăn	*Barcelona*	liquid capacity	1,9625	gallons.
"	....,,........	dry capacity....	0,17061	bushels.
" *for oil; mean.*	....,,........	liquid capacity	1,05671	gallons.
Coss	*Calcutta*........	itinerary.......	1,2273	miles.
"	*Seringapatam*....	....,,.......	3,6458	"
Cottah...................	*Calcutta*........	superficial	0,0158	acres.
Cotyla...................	*Ancient Greeks*..	liquid capacity	0,07126	gallons.
"	....,,........	dry capacity ...	0,00765	bushels.
Coupe	*Geneva*..........	....,,.........	2,20365	"
"	*Lyons*	....,,.........	0,24319	"
Coupʿe	*Bresse*..........	superficial......	0,1629	acres.

Acre = 4840 square yards. Bushel = 2150,42 cubic inches. Cubic foot = 1728 cubic inches. Gallon = 231 cubic inches. Mile = 1760 yards. Pound = 7000 grains. Yard = 36 inches.

NAME.	LOCALITY.	CHARACTER.	VALUE.	
Covãdo	Goa	length	0,74436	yards.
"	Lisbon	....,,....	0,71717	"
"	Morocco	....,,....	0,55141	"
"	Rio Janeiro	....,,....	0,71328	"
Covid	Bombay	....,,....	0,50329	"
"	Culcutta	....,,....	0,48910	"
"	Ceylon	....,,....	0,51390	"
"	China	....,,....	0,39067	"
" average	English India	....,,....	0,5	"
"	Java	....,,....	0,75	"
"	Madras	....,,....	0,51805	"
"	Malacca	....,,....	0,50147	"
"	Mocha	....,,....	0,52778	"
"	Pondichery	....,,....	0,50012	"
"	Siam	....,,....	0,5	"
Coyang	Amboyna	dry capacity	55,33710	bushels.
" for rice	Bantam	....,,....	147,56560	"
" "	Batavia	....,,....	62,43160	"
"	Malacca	....,,....	90,80960	"
"	Siam	....,,....	90,80960	"
" minimum	Sumatra	....,,....	49,51961	"
" maximum	....,,....	....,,....	149,83584	"
Crat	Mocha	weight	3.——	grains.
Crazïa	Tuscany	length	1,9130	inches.
Cuartal	Aragon	dry capacity	0,21341	bushels.
Cuartëron; for oil	Madrid	liquid capacity	0,03374	gallons.
Cuartïlla	Aragon	dry capacity	0,07701	bushels.
"	Madrid	....,,....	0,38877	"
" for wine	Spain; generally	liquid capacity	1,06570	gallons.
" for oil	....,,....	....,,....	0,82978	"
"	Aragon	weight	0,016077	pounds.
Cuartïllo; minimum for wine	Spain; Saragossa	liquid capacity	0,08215	gallons.
" maximum "	....,,....Alicant	....,,....	0,18967	"
" minimum	....,,....Benicarlo	dry capacity	0,02955	bushels.
" maximum	....,,...Oviedo	....,,....	0,04456	"
"	....,,....	superficial	0,0331	acres.
Cuarto	Madrid	weight	0,015877	pounds.
"	Alicant	liquid capacity	0,76294	gallons.
" for oil	Barcelona	....,,....	0,27211	"
"	Corsica	....,,....	0,08559	"
"	Valencia	....,,....	0,77828	"
"	Madeira	dry capacity	0,11290	bushels.

Acre = 4840 square yards.   Bushel = 2150,42 cubic inches.   Cubic foot = 1728 cubic inches.   Gallon = 231 cubic inches.   Mile = 1760 yards.   Pound = 7000 grains.   Yard = 36 inches.

NAME.	LOCALITY.	CHARACTER.	VALUE.	
Cuarto.................	Tortosa.........	dry capacity ...	2,52016	bushels.
Cuba	Abyssinia.......	liquid capacity	0,26840	gallons.
Cube-foot.................	England........	solid..........	1.——	cub. feet.
"	United States....	..,,.............	1.——	"
Cube-yard	England........	..,,.............	27.——	"
"	United States....	..,,.............	27.——	"
Cubit	Anc. Babylonians	length	0,57888	yards.
" royal Persian	........,,........	........,,........	0,50572	"
" great...........	Anc. Egyptians..	..·..,,..........	0,57888	"
" pachys metrios....	........,,........	......,,........	0,50572	"
"	Batavia.........	......,,........	0,75	"
"	Masulipatan.....	......,,........	0,53125	"
" for matting.......	Surat..........	....,,........	0,58056	"
Cubïtus..................	Ancient Rome....	....,,........	0,48533	"
Cucchiãro.................	Turin..........	dry capacity...	0,00340	bushels.
Cuerda	Spain..	length	7,65074	yards.
"	Valencia	....,,........	39,67667	"
Cugnatëlla ; for oil.........	Rome	liquid capacity	2,16930	gallons.
Cuiller ; old measure.......	Brussels.........	dry capacity ...	0,27671	bushels.
Culah....................	Sumatra.........	......,,........	0,06187	"
Culëus...................	Ancient Romans .	liquid capacity	136,820	gallons.
Cuttra....................	Bassora.........	weight.........	136,5	pounds.
Cwierzec.................	Cracow	dry capacity...	0,85205	bushels.
"	....,,........	length.........	6,0728	inches.
"	Warsaw	dry capacity...	0,90810	bushels.
" since 1819.........	....,,........	length.........	5,6695	inches.
Cyäthos..............	Ancient Greeks ..	liquid capacity	0,01188	gallons.
"	........,,........	dry capacity...	0,00128	bushels.
Cyäthus	Ancient Romans .	liquid capacity	0,01188	gallons.
"	........,,........	dry capacity...	0,00128	bushels.
Czëber.................	Hungary........	liquid capacity	22,01923	gallons.
Dactylos	Ancient Greeks ..	length.........	0,7586	inches.
Dain....................	Rangoon........	itinerary........	2,4306	miles.
Dam....................	An-nam.........	......,,........	0,5523	"
Dang ; for gold and silver...	Persia	weight.........	11,96	grains.
Danik	Arabia.........	......,,........	7,86	"
Danrée	Chalons s. Marne.	superficial......	0,1448	acres.
Decagramme	France..........	weight	0,022047	pounds.
Decalitre...............	....,,........	liquid capacity	2,64178	gallons.
"	....,,........	dry capacity ..	0,28378	bushels.
Decamètre...............	....,,........	length.........	10,93633	yards.

Acre = 4840 square yards. Bushel = 2150,42 cubic inches. Cubic foot = 1728 cubic inches.
Gallon = 231 cubic inches. Mile = 1760 yards. Pound = 7000 grains. Yard = 36 inches.

NAME.	LOCALITY.	CHARACTER.	VALUE.	
Decapŏdon.................	*Ancient Greeks* ..	itinerary.......	0,0019	miles.
Decăre ; *not used*...........	......,,.........	superficial.....	0,2471	acres.
Decastère.................	......,,.........	solid..........	353,166	cub. feet
Decēmpeda	*Ancient Rome*....	length........	3,23555	yards.
Deciăre ; *not used*	*France*..........	superficial.....	0,0025	acres.
Deciătine................	*S. Petersburg*....	......,,.........	2,7015	"
Decigrămme...............	*France*..........	weight........	1,54	grains.
Decilītre.................	...,,.........	liquid capacity	0,02642	gallons.
"	...,,.........	dry capacity...	0,00234	bushels.
Decimètre.................	...,,.........	length........	3,9371	inches.
Decĭmo..................	*Rome*.........	......,,.........	0,0733	"
Decīna..................	...,,.........	weight........	7,4756	pounds.
Decistère	*France*	solid..........	3,532	cub. feet
Decŭssis................	*Ancient Rome*....	weight........	7,218971	pounds.
Dedo...................	*Portugal*.......	length........	0,7218	inches.
"	*Spain*..........	...,,.........	0,6849	"
Demi-boisseau ; 1812-1840...	*France*..........	dry capacity...	0,17736	bushels.
Demi-hectogramme........	...,,.........	weight........	0,110237	pounds.
Demi-hectolitre	...,,.........	liquid capacity	13,20890	gallons.
Demi-litre...............	...,,.........	......,,.........	0,13209	"
"	...,,.........	dry capacity...	0,01419	bushels.
Demi-minot ; *old m. for coal*	...,,.........	......,,.........	1,13744	"
Demi-queue ; *for wine*......	*Burgundy*.......	liquid capacity	53,14205	gallons.
"	*Champagne*......	......,,.........	47,23766	"
Demi-setier................	*France*..........	......,,.........	0,06151	"
Denăr...................	*Breslau*	weight........	12,33	grains.
Denărius ; *republican*........	*Ancient Romans*.	......,,.........	60,16	"
" *imperial*........	......,,.........	......,,.........	52,64	"
Denăro..................	*Florence*........	......,,.........	18,19	"
"	....,,.........	length........	0,0956	inches.
" *metrical ; since* 1803..	*Italy*............	weight........	15,43	grains.
"	*Lucca*..........	......,,.........	19,94	"
"	*Milan*.........	......,,.........	18,90	"
"	*Parma*.........	......,,.........	17,49	"
"	*Rome*..........	......,,.........	18,17	"
"	*Turin*..........	......,,.........	19,77	"
Denier ; *esterlin*	*France, A. D.*800	....,,.........	23,61	"
"	....,,.........	......,,.........	19,67	"
" *forbidden*...........	...,,........1799	....,,.........	15,43	"
"	*Geneva*	......,,.........	18,27	"
Derah	*Cairo*..........	length	0,708	yards.
Derech-yôm ; *day's journey*	*Ancient Hebrews*.	itinerary.......	16,9540	miles.

Acre = 4840 square yards.　Bushel = 2150,42 cubic inches.　Cubic foot = 1728 cubic inches.
Gallon = 231 cubic inches.　Mile = 1760 yards.　Pound = 7000 grains.　Yard = 36 inches.

NAME.	LOCALITY.	CHARACTER.	VALUE.	
Desatine.................	*S. Petersburg*	superficial	2,7015	acres.
Deünx...................	*Ancient Romans.*	weight........	0,661739	pounds.
Deusken.................	*Amsterdam*.....	....,,.........	1,48	grains.
Dextans	*Ancient Romans.*	....,,..........	0,601581	pounds.
Dhan ; *for gold and silver*...	*Calcutta*........	....,,..........	0,56	grains.
Dhurra ; *minimum*	*Hindostan*......	....,,..........	6,171	pounds.
" *maximum*	....,,.........	....,,..........	19,714	"
" *mean of* 16........	....,,.......	....,,..........	10,047190	"
Diaŭlos.................	*Ancient Greeks.*.	itinerary......	0,2299	miles.
Dichălcos................	....,,.........	weight	2,81	grains.
Dichas..................	....,,.........	length........	6,0686	inches.
Didrăchmon..............	*Ancient Œgina.*.	weight........	0,032086	pounds.
"	*Ancient Attica*...	....,,..........	0,019252	"
"	*Babylon*.......	....,,..........	0,032086	"
"	*Eubœa*.........	....,,..........	0,026738	"
Diemt..................	*Emden*.........	superficial	1,4014	acres.
Diethaufe...............	*Nürnberg*	dry capacity ..	0,28213	bushels.
Digitus.................	*Ancient Romans* .	length........	0,7530	inches.
Dilöchos................	*Ancient Greeks.*.	itinerary......	1,3792	miles.
Dimerle	*Bucharest*	dry capacity....	0,69810	bushels.
Dinĕro.................	*Spain*..........	weight........	0,002646	pounds.
Dinheïro...............	*Portugal*.......	....,,..........	0,002635	"
Diŏbolon	*Ancient Greeks* ..	....,,..........	22,46	grains.
Diŏta..................	....,,.........	liquid capacity	5,13075	gallons.
Dirhem................	*Abyssinia*......	weight........	40,13	grains.
"	*Constantinople*...	....,,..........	49,50	"
"	*Shiraz*.........	....,,..........	23,62	"
"	*Tauris*.........	....,,..........	11,81	"
Dito ; *since* 1803..........	*Italy*..........	length........	0,3937	inches.
Dodrans................	*Ancient Romans.*	weight........	0,541423	pounds.
Doigt ; *not used*	*France*.........	length	0,3937	inches.
Doit ; "	*England*	weight........	0,002	grains.
Doli...................	*Russia*.........	....,,..........	0,09	"
Dolïchos ; *Delphic*	*Ancient Greeks* ..	itinerary......	1,1049	miles.
" *Olympic*........	....,,.........	....,,..........	1,3792	"
" *Philetairic or Syrian*	....,,.........	....,,..........	1,5781	"
Dong..................	*An-nam*........	weight........	60,27	grains.
Doppelmäss..............	*Solothurn*......	dry capacity ...	0,75174	bushels.
Doron	*Ancient Greeks* ..	length........	3,0343	inches.
Double-boisseau..........	*France*.........	dry capacity...	0,70945	bushels.
Double-stére	....,,.........	solid..........	70,633	cub. feet.
Dra mesrour.............	*Aleppo*........	length........	0,60686	yards.

Acre = 4840 square yards.   Bushel = 2150,42 cubic inches.   Cubic foot = 1728 cubic inches.
Gallon = 231 cubic inches.   Mile = 1760 yards.   Pound = 7000 grains.   Yard = 36 inches.

NAME.	LOCALITY.	CHARACTER.	VALUE.
Dra stambouli	Aleppo..........	length........	0,708 yards.
Drachm; *apothecaries*'......	*England*.......	weight........	60.— grains.
" "	*United States*....	...,,..........	60.— "
Drachma.................	*Ancient Œgina*..	...,,..........	112,30 "
"	*Ancient Attica*...	...,,..........	67,38 "
"	*Babylon*........	...,,..........	112,30 "
"	*Eubœa*......	...,,..........	93,58 "
"	*Ancient Romans*.	...,,..........	52,64 "
"	*Aix-la-Chapelle*..	...,,..........	56,31 "
"	*Berlin*..........	...,,..........	56,40 "
" *apothecaries*'......	...,,...........	...,,..........	57,47 "
"	*Berne*.........	...,,..........	62,71 "
" *apothecaries*'......	..,,.......	...,,..........	57,34 "
"	*Cairo*........	...,,..........	48,60 "
"	*Cologne*........	...,,..........	56,35 "
"	*Dresden*........	...,,..........	56,29 "
"	*Frankfort*......	...,,..........	60,93 "
" *light*.	...,,.......	...,,..........	56,41 "
" *apothecaries*'......	...,,.......	...,,..........	57,54 "
" "	*Germany; gen'ry*	...,,..........	57,53 "
"	*Greece*..........	...,,..........	59.— "
"	*Hamburg*.......	...,,..........	58,40 "
"	*Hanover*.......	...,,..........	59,03 "
"	*Hungary*.......	...,,..........	48,62 "
"	*Ionian Isles*.....	...,,..........	47,25 "
"	*Leipsic*........	...,,..........	56,36 "
"	*Lübec*........	...,,..........	58,45 "
"	*Morea*..........	..,,,.......	46,26 "
"	*Mecklenburg*....	...,,..........	61,27 "
"	*Nürnberg*.......	...,,..........	57,53 "
"	*Smyrna*........	...,,..........	49,21 "
"	*Tripoli in Africa*	...,,..........	48.— "
"	*Tripoli in Syria*.	...,,..........	46,73 "
"	*Vienna*........	... ,,.......	67,69 "
"	*Weimar*........	...,,.......	56,36 "
"	*Würtemberg*....	...,,......	56,38 "
Drachme................	*Antwerp*........	...,,.......	45,34 "
Dracma..........:......	*Madrid*........	...,,.......	55,57 "
Dragma..............	*Amsterdam*......	...,,.......	59,32 "
" *commercial*......	...,,.......	...,,.......	59,49 "
"	*Poland*........	...,,.......	48,90 "
Drakme...............	*Copenhagen*.....	...,,.......	60,20 "

Acre = 4840 square yards. Bushel = 2150,42 cubic inches. Cubic foot = 1728 cubic inches.
Gallon = 231 cubic inches. Mile = 1760 yards. Pound = 7000 grains. Yard = 36 inches.

NAME.	LOCALITY.	CHARACTER.	VALUE.	
Dram......................	*England*	weight........	27,34	grains.
Dramma...................	*Florence*..........	...,,..........	54,58	"
"	*Rome*............	...,,..........	54,51	"
"	*Turin*............	...,,..........	49,40	"
Dreiling...................	*Vienna*..........	liquid capacity	448,57410	gallons.
"	*Rhenish Prussia*.	dry capacity...	0,22163	bushels.
Dreissiger.................	*Bavaria*..........	...,,..........	0,03287	"
Drittel...................	*Hanover*	...,,..........	0,29428	"
Drömt; *for wheat and rye* ...	*Lübec*............	,,..........	11,37674	"
" *for oats*...........	...,,............	...,,..........	13,36036	"
" *for wheat, etc*.......	*Rostock*	...,,..........	13,24305	"
" *for oats*...........	...,,............	...,,..........	14,92115	"
" *old measure*	*Stettin*	...,,..........	17,58868	"
" *legal measure*.......	...,,............	...,,..........	18,71529	"
Ducat; *of gold*............	*Germany*........	weight........	53,86	grains.
Duëlla....................	*Ancient Romans*.	...,,..........	0,020053	pounds.
Duim; *Netherlandic*........	*Holland*..........	length..........	0,3937	inches.
Dumplachter...............	*Bohemia*.........	,,..........	2,59833	yards.
Duöng....................	*An-nam*.........	...,,..........	7,10512	"
Dupõndius	*Ancient Romans*.	weight........	1,443794	pounds.
Ecklein...................	*Würtemberg*.....	dry capacity...	0,01965	bushels.
"	...,,............	solid..........	7,479	cub. feet.
Eggčba	*Guinea*	weight........	0,047119	pounds.
Eimer....................	*Aarau*	liquid capacity	9,51410	gallons.
"	*Appenzell*.......	...,,........	11,06758	"
"	*Altona*...........	...,,........	7,65059	"
"	*Augsburg*	...,,........	19,90336	"
" *for wine*............	*Bavaria*..........	...,,........	16,94433	"
" *for beer*...........	...,,............	...,,........	18,07505	"
" *old measure*	*Berlin*..........	...,,........	24,90983	"
"	...,,............	...,,........	18,14638	"
"	*Bohemia*.........	...,,........	16,14128	"
" *old measure*	*Breslau*..........	...,,........	14,67244	"
" *for wine*...........	...,,............	...,,........	18,14902	"
"	*Courland*........	...,,........	20,83043	"
"	*Dantzic*........	...,,........	18,14902	"
"	*Dresden*	...,,........	17,81352	"
" *for wine*............	*Erfurt*	...,,........	18,73315	"
" *for beer*...........	...,,............	...,,........	19,45671	"
"	*Glaris*	...,,........	23,20343	"
"	*Gotha*..........	...,,........	19,22418	"

Acre = 4840 square yards. Bushel = 2150,42 cubic inches. Cubic foot = 1728 cubic inches.
Gallon = 231 cubic inches. Mile = 1760 yards. Pound = 7000 grains. Yard = 36 inches.

NAME.	LOCALITY.	CHARACTER.	VALUE.
Eimer....................	Hamburg........	liquid capacity	7,62946 gallons.
"	Hanover	....,,.........	16,43452 "
"	Lower Hungary..	....,,.........	15,02935 "
"	Upper Hungary..	....,,.........	19,36847 "
"	Lausanne........	....,,.........	10,69921 "
"	Leipsic..........	....,,.........	20,03843 "
"	Lübec..........	....,,.........	7,91472 "
"	Mecklenburg....	....,,.........	7,65482 "
"	Munich..........	....,,.........	18,074 "
" schenk-mass..........	Nürnberg	....,,.........	18,22338 "
" visir-mass	....,,.........	....,,.........	19,36234 "
"	Prague	....,,.........	16,95151 "
"	Ratisbon........	....,,.........	13,20890 "
" ....●....	Rostock.........	....,,.........	7,65059 "
"	S. Gall..........	....,,.........	11,09275 "
"	Schaffhausen....	....,,.........	11,11280 "
"	Vienna..........	....,,.........	14,95247 "
"	Weimar..........	....,,.........	19,36430 "
" hell eich-mass,(refined)	Würtemberg....	....,,.........	77,64944 "
" trüb eich-mass,(on lees)	....,,.........	....,,.........	81,04624 "
" schenk-mass..........	....,,.........	....,,.........	70,59040 "
" for lime and charcoal..	....,,.........	dry capacity....	8,34114 bushels.
" lauter-mass	Zurich..........	liquid capacity	28,92749 gallons.
" trüber-mass	....,,.........	....,,.........	30,86599 "
El ; old measure	Amsterdam......	length..........	0,75219 yards.
" of Brabant.............	....,,.........	....,,.........	0,75931 "
" of Flanders	....,,.........	....,,.........	0,77714 "
"	Bergen-op-Zoom.	....,,.........	0,75739 "
"	Breda..........	....,,.........	0,75739 "
" wholesale..............	Dendermonde....	....,,.........	0,79944 "
" retail	....,,.........	....,,.........	0,76117 "
"	Dordrecht.......	....,,.........	0,74728 "
"	Groningen	....,,.........	0,75822 "
" ....+.........	Harlaem	....,,.........	0,79586 "
" Netherlandic ....,....	Holland.........	....,,.........	1,09363 "
" old measure	Nimeguen......	....,,.........	0,74753 "
" "	Zealand.........	....,,.........	0,75492 "
Ell....·..............	England	....,,.........	1,25 "
"	Ireland.........	....,,.........	1,25 "
"	Scotland	....,,.........	1,03333 "
Elle......	Aarau..........	....,,.........	0,64948 "
"	Aix-la-Chapelle..	....,,.........	0,73135 "

Acre = 4840 square yards. Bushel = 2150,42 cubic inches. Cubic foot = 1728 cubic inches.
Gallon = 231 cubic inches. Mile = 1760 yards. Pound = 7000 grains. Yard = 36 inches.

NAME.	LOCALITY.	CHARACTER.	VALUE.
Elle ; of Hamburg	Altona	length	0,62664 yards.
" of Brabant	.,,.	.,,.	0,75614 "
"	Anhalt Coethen ..	.,,.	0,69544 "
" for cloth	Antwerp	.,,.	0,74848 "
" for silk	.,,.	.,,.	0,75931 "
" for linen	Appenzell	.,,.	0,87677 "
" for woollens	.,,.	.,,.	0,67375 "
"	Augsburg	.,,.	0,64780 "
" mercers'	.,,.	.,,.	0,66657 "
" legal	Austria	.,,.	0,85216 "
"	Upper Austria	.,,.	0,87458 "
" legal	Baden	.,,.	0,65617 "
"	Basel	.,,.	1,23372 "
" legal	Bavaria	.,,.	0,91100 "
"	Rhenish Bavaria	.,,.	1,31236 "
" minimum	Bavaria ; Speyer	.,,.	0,60197 "
" maximum	.,,. Amberg	.,,.	0,91331 "
" mean of 36	.,,.	.,,.	0,72553 "
" legal	Berlin	.,,.	0,72934 "
" old measure	.,,.	.,,.	0,73022 "
"	Berne	.,,.	0,59330 "
"	Bohemia	.,,.	0,64962 "
"	Brabant	.,,.	0,76072 "
"	Bremen	.,,.	0,64382 "
" of Prussia	Breslau	.,,.	0,72934 "
" of Silesia	.,,.	.,,.	0,62983 "
"	Brunswic	.,,.	0,62416 "
" old measure	Carlsruhe	.,,.	0,60589 "
"	Coblentz	.,,.	0,62689 "
"	Coburg	.,,.	0,64142 "
" old measure	Cologne	.,,.	0,62910 "
"	Courland	.,,.	0,66781 "
" legal	Dantzic	.,,.	0,72934 "
" old measure	.,,.	.,,.	0,62750 "
"	Dresden	.,,.	0,61958 "
" old measure	Düsseldorf	.,,.	0,64586 "
" "	.,,.	.,,.	0,74936 "
"	Frankfort, a. M.	.,,.	0,59856 "
" of Brabant	.,,.	.,,.	0,76467 "
"	Frankfort, a.d.O.	.,,.	0,72556 "
"	Giessen	.,,.	0,60092 "
"	.,,.	.,,.	0,62689 "

Acre = 4840 square yards. Bushel = 2150,42 cubic inches. Cubic foot = 1728 cubic inches. Gallon = 231 cubic inches. Mile = 1760 yards. Pound = 7000 grains. Yard = 36 inches.

NAME.	LOCALITY.	CHARACTER.	VALUE.
Elle....................	Gotha..........	length..........	0,62910 yards.
"	Gueldres	...,,...........	0,72561 "
"	Halle...........	...,,...........	0,62467 "
" for silks, etc...........	Hamburg........	...,,...........	0,62663 "
" for woollens and prints ..	....,,..........	...,,...........	0,75615 "
"	Hanover........	...,,...........	0,63867 "
"	Hesse Cassel.....	...,,...........	0,62318 "
"	Hesse Darmstadt	...,,...........	0,59898 "
"	Holstein........	...,,...........	0,62663 "
"	Hungary........	...,,.	0,85216 "
"	...,, ...	...,,...........	0,87458 "
"	Königsberg......	...,,...........	0,62862 "
"	Leipsic..........	...,,...........	0,61824 "
"	Lippe...........	...,,...........	0,63324 "
"	Lübec...........	...,,...........	0,62972 "
"	Lucerne.........	...,,...........	0,68648 "
"	Mannheim.......	...,,...........	0,61036 "
"	Mecklenburg.....	...,,...........	0,62664 "
"	Moravia	...,,...........	0,86474 "
"	Munich.........	...,,...........	0,91100 "
" old measure...........	Munster.........	...,,...........	0,88419 "
"	Neufchâtel......	...,,...........	0,60758 "
"	Nürnberg........	...,,...........	0,71786 "
"	Oldenburg.......	...,,...........	0,63206 "
"	Osnabrück.......	...,,...........	0,69817 "
"	Pomerania	...,,...........	0,71175 "
" of Bohemia...........	Prague..........	...,,...........	0,64962 "
" of Moravia...........	...,,........	...,, ...	0,86474 "
"	Presburg........	...,,...........	0,61036 "
"	Ragusa..........	...,,...........	0,56125 "
" old measure...........	Ratisbon	...,,...........	0,88704 "
"	Rostock.........	...,,...........	0,63254 "
"	S. Gall..........	...,,...........	0,66854 "
"	...,,........	...,,...........	0,80426 "
"	Schaffhausen.....	...,,...........	0,65126 "
"	Schweitz	...,,...........	0,65617 "
"	Silesia; Austrian	...,,...........	0,63254 "
"	...,,.... Prussian	...,,...........	0,62983 "
"	Solothurn........	...,,...........	0,59581 "
" old measure...........	Strasburg	...,,...........	0,58864 "
" for linens.............	Thurgau........	...,,...........	0,87677 "
" for woollens...........	....,,..........	...,,...........	0,67375 "

Acre = 4840 square yards. Bushel = 2150,42 cubic inches. Cubic foot = 1728 cubic inches.
Gallon = 231 cubic inches. Mile = 1760 yards. Pound = 7000 grains. Yard = 36 inches.

31

NAME.	LOCALITY.	CHARACTER.	VALUE.	
Elle	Transylvania....	length	0,68139	yards.
"	Tyrol	...,,...	0,87950	"
" old measure	Ulm	...,,...	0,62169	"
"	Uri and Vaud...	...,,...	0,65629	"
"	Vienna	...,,...	0,85216	"
"	Weimar	...,,...	0,61676	"
"	Würtemberg	...,,...	0,67175	"
"	Zurich	...,,...	0,65629	"
Embar	Sweden	liquid capacity	20,73268	gallons.
Eminne; old meas. minimum	France	dry capacity ...	0,73783	bushels.
" maximum	...,,...	...,,...	13,50992	"
"	Lausanne	...,,...	0,03831	"
"	Montpellier	liquid capacity	4,91071	gallons.
"	Neufchâtel	dry capacity...	0,43232	bushels.
"	Vaud	...,,...	0,03831	"
Eminée; old measure	Avignon	superficial	0,2108	acres.
"	Gap	...,,...	0,1642	"
"	Nismes	...,,...	0,1389	"
Emmer	Antwerp	liquid capacity	8,80593	gallons.
Endēsi; for cloths	Bucharest	length	0,72433	yards.
Endrāsi "	Constantinople...	...,,...	0,75167	"
Engel; for gold, etc	Amsterdam	weight	23,73	grains.
Epha	Ancient Hebrews.	dry capacity ...	1,10300	bushels.
Es	Copenhagen	weight	0,89	grains.
Escandāl	Marseilles	liquid capacity	4,22684	gallons.
Esche	Cologne	weight	0,83	grains.
Escrōpulo ; for gold	Oporto	...,,...	18,45	"
" for precious stones	Portugal	...,,...	9,53	"
Escrûpulo ; apothecaries'	Spain	...,,...	18,51	"
Estadāle; since 1801	...,,...	length	3,70944	yards.
" old measure	...,,...	...,,...	3,40033	"
" for vineyards	...,,...	superficial	0,0024	acres.
Estādio	Portugal	itinerary	0,1594	miles.
Estādo	Spain	length	1,85472	yards.
Estërlin; for gold, etc.; old m.	France	weight	23,61	grains.
"	Holland	...,,...	15,43	"
" for gold, etc.; old m.	Netherlands	...,,...	23,74	"
Etto	Sumatra	length	0,52	yards.
Etzba	Ancient Hebrews	...,,...	0,01992	"

Acre = 4840 square yards. Bushel = 2150,42 cubic inches. Cubic foot = 1728 cubic inches.
Gallon = 231 cubic inches. Mile = 1760 yards. Pound = 7000 grains. Yard = 36 inches.

NAME.	LOCALITY.	CHARACTER.	VALUE.	
Faden	*Amsterdam*	length	1,85736	yards.
"	*Bremen*	solid	61,599	cub. feet.
" *legal*	*Copenhagen*	...,,, ...	78,611	"
" *ordinary*	....,,, ...	...,,, ...	235,833	"
"	*Dantzic*	...,,, ...	50,038	"
"	*Holstein*	...,,, ...	59,798	"
"	*Lübec*	...,,, ...	74,912	"
"	*Rostock*	...,,, ...	82,590	"
" *old measure*	*Stettin*	...,,, ...	130,346	"
" *legal*	..,,, ...	...,,, ...	150,499	"
Fall	*Scotland*	length	6,2	yards.
Famn	*Sweden* ..	...,,, ...	1,94289	"
"	....,,, ...	solid	99,790	cub. feet.
Fan ; *architects'*	*An-nam*	length	0,1918	inches.
" *mercers'*	...,,, ...	...,,, ...	0,2558	"
"	*Canton*	...,,, ...	0,1313	"
"	*Pekin*	...,,, ...	0,1476	"
Fanăm ; *gold and silver, mean*	*E. Indies*	weight	5,84	grains.
Fanēga	*Aragon*	dry capacity ...	0,64021	bushels.
"	*Asturias*	...,,, ...	2,07358	"
"	*Buenos Ayres*	...,,, ...	3,74988	"
" *struck*	*Canary Islands* ..	...,,, ...	1,77679	"
" *heaped*	...,,, ...	...,,, ...	2,5	"
"	*Castille*	...,,, ...	1,59914	"
" *struck for wheat*	*Gibraltar*	...,,, ...	1,6	"
" *heaped for maize*	...,,, ...	...,,, ...	2,06250	"
"	*Havana*	...,,, ...	3,11023	"
"	*Madeira*	...,,, ...	1,60080	"
"	*Mexico*	...,,, ...	1,60307	"
"	*Montevideo*	...,,, ...	3,86792	"
"	*Teruel ; Aragon* ..	...,,, ...	1,23217	"
"	*Valparaiso*	...,,, ...	2,57530	"
Fanegāda	*Canary Islands* ..	superficial	0,5	acres.
"	*Spain*	...,,, ...	1,1945	"
" *minimum*	..,,, ...	...,,, ...	0,9261	"
" *max. legal since* 1801	..,,, ...	...,,, ...	1,5871	"
"	*Valencia*	...,,, ...	0,1710	"
Fanga	*Azores*	dry capacity ...	1,35959	bushels.
"	*Faro*	...,,, ...	1,87465	"
"	*Lisbon*	...,,, ...	1,53468	"
" *for coal*	...,,, ...	...,,, ...	21,1667	"
"	*Oporto*	...,,, ...	1,93737	"

Acre = 4840 square yards.　Bushel = 2150,42 cubic inches.　Cubic foot = 1728 cubic inches.
Gallon = 231 cubic inches.　Mile = 1760 yards.　Pound = 7000 grains.　Yard = 36 inches.

NAME.	LOCALITY.	CHARACTER.	VALUE.	
Fanga....................	*Rio Janeiro*	dry capacity....	1,53468	bushels.
Fass......................	*Berlin*	liquid capacity	60,49675	gallons.
"	*Berne*...........	......,,........	176,60035	"
"	*Bohemia*	......,,........	64,55981	"
"	*Brunswic*	......,,........	106,70449	"
"	*Dantzic*.........	......,,........	60,49940	"
" *for wine*..............	*Dresden*.........	......,,........	89,04384	"
" *for beer*..............	...,,...........	......,,........	103,88535	"
"	*Friburg*.........	......,,........	164,95048	"
"	*Gotha*...........	......,,........	52,86995	"
" *for whale oil*..........	*Hamburg*.........	......,,........	38,25561	"
"	*Hanover*	......,,........	165,05840	"
" *for wine*.............	*Leipsic*..........	......,,........	100,17366	"
" *for beer*..............	...,,............	......,,........	95,40524	"
" *for brandy*...........	*Lübec*...........	......,,........	57,38211	"
" *for beer*.............	...,,...........	......,,........	38,25561	"
"	*Magdeburg*.......	......,,........	60,49675	"
"	*Prague*	......,,........	67,80604	"
" *for beer*..............	*Presburg*........	......,,........	56,36765	"
" *for Tokay*	...,,............	......,,........	38,75228	"
" *for wine*.............	*Vienna*..........	......,,........	153,26287	"
" *for beer*.............	...,,............	......,,........	31,77269	"
" *for wheat, etc*..........	*Aix-la-Chapelle*..	dry capacity ...	0,70117	bushels.
" *for oats and barley*.....	...,,.........	......,,........	1,05176	"
"	*Altona*..........	......,,........	1,49694	"
"	*Cologne*.........	......,,........	0,50918	"
"	*Hamburg*.........	......,,........	1,49406	"
"	*Lübec*...........	......,,........	0,25242	"
"	*Rostock*	......,,........	0,27583	"
" *for oats*..............	...,,...........	......,,........	0,30774	"
" *for charcoal*...........	*Tréves*	......,,........	7,61155	"
Fässli ; *for lime*	*Berne*...........	......,,........	9,66186	"
Fathom....................	*England*........	length.........	2.——	yards.
"	*United States*....	......,,........	2.——	"
Faucheur..................	*Gap*............	superficial	0,7518	acres.
Faux......................	*Neufchâtel*	......,,........	1,3353	"
Favn.....................	*Denmark*........	length	2,05933	yards.
Fedan.....................	*Cairo*...........	......,,........	1,4651	"
Felin ; *old measure; jewelry*.	*Brussels*.........	weight.........	5,93	grains.
"	*Paris*	......,,.........	5,90	"
Ferlino...................	*Bologna*.........	......,,........	29,11	"
"	*Modena*.........	......,,........	25,68	"

Acre = 4840 square yards. Bushel = 2150,42 cubic inches. Cubic foot = 1728 cubic inches.
Gallon = 231 cubic inches. Mile = 1760 yards. Pound = 7000 grains. Yard = 36 inches.

NAME.	LOCALITY.	CHARACTER.	VALUE.	
Ferrädo	Gallicia	dry capacity	0,53305	bushels.
Feuillette	Bordeaux	liquid capacity	29,87853	gallons.
"	Champagne	"	35,18446	"
Fiäsco	Modena	"	0,55028	"
" for wine	Tuscany	"	0,60211	"
" for oil	"	"	0,55187	"
Firkin ; for ale	England	"	9,76624	"
" for beer	"	"	10,98702	"
" for butter	"	weight	56.——	pounds.
" " mean	Goshen ; N. Y.	"	56.——	"
" " "	Glades ; Penn'a	"	110.——	"
Firlot ; for barley	Scotland	dry capacity	1,49064	bushels.
" for wheat, etc.	"	"	1,02182	"
Fjerding	Denmark	"	0,98690	"
"	Finland	liquid capacity	8,29308	gallons.
"	Sweden	"	8,28990	"
"	"	dry capacity	0,51964	bushels.
Fod	Denmark	length	0,34325	yards.
Fodder ; for lead	England	weight	2184.——	pounds.
" "	Newcastle	"	2352.——	"
" "	Stockton-'on-Tees	"	2464.——	"
Fogliëtta	Ancona	liquid capacity	0,11835	gallons.
"	Bologna	"	0,08651	"
"	Genoa	"	0,39217	"
"	Milan	"	0,41582	"
" for wine	Rome	"	0,12041	"
" for oil	"	"	0,13558	"
"	Turin	"	0,41340	"
Foot	England	length	12.——	inches.
"	United States	"	12.——	"
Fortin	Constantinople	dry capacity	3,77140	bushels.
"	Smyrna	"	5,824	"
Fossöreé ; mean	H. Alpes; France.	superficial	0,0964	acres.
Fossörier	Lausanne	"	0,1112	"
Fossöyée	Geneva	"	0,0834	"
Fot	Sweden	length	11,6573	inches.
Frasco	Brazil	liquid capacity	0,56250	gallons.
Frazïl	Bet-el-faki	weight	20,390625	pounds.
" of Mocha	"	"	14,273438	"
"	Jidda	"	18,300780	"
"	Mocha	"	30.——	"
Frohngewïcht	Augsburg	"	1,082621	"

Acre = 4840 square yards. Bushel = 2150,42 cubic inches. Cubic foot = 1728 cubic inches.
Gallon = 231 cubic inches. Mile = 1760 yards. Pound = 7000 grains. Yard = 36 inches.

NAME.	LOCALITY.	CHARACTER.	VALUE.
Fuder......................	Augsburg	liquid capacity	238,74500 gallons.
"	Altona.....,......	.....,,,.........	229,51775 "
"	Baden	.....,,,.........	396,26700 "
"	Berlin	.....,,,.........	217,78834 "
"	Bremen.........	.....,,,.........	229,77905 "
"	Brunswic.......	.....,,,.........	237,12108 "
"	Coblentz	.....,,,.........	241,19451 "
"	Copenhagen......	.....,,,.........	237,33751 "
"	Dantzic.........	.....,,,.........	217,78834 "
"	Dresden.........	.....,,,.........	213,69358 "
"	Frankfort a. M..	.....,,,.........	227,34624 "
"	Gotha..........	.....,,,.........	230,70664 "
"	Graubündten	.....,,,.........	224,70981 "
"	Hamburg	.....,,,.........	229,77905 "
"	Hanover	.....,,,.........	246,50449 "
"	Hesse Cassel.....	.....,,,.........	251,52388 "
"	Hesse Darmstadt.	.....,,,.........	253,61088 "
"	Leipsic..........	.....,,,.........	240,46116 "
"	Lübec...........	.....,,,.........	229,51775 "
" schenk-mass..........	Nürnberg.......	.....,,,.........	218,92430 "
" visir-mass...........	....,,,.......	.....,,,.........	232,34813 "
"	Oldenburg.......	.....,,,.........	241,98705 "
"	Rostock	.....,,,.........	229,51775 "
"	S. Gall........	.....,,,.........	332,78502 "
"	Sweden.........	.....,,,.........	258,80284 "
" schenk-mass..........	Ulm...........	.....,,,.........	698,77723 "
" visir-mass...........	....,,,.......	.....,,,.........	776,11447 "
"	Vaud...........	.....,,,.........	171,18734 "
"	Vienna.........	.....,,,.........	478,47900 "
"	Würtemberg....	.....,,,.........	465,90372 "
" for charcoal.........	Hamburg........	dry capacity...	179,63274 bushels
"	Hanover	.....,,,.........	63,54969 "
"	Osnabrück.......	.....,,,.........	58,66679 "
Fudermässel.............	Vienna.........	.....,,,.........	0,05454 "
Funt	Cracow....:.....	weight.........	0,894929 pounds.
" old measure...........	Poland.........	.....,,,.........	0,894929 "
" since 1819............	....,,,.......	.....,,,.........	0,894089 "
" of Warsaw...........	....,,,.......	.....,,,.........	0,825236 "
"	Russia.........	.....,,,.........	0,901691 "
" apothecaries'.........	....,,,.......	.....,,,.........	0,788974 "
Furlong..............	England	itinerary.......	0,1250 miles.
" old measure........	Ireland..........	.....,,,.........	0,1500 "

Acre = 4840 square yards. Bushel = 2150,42 cubic inches. Cubic foot = 1728 cubic inches.
Gallon = 231 cubic inches. Mile = 1760 yards. Pound = 7000 grains. Yard = 36 inches.

NAME.	LOCALITY.	CHARACTER.	VALUE.	
Furlong; *old measure*	Scotland	itinerary.	0,1409	miles.
"　　　*not used*	United States	...,,...	0,1250	"
Fuss	Aarau	length	0,32072	yards.
"　*builders'*	Aix-la-Chapelle	...,,...	0,31573	"
"　*surveyors'*	...,,...	...,,...	0,30838	"
"	Altona	...,,...	0,31331	"
"	Antwerp	...,,...	0,31232	"
"　*Rhine foot*	Anhalt	...,,...	0,34324	"
"	Appenzell	...,,...	0,34416	"
"	Augsburg	...,,...	0,32390	"
"	Baden	...,,...	0,32809	" ₁
"　*old measure*	Bamberg	...,,...	0,33214	"
"	Basel	...,,...	0,33305	"
"　*since 1809*	Bavaria	..,,...	0,31919	"
"	Rhenish Bavaria.	...,,...	0,36456	"
"　*since 1816*	Berlin	...,,...	0,34324	"
"　*surveyors'*	...,,...	...,,...	0,41189	"
"	Berne	...,,...	0,32072	"
"　*quarry*	...,,...	...,,...	0,34744	"
"　*of Schweitz*	...,,...	...,,...	0,32809	"
"　*old measure*	Bohemia	...,,...	0,32414	"
"　*imperial*	...,,...	...,,...	0,34571	"
"	Bremen	...,,...	0,31628	"
"	Brunswic	...,,...	0,31208	"
"　*old measure*	Carlsruhe	..,,...	0,36454	"
"	Cleves	...,,...	0,32318	"
"	Coblentz	...,,...	0,31783	"
"　*old measure*	Cologne	...,,...	0,31455	"
"　*Rhine foot*	Courland	...,,...	0,34324	"
"　*old measure*	Dantzic	...,,...	0,31375	"
"	Dresden	...,,...	0,30978	"
"	Frankfort	...,,...	0,31126	"
"　*surveyors'*	...,,...	...,,...	0,38917	"
"	Friburg	...,,...	0,32072	"
"	Glaris	...,,...	0,32811	"
"	Göttingen	...,,...	0,31824	"
"	Gotha	...,,...	0,31455	"
"	Hamburg	...,,...	0,31332	"
"　*surveyors'; Rhine foot*	...,,...	...,,...	0,34324	"
"	Hanover	...,,...	0,31934	"
"　*old measure*	Heidelberg	...,,...	0,30550	"
"	Hesse Cassel	...,,...	0,31455	"

Acre = 4840 square yards. Bushel = 2150,42 cubic inches. Cubic foot = 1728 cubic inches.
Gallon = 231 cubic inches. Mile = 1760 yards. Pound = 7000 grains. Yard = 36 inches.

NAME.	LOCALITY.	CHARACTER.	VALUE.	
Fuss ; *surveyors'*	*Hesse Cassel*	length	0,31159	yards.
" *old measure*	*Hesse Darmstadt.*	..,,.	0,31455	"
" *since* 1818	..,,.	..,,.	0,27341	"
"	*Holstein*	..,,.	0,32649	"
"	*Hungary*	..,,.	0,34571	"
" *common*	*Leipsic*	..,,.	0,30863	"
" *builders'*	..,,.	..,,.	0,30912	"
"	*Lippe*	..,,.	0,31662	"
"	*Lübec.*	..,,.	0,31486	"
" *old measure*	*Luneburg*	..,,.	0,31825	"
" "	*Mannheim*	..,,.	0,31745	"
"	*Mecklenburg*	..,,.	0,31825	"
"	*Moravia*	..,,.	0,32367	"
"	*Munich*	..,,.	0,31919	"
"	*Neufchâtel*	..,,.	0,32072	"
" *surveyors'*	..,,.	..,,.	0,31403	"
" *old measure*	*Nürnberg*	..,,.	0,33224	"
"	*Oldenburg*	..,,.	0,32358	"
"	*Osnabrück*	..,,.	0,30542	"
"	*Rostock*	..,,.	0,31486	"
"	*Schweitz*	..,,.	0,32809	"
"	*Solothurn*	..,,.	0,32072	"
" *Rhine foot*	*Thurgau*	..,,.	0,34324	"
"	*Trent.*	..,,.	0,40017	"
"	*Vaud.*	..,,.	0,32809	"
" *imperial*	*Vienna*	..,,.	0,34571	"
"	*Weimar*	..,,.	0,30838	"
" *surveyors'*	..,,.	..,,.	0,49342	"
" *old measure*	*Wesel*	..,,.	0,25706	"
"	*Würtemberg*	..,,.	0,31332	"
"	*Zurich*	..,,.	0,32811	"
" *builders';since* 1820	..,,.	..,,.	0,32960	"
Gässel ; *for rye, etc.*	*Bamberg*	dry capacity	0,05515	bushels.
" *for oats and barley.*	..,,.	..,,.	0,06828	"
Gallon ; *imperial ; since* 1825	*Great Britain*	liquid capacity	1,20060	gallons.
" *for wine ; Saxon*	*England;* ... 1000	..,,.	0,93506	"
" *for wine ; Rumford.*	..,,. 1266	..,,.	0,93506	"
" " *Winchester*	..,,. 1266	..,,.	1.——	"
" " *Guildhall*	..,,. *after* 1496	..,,.	0,96970	"
" *for ale and beer;* 1803	..,,. *till* 1825	..,,.	1,22078	"
" *for wine*	*Ireland*	..,,.	0,94199	"

Acre = 4840 square yards. Bushel = 2150,42 cubic inches. Cubic foot = 1728 cubic inches.
Gallon = 231 cubic inches. Mile = 1760 yards. Pound = 7000 grains. Yard = 36 inches.

NAME.	LOCALITY.	CHARACTER.	VALUE.	
Gallon	Scotland	liquid capacity	3,58109	gallons.
" for wine	E. and W. Indies	,,	1.——	"
"	United States	,,	1.——	"
" for corn, Saxon	England	dry capacity	0,12556	bushels.
" " Rumford	,,	,,	0,12359	"
" " Winchester	,,	,,	0,12451	"
" " Guildhall	,,	,,	0,12660	"
" imperial since 1825	Great Britain	,,	0,12894	"
"	United States	,,	0,12500	"
Gántang	Bantam	,,	0,36891	"
"	Borneo	,,	0,73782	"
" minimum	East Indies	,,	0,03406	"
" maximum	,,	,,	0,27243	"
" mean of 11	,,	,,	0,14628	"
Gárave	Syria	,,	41,14810	"
Garce	Madras	,,	139,53488	"
"	Pondichery	,,	103,96700	"
Garnetz	Russia	,,	0,09300	"
Garnitz	Lemberg	liquid capacity	1,01523	gallons.
"	,,	dry capacity	0,10906	bushels.
Garniëc	Cracow	liquid capacity	0,99145	gallons.
"	,,	dry capacity	0,10763	bushels.
"	Lublin	,,	0,05179	"
" since 1819	Warsaw	liquid capacity	1,05671	gallons.
" old measure	,,	,,	0,99568	"
" since 1819	,,	dry capacity	0,11351	bushels.
" old measure	,,	,,	0,10763	"
Garráfa	Rio Janeiro	liquid capacity	0,18337	gallons.
Gasab	Cairo	length	4,21049	yards.
Gaváda	Mysore	itinerary	14,5833	miles.
Geestruthe	Hamburg	length	5,01304	yards.
Geîra	Portugal	superficial	1,4287	acres.
Gelte	Brussels	liquid capacity	0,71560	gallons.
"	,,	dry capacity	0,07687	bushels.
Gelt	Vaud	liquid capacity	3,56640	gallons.
"	,,	dry capacity	0,38310	bushels.
Gerah	Ancient Hebrews.	weight	22,46	grains.
"	Mysore	length	2,3875	inches.
Gerle	Neufchâtel	liquid capacity	26,15976	gallons.
Gerrah	Minorca	,,	3,18599	"
Gescheid	Frankfort	dry capacity	0,04979	bushels.
"	Hesse Darmstadt.	,,	0,04981	"

Acre = 4840 square yards.   Bushel = 2150,42 cubic inches.   Cubic foot = 1728 cubic inches.
Gallon = 231 cubic inches.   Mile = 1760 yards.   Pound = 7000 grains.   Yard = 36 inches.

NAME.	LOCALITY.	CHARACTER.	VALUE.	
Gescheid..................	*Mentz & Nassau*	dry capacity ...	0,04852	bushels.
Gez.......................	*Mocha*..........	length.........	0,69444	yards.
Gheria....................	*Calcutta*	....,,...........	2,2147	inches.
Ghes	....,,..........	....,,..........	1.——	yards.
Gill ; *imperial*..............	*Great Britain* ...	liquid capacity	0,03752	gallons.
" *old measure*	.....,,.........	......,,.......	0,03125	"
"	*Ireland*..........	......,,.......	0,02694	"
"	*Scotland*	......,,.......	0,02798	"
"	*United States*....	......,,.......	0,03125	"
Giornăta..................	*Turin*...........	superficial	0,9393	acres.
Goelak	*Java*............	weight........	2,033888	pounds.
"	*Sumatra*........	....,,..........	1,694906	"
Gombĕtta	*Genoa*	dry capacity ...	0,03568	bushels.
Gonje ; *for gold and silver* ...	*Aurengabad*.....	weight........	1,96	grains.
Gonze " " ..	*Bombay*.........	....,,..........	1,79	"
Goondŏminy " ...	*Mysore*	....,,..........	1,96	"
Gradus....................	*Ancient Romans.*	length	0,80889	yards.
Grain ; *gold and silver ; Troy*	*Great Britain* ...	weight........	1.——	grains.
" *apothecaries'*.......	.....,,.........	......,,.......	1.——	"
" *avoirdupois*..........	....,,..........	....,,........	1.——	"
" *for diamonds*	....,,..........	;....,,.......	0,79	"
" *for pearls*..........	....,,..........	...,,.......	0,80	"
" *poids de marc*.......	*France*..........	....,,........	0,82	"
" *until* 1840..........	....,,..........	....,,.......	0,84	"
" *for precious stones*...	....,,..........	....,,.......	0,79	"
" *of Charlemagne*.....	....,,..........	....,,.......	0,98	"
"	*Geneva*	....,,.......	0,82	"
"	*Liège*...........	....,,.......	0,75	"
"	*Marseilles*.......	....,,.......	0,68	"
"	*Neufchâtel*	....,,.......	0,82	"
"	*Vaud*...........	....,,.......	0,84	"
Gramme...................	*France*..........	....,,.......	15,43	"
Gran ; *apothecaries'*........	*Austria*	....,,.......	1,13	"
" " *since* 1811	*Bavaria*.........	....,,.......	0,96	"
" *ap. o. m. of Nürnberg*	...,,..........	....,,.......	0,96	"
"	*Denmark*........	....,,.......	0,11	"
" *apothecaries'*........	....,,..........	....,,.......	0,96	"
" "	*Prussia*	.·...,,.......	0,94	"
" *ap. o. m. of Nürnberg*.	...,,..........	....,,.......	0,96	"
"	*Saxony*	....,,.......	0,94	"
Granikow	*Poland*	....,,.......	0,12	"
Grano ; *new Italian*........	*Italy*...........	....,,..........	1,54	"

Acre = 4840 square yards.   Bushel = 2150,42 cubic inches.   Cubic foot = 1728 cubic inches.
Gallon = 231 cubic inches.   Mile = 1760 yards.   Pound = 7000 grains.   Yard = 36 inches.

NAME.	LOCALITY.	CHARACTER.	VALUE.	
Grano	Spain	weight	0,77	grains.
" for gold	..,..	..,..	0,74	"
Granottino	Piedmont	..,..	0,03	"
Granow	Poland	..,..	0,68	"
Grao	Brazil	..,..	0,77	"
"	Portugal	..,..	0,77	"
" barley-corn; (imaginary)	..,..	length.	0,1804	inches.
Grave; disused	France	weight	2,204737	pounds.
Gravet "	..,..	..,..	15,43	grains.
Grein	Holland	..,..	1,54	"
Gressus	Ancient Romans	length.	0,80889	yards.
Gros	France	weight	59,02	grains.
"	Lausanne	..,..	60,29	"
"	Neufchâtel	..,..	62,71	"
"	Vaud	..,..	60,29	"
Grosso; metrical; since 1803.	Venet. Lombardy.	..,..	0,022047	pounds.
Ground	Madras	superficial	0,0551	acres.
Gujah	Mysore	length	1,06944	yards.
Gueza	Gambroon	..,..	1,07528	"
"	Ispahan	..,..	1,03853	"
" monkelser or royal	Persia	..,..	1,03398	"
" ordinary	..,..	..,..	0,68932	"
Guz	Bagdad	..,..	0,87963	"
"	Bassora	..,..	0,87963	"
"	Bet-el-faki	..,..	0,69444	"
"	Bushire	..,..	0,55556	"
" minimum	E. Indies; Gujerat	..,..	0,64815	"
" maximum	..,.. Patna.	..,..	1,18056	"
" mean of 67	..,..	..,..	0,91447	"
Hadid; for muslins	Bassora	length	0,95	yards.
Hærēdium	Ancient Romans.	superficial	2,4917	acres.
Hafer-metze; for oats	Nürnberg	dry capacity	0,52176	bushels.
Hafer-scheffel "	Lippe	..,..	1,46897	"
Hafer-simmer	Nürnberg	..,..	16,69639	"
Hailoh	Sumatra	length	1.——	yards.
Haken	Berlin	superficial	2,8030	acres.
"	Dantzic	..,..	27,4439	"
"	Königsberg	..,..	31,5698	"
"	Poland	..,..	27,6576	"
"	Pomerania	..,..	24,2831	"
Halbe; since 1808	Hungary	liquid capacity	0,22019	gallons.

Acre = 4840 square yards. Bushel = 2150,42 cubic inches. Cubic foot = 1728 cubic inches. Gallon = 231 cubic inches. Mile = 1760 yards. Pound = 7000 grains. Yard = 36 inches.

NAME.	LOCALITY.	CHARACTER.	VALUE.	
Halbe; *since* 1803	*Hungary*	dry capacity ...	0,02365	bushels.
Halēbi	*Constantinople*...	length	0775	yards.
"	*Crimea*	...,,	0,79933	"
Hali	*Malacca*	weight	32.——	pounds.
Halĭbin	*Bucharest*	length	0,76694	yards.
Halster	*Brussels*	dry capacity ...	0,69185	bushels.
" *for oats*	...,,	.....,,	0,73016	"
"	*Ghent*	.....,,	1,49893	"
"	*Louvain*	.....,,	0,85134	"
" *for oats*	...,,	.....,,	0,99323	"
Hamma	*Ancient Greeks* ..	itinerary	0,0115	miles.
Hand	*England*	length	4.——	inches.
"	*Calcutta*	...,,	3.——	"
Hao	*An-nam*	weight	0,06	grains.
Hardăry	*Mysore*	itinerary	2,7344	miles.
Harsēla; *for silk*	*Cairo*	weight	2,6361	pounds.
Hartkorn-scheffel	*Leipsic*	dry capacity ...	1,25692	bushels.
Hasta	*Singapore*	length	0,5	yards.
Hath	*Ahmednuggur*...	...,,	0,38889	"
" *mean of* 4	*Doab*	...,,	0,52605	"
" *for matting*	*Surat*	...,,	0,58056	"
Haut	*Bombay*	...,,	0,50329	"
"	*Calcutta*	...,,	0,48910	"
"	*Mysore*	...,,	0,53056	"
Havot; *old measure*	*Lille*	dry capacity ...	0,49790	bushels.
Hectare	*France*	superficial	2,4711	acres.
Hecteus	*Ancient Greeks*..	dry capacity...	0,24496	bushels.
Hectogramme	*France*	weight	0,220474	pounds.
Hectolitre	...,,	liquid capacity	26,4178	gallons.
"	...,,	dry capacity....	2,83782	bushels.
Hectometre	...,,	itinerary	0,0621	miles.
Hectos	*Ancient Greeks*..	superficial	0,0391	acres.
Hellēich-mass	*Würtemberg*	liquid capacity	0,48531	gallons.
Heller; *Cologne weight*	*Prussia*	weight	7,04	grains.
" *old measure*	*Silesia*	...,,	6,17	"
Hemiēcteus	*Ancient Greeks*..	dry capacity....	0,12248	bushels.
Hemīna	*Ancient Romans*.	liquid capacity	0,07126	gallons.
"	...,,	dry capacity ...	0,00765	bushels.
Hemi-obŏlon	*Ancient Greeks*..	weight	5,62	grains.
Hemi-podion	...,,	length	6,0686	inches.
Henkemann; *beer and milk*..	*Oldenburg*	liquid capacity	10,12435	gallons.
" *for grain*	...,,	dry capacity ...	1,08755	bushels.

Acre = 4840 square yards. Bushel = 2150,42 cubic inches. Cubic foot = 1728 cubic inches. Gallon = 231 cubic inches. Mile = 1760 yards. Pound = 7000 grains. Yard = 36 inches.

NAME.	LOCALITY.	CHARACTER.	VALUE.	
Hexapŏdon ; *Olympic*	*Ancient Greeks* ..	length	2,02287	yards.
Hide	*England*	superficial	100.——	acres.
Himt	*Altona*	dry capacity ...	0,74833	bushels.
"	*Brunswic*	......,,........	0,88446	"
"	*Hamburg*	......,,........	0,74703	"
"	*Hanover*	......,,........	0,88427	"
"	*Hesse Cassel*	......,, ...	1,14037	"
"	*Hesse Homberg* ..	......,,.......	1,26594	"
" *old measure*	*Merseburg*	......,, ...	2,47684	"
Hin	*Ancient Hebrews*	liquid capacity	1,71025	gallons.
Hippïcon	*Ancient Greeks* ..	itinerary	0,4597	miles.
Hoed ; *old measure*	*Bruges*	dry capacity ...	4,72806	bushels.
" " *minimum*	*Holland ; Dort* ...	......,,........	27,57831	"
" " *maximum*	....,,.... *Gorcum*	......,,........	37,09119	"
" " *mean of 6*	....,, ...	......,,........	31,55917	"
" " *for coal* ..	*Amsterdam*	......,,........	66,22601	"
Hoeschen ; *for butter*	*Saxony*	weight	24,734352	pounds.
Hogshead ; *for wine, etc*	*England*	liquid capacity	63.——	gallons.
" *of claret*	....,,.........	......,,........	58.——	"
" *for ale*	....,,.........	......,,........	58,59744	"
" *for beer*	....,,.........	......,,........	65,92212	"
" *old measure*	*Scotland*	......,,........	57,29745	"
"	*United States*	......,,........	63.——	"
" *for tobacco, nett* ..	*Kentucky ; mean* .	weight	1200.——	pounds.
" " " ..	*Maryland* ..,,...	....,,.........	800.——	"
" " " ..	*Missouri* ....,,..	....,,.........	1200.——	"
" " " ..	*Ohio* ......,,...	....,,.........	750.——	"
" " " ..	*Virginia* ....,,...	....,,.........	1200.——	"
Hok	*China*	dry capacity ...	1,03867	bushels.
Holzstoss ; *for firewood*	*Breslau*	solid	550,470	cub. feet.
Hot	*An-nam*	weight	0,006	grains.
Hotteau ; *mean of* 8	*Hainault*	dry capacity ...	0,44556	bushels.
Hubla ; *for diam. and pearls* .	*Sindh*	weight	2.——	grains.
Hufe	*Mecklenburg*	superficial	214,1848	acres.
"	*Pomerania*	......,,........	48,5659	"
" *Wendish*	....,,.........	......,,........	24,2828	"
" *legal*	*Prussia*	......,,........	18,9195	"
"	*Silesia*	......,,........	41,4740	"
Hund	*Oldenburg*	......,, ...	0,5151	"
Hundred weight ; *nett*	*England : 1300* ..	weight	100.——	pounds.
" *for sugar and wax* ..	....,,......,,..	....,,.........	108.——	"
" *for wool*	....,,......,,..	....,,.........	110.——	"

Acre = 4840 square yards. Bushel = 2150,42 cubic inches. Cubic foot = 1728 cubic inches.
Gallon = 231 cubic inches. Mile = 1760 yards. Pound = 7000 grains. Yard = 36 inches.

NAME.	LOCALITY.	CHARACTER.	VALUE.	
Hundred weight; *for iron* ..	*England :* 1300..	weight........	120.——	pounds.
"	*Great Britain*....	....,,..........	112.——	"
"	*Maryland*	....,,,..........	100.——	"
" *for coal*...	....,,..........	....,,,..........	112.——	"
"	*United States*....	....,,,..........	112.——	"
Icze	*Hungary*........	liquid capacity	0,22019	gallons.
"	....,,..........	dry capacity...	0,02365	bushels.
Ikje	*Japan*..........	length........	2,31653	yards.
Imal...	*Nancy*..........	dry capacity....	0,64216	bushels.
Imbūto..................	*Sardinia*.......	....,,..........	0,08679	"
"	....,,..........	superficial	0,0612	acres.
Immel..................	*Heidelberg*.......	dry capacity ..	0,09878	bushels.
"	*Mannheim*.......	....,,..........	0,09851	"
Immi..................	*Berne*..........	....,,..........	0,09940	"
"	*Friburg*........	weight........	0,018881	pounds.
"	....,,..........	dry capacity...	0,03777	bushels.
"	*Glaris*	....,,..........	0,01646	"
"	*Lucerne*........	....,,..........	0,09862	"
"	*Schweitz* and *Uri*	....,,..........	0,01646	"
"	*Solothurn*.......	....,,..........	0,09396	"
"	*Ulm*	....,,..........	6,52069	"
"	*Unterwalden*.....	....,,..........	0,09862	"
" *hell eich-mass*..........	*Würtemberg*.....	liquid capacity	4,85309	gallons.
" *schenk-mass*..........	....,,..........	....,,..........	4,41190	"
" *trüb eich-mass*........	....,,..........	....,,..........	5,06539	"
" *for charcoal and lime*...	....,,..........	dry capacity....	0,52130	bushels.
"	*Zurich*..........	....,,..........	0,01646	"
Inch..................	*England*	length	1.——	inches.
"	*Scotland*	....,,..........	1,0054	"
"	*United States*....	....,,..........	1.——	"
Indīse..................	*Smyrna*.	....,,..........	0,68461	yards.
Ingistāra.................	*Verona*.,........	liquid capacity	2,48674	gallons.
"	*Vicenza*.........	....,,..........	2,40749	"
Inion	*Anct. Egyptians.*	liquid capacity	0,14252	"
"	....,,..........	dry capacity ...	0,01531	bushels.
Ink..................	*Japan*..........	length........	2,07845	yards.
Invel	*Mannheim*.......	dry capacity....	0,09851	bushels.
Jaktān ; *for cloth*..........	*Guinea*..........	length........	4.——	yards. ?
Jallois ; *old measure*	*Guise*..........	dry capacity....	1,84576	bushels.
"	*Ribemont*........	....,,..........	1,47661	"

Acre = 4840 square yards. Bushel = 2150,42 cubic inches. Cubic foot = 1728 cubic inches.
Gallon = 231 cubic inches. Mile = 1760 yards. Pound = 7000 grains. Yard = 36 inches.

NAME.	LOCALITY.	CHARACTER.	VALUE.	
Jallois ; *old m. for vineyards*	*Laon*	superficial	1,5138	acres.
"	*Vervins*	....,,.........	0,7420	"
Jankal....................	*Sumatra*........	length........	0,25	yards.
Jaob......................	*Calcutta*........	....,,.........	0,2461	inches.
Jauchärt ; *old measure*......	*Augsburg*........	superficial......	0,3467	acres.
" *legal since 1809*...	*Bavaria*.........	....,,.........	0,8416	"
"	*Lausanne*........	....,,.........	1,1115	"
" ....,..........	*Tyrol*.......	....,,.........	0,8889	"
"	*Vaud*.......	....,,.........	0,1115	"
Jez ; *old measure*	*Augsburg*........	liquid capacity	29,84313	gallons.
Joch *or* Jochart ; *legal*......	*Austria*........	superficial......	1,4223	acres.
Jod...:...............	*Siam*	itinerary.......	0,0956	miles.
Journal..................	*Aix in Provence*..	superficial......	1,4625	acres.
"	*Alpes (Basses)* ..	....,,.........	0,4877	"
"	*Amiens*........	....,,.........	1,0430	"
"	*Besançon*.......	....,,.........	0,7138	"
"	*Bordeaux*	....,,.........	0,7890	"
"	*Burgundy*.......	....,,.........	0,8807	"
"	*Finistère*.......	....,,.........	1,2016	"
"	*Lorraine*	....,,.........	0,5051	"
"	*Rheims*.........	....,,.........	1,2535	"
"	*Rochelle*.......	....,,.........	2,5241	"
"	*Tremblade*......	....,,.........	1,6897	"
Journé...................	*Vannes*	....,,.........	0,9012	"
Journel..................	*Châlons s. Marne*	....,,.........	1,2522	"
Juchart..................	*Basel*..........	....,,.........	0,8250	"
"	*Baden*..........	....,,.........	0,8199	"
" *tillage*	*Berne*..........	....,,.........	0,8503	"
" *meadow*...........	....,,........	....,,.........	0,7440	"
" *woodland*...........	....,,........	....,,.........	0,9566	"
"	*Friburg*........	....,,.........	1,0621	"
" *greater*...........	*Lucerne*........	....,,.........	0,8984	"
" *small*...........	....,,........	....,,.........	0,6239	"
"	*Solothurn*.......	....,,.........	0,8497	"
" *for vines*...........	*Strasburg*.......	....,,.........	0,1860	"
"	*Würtemberg*.....	....,,.........	1,1683	"
" *tillage*............	*Zurich*.........	....,,.........	0,8080	"
" *vineyard*...........	....,,........	....,,.........	0,7183	"
" *woodland*...........	....,,........	....,,.........	0,8978	"
Juck ; *old measure*.........	*Oldenburg*......	....,,.........	1,3854	"
" *new measure*........	....,,........	....,,.........	1,1196	"
Jugërum	*Ancient Romans*.	....,,.........	0,6229	"

Acre = 4840 square yards. **Bushel** = 2150,42 cubic inches. **Cubic foot** = 1728 cubic inches.
Gallon = 231 cubic inches. **Mile** = 1760 yards. **Pound** = 7000 grains. **Yard** = 36 inches.

45

NAME.	LOCALITY.	CHARACTER.	VALUE.	
Jumba......................	Malacca.......	length........	4.——	yards.
Jungfru..................	Sweden.........	liquid capacity	0,02157	gallons.
Jütte ; old measure..........	S. Malo........	dry capacity...	1,62160	bushels.
Kab......................	Ancient Hebrews.	dry capacity....	0,06124	bushels.
Kahōon....................	Calcutta........	......,,........	37,40480	"
Kalämos..................	Ancient Greeks..	itinerary......	0,0019	miles.
Kalkvat ; for lime ; old meas.	Brussels........	dry capacity....	0,80713	bushels.
Kamīnieck................	Poland.........	weight........	22,356033	pounds.
Kan......................	China..........	......,,.......	1,333333	"
"	Holland; generally	liquid capacity	0,26418	gallons.
" old measure............	Rotterdam......	......,,.......	0,32789	"
Kande....................	Denmark,Norway	......,,.......	0,51040	"
Kaneh....................	Ancient Hebrews.	length........	2,86795	yards.
Kanna....................	Finland & Sweden	liquid capacity	0,69083	gallons.
"	....,,......,,...	dry capacity...	0,07423	bushels.
Kanne ; for wine............	Aix-la-Chapelle..	liquid capacity	0,28162	gallons.
" for beer............	.....,,.........	......,,.......	0,29932	"
"	Altona.........	......,,.......	0,47816	"
"	Batavia........	......,,.......	0,39394	"
" for wine............	Clèves.........	......,,.......	0,31411	"
" for beer............	....,,.........	......,,.......	0,47420	"
"	Dresden........	......,,.......	0,24741	"
"	Gotha..........	......,,.......	0,48060	"
"	Hamburg........	......,,.......	0,47816	"
"	Hanover........	......,,.......	0,51800	"
"	Leipsic.........	......,,.......	0,31808	"
" visir-mass........	....,,.........	......,,.......	0,37092	"
"	Lippe..........	......,,.......	0,36356	"
"	Lübec..........	......,,.......	0,49467	"
"	Mecklenburg.....	......,,.......	0,47843	"
" for wine............	Oldenburg......	......,,.......	0,38808	"
" for beer............	....,,.........	......,,.......	0,36166	"
" old measure........	Rostock........	......,,.......	0,43485	"
" "	Thuringia......	......,,.......	0,49427	"
"	Vienna.........	......,,.......	0,18703	"
" for oil.....	Weimar........	......,,.......	0,26895	"
" for wine............	....,,.........	......,,.......	0,24199	"
"	Clèves..........	dry capacity...	0,03168	bushels.
"	Oldenburg......	......,,.......	0,03884	"
"	Weimar.........	......,,.......	0,02952	"
" for butter..........	Saxony.........	weight........	24,734352	pounds.

Acre = 4840 square yards.   Bushel = 2150,42 cubic inches.   Cubic foot = 1728 cubic inches.
Gallon = 231 cubic inches.   Mile = 1760 yards.   Pound = 7000 grains.   Yard = 36 inches.

NAME.	LOCALITY.	CHARACTER.	VALUE.	
Kannland................	Sweden.........	superficial......	0,0217	acres.
Kapp...................	Narva..........	dry capacity ...	0,14376	bushels.
Kappe.................	Sweden..........	......,,.........	0,12991	"
Kappland.............	...,,...........	superficial	0,0379	acres.
Kara..................	Constantinople...	weight........	3,09	grains.
Karaat................	Amsterdam......	......,,........	3,17	"
"	Russia..........	......,,........	3,17	"
Karat.................	Cologne.........	......,,........	3,17	"
"	Frankfort.......	......,,........	3,18	"
" of Cologne..........	Germany, gen'y..	......,,........	3,17	"
"	Vienna.........	......,,........	3,18	"
Karch.................	...,,...........	......,,........	493,870840	pounds.
Karob................	Algiers & Tripoli	......,,........	3.———	grains.
Kassāba	Arabia.........	length.........	4,1	yards.
Kasten...............	Würtemberg.....	dry capacity ...	4,00474	bushels.
Keel.................	Newcastle.......	weight........	47488.——	pounds.
Kella................	Bet-el-faki......	......,,........	4,2	"
Ken.................	Siam...........	length........	1,05097	yards.
Keping ; for gold and silver..	Sumatra........	weight........	53,17	grains.
Kerāmion.............	Ancient Greeks..	liquid capacity	10,26150	gallons.
Kerātion.............	......,,........	weight........	3,74	grains.
"	Ancient Romans..	......,,........	2,92	"
Keub................	Siam...........	length.........	9,4590	inches.
Khancha ; bazar..........	Calcutta........	weight........	0,032083	pounds.
Khoullé.............	Algiers..........	liquid capacity	4,40270	gallons.
Kibrath-aretz...........	Ancient Hebrews.	itinerary......	2,4220	miles.
Kichkar.............	......,,........	weight........	96,258287	pounds.
Kilderkin ; for ale, old meas.	England.......	liquid capacity	19,53248	gallons.
" for beer, " ..	...,,...........	......,,........	21,97404	"
Kiliare ; disused...........	France..........	superficial......	24,7114	acres.
Killot................	Constantinople...	weight........	3,09	grains.
Kilo.................	Bucharest.......	dry capacity ...	11,16929	bushels.
"	Cerigo..........	......,,........	1.——	"
"	Salonica........	......,,........	5,50249	"
"	Smyrna.........	......,,........	1,45579	"
Kilogramme.............	France..........	weight........	2,204737	pounds.
Kilolītre............	......,,........	dry capacity ...	28,37820	bushels.
Kilomētre.............	......,,........	itinerary......	0,6214	miles.
" carré............	......,,........	superficial......	247,1134	acres.
Kiloz................	Constantinople...	dry capacity ...	0,94285	bushels.
Kip ; for tin.............	Malacca........	weight........	40,677750	pounds.
Kisloz................	Alexandria......	dry capacity ...	4,84100	bushels.

Acre = 4840 square yards.   Bushel = 2150,42 cubic inches.   Cubic foot = 1728 cubic inches.   Gallon = 231 cubic inches.   Mile = 1760 yards.   Pound = 7000 grains.   Yard = 36 inches.

NAME.	LOCALITY.	CHARACTER.	VALUE.
Kisloz....................	*Negropont.......*	dry capacity ...	0,86080 bushels.
Klafter	*Basel............*	length	1,28928 yards.
"	*Berlin..........*	...,,...........	2,05945 "
"	*Berne..........*	...,,...........	1,92430 "
"	*Bremen..........*	...,,...........	1,89765 "
"	*Gotha..........*	...,,...........	1,88730 "
"	*Hamburg........*	...,,...........	1,87989 "
"	*Leipsic........*	...,,...........	1,85473 "
"	*Vienna.........*	...,,...........	2,07424 "
"	*Weimar........*	...,,...........	1,85029 "
"	*Würtemberg....*	...,,...........	1,87989 "
"	*Baden ....*	solid..........	137,311 cub. feet.
"	*Basel..........*	..,,...........	128.— "
"	*Bavaria........*	..,,...........	110,630 "
"	*Berlin ....*	..,,...........	117,907 "
"	*Berne..........*	..,,...........	192,388 "
"	*Frankfort.......*	..,,...........	102,595 "
"	*Hesse Cassel.....*	..,,...........	126,141 "
"	*Hesse Darmstadt.*	..,,...........	120,955 "
"	*Leipsic..........*	..,,...........	100,490 "
"	*Nassau..........*	..,,...........	137,311 "
"	*Würtemberg.....*	..,,...........	119,583 "
Kleuder...................	*Hesse Cassel.....*	weight.........	22,422175 pounds.
Kloda ; *old measure*........	*Poland..........*	dry capacity...	6,67394 bushels.
Köpfchen..................	*Hesse Cassel....*	.....,,.........	0,03994 "
Köpfel ; *old measure*	*Ratisbon ....*	liquid capacity	0,22015 gallons.
" "	....,,...........	dry capacity...	0,02365 bushels.
Köpflein	*Basel...........*	.....,,.........	0,12119 "
Kole.....................	*Travancore......*	length	0,80736 yards.
Kong-pu..................	*China..........*	....,,..........	0,33497 "
Koolah...................	*Sumatra ....*	dry capacity...	0,11727 bushels.
Koonke...................	*Calcutta ....*	.....,,.........	0,00183 "
Koorah	*Mahrattas.......*	.....,,.........	4,06146 "
Kop shi..................	*China..........*	....,,..........	0,00218 "
" tsong...................	..,,...........	liquid capacity	0,01318 gallons.
" legal..................	*Holland.........*	dry capacity...	0,02838 bushels.
" *old measure*..............	...,,...........	.....,,.........	0,02463 "
Kopf......................	*Aix-la-Chapelle..*	.....,,.........	0,17529 "
"	*Glaris ....*	liquid capacity	0,94011 gallons.
"	*Zurich..........*	.....,,.........	0,96425 "
" *standard*..............	....,,...........	.....,,.........	0,86754 "
Kopfen	*Vienna..........*	.....,,.........	0,21361 "

Acre = 4840 square yards. Bushel = 2150,42 cubic inches. Cubic foot = 1728 cubic inches.
Gallon = 231 cubic inches. Mile = 1760 yards. Pound = 7000 grains. Yard = 36 inches.

48

NAME.	LOCALITY.	CHARACTER.	VALUE.	
Korb ; *for charcoal*	*Osnabrück*	dry capacity....	0,32722	bushels.
" "	*Zurich*	......,, ...	10,53789	"
Korrel	*Holland*	weight	1,54	grains.
Korzec	*Cracow*	dry capacity....	3,40820	bushels.
" *since* 1819	*Warsaw*	......,, ...	3,63238	"
" *old measure*	....,, ...	......,, ...	3,42267	"
Krinne ; *large*	*Graubündten*	weight	1,529657	pounds.
" *small*	....,, ...	....,, ...	1,147243	"
" *for milk*	....,, ...	liquid capacity	0,17555	gallons.
Krooskänne	*Oldenburg*	dry capacity....	0,03767	bushels.
Krüs	*Hanover*	....,, ...	0,03767	"
Krukke	*Bergen*	......,, ...	0,02741	"
Kuba	*Abyssinia*	liquid capacity	0,26840	gallons.
Kübel ; *for coal*	*Bavaria*	dry capacity....	1,05822	bushels.
" *for coal at the mines* ..	*Saxony*	......,, ...	9,14623	"
" *for mortar*	*Würtemberg*	......,, ...	0,20881	"
Küchenmass ; *for flour*	*Leipsic*	......,, ...	0,07237	"
Kuhl	*Russia*	......,, ...	7,43958	"
Kullanjey ; *for gold and silver*	*Carnatic*	weight	0,011610	pounds.
" *mean of* 6	*Travancore*	....,, ...	0,011138	"
Kullmitz	*Pernau ; Russia* .	dry capacity....	0,44922	bushels.
Kulmet	*Reval*	......,, ...	0,37289	"
"	*Riga*	......,, ...	0,32294	"
Kumme ; *for stone*	*Berlin*	solid	26,841	cub. feet.
Kumpf	*Heidelberg*	dry capacity...	0,19760	bushels.
"	*Hesse Darmstadt.*	....,, ...	0,22703	"
"	*Mannheim*	....,, ...	0,19703	"
"	*Mentz*	....,, ...	0,19399	"
Kwan	*China*	weight	40.——	pounds.
Kwarti	*Cracow*	liquid capacity	0,25044	gallons.
" *since* 1819	*Warsaw*	......,, ...	0,26418	"
" *old measure*	....,, ...	......,, ...	0,25044	"
" *minimum*	*Lublin*	......,, ...	0,12046	"
" *maximum*	*Czernowitz*	......,, ...	0,25397	"
" *mean of* 8	*Poland*	......,, ...	0,21134	"
"	*Cracow*	dry capacity....	0,02662	bushels.
" *since* 1819	*Warsaw*	......,, ...	0,02838	"
" *old measure*	....,, ...	......,, ...	0,02671	"
Kwatērki	*Cracow*	liquid capacity	0,06261	gallons.
"	*Warsaw*	......,, ...	0,06605	"
"	*Cracow*	dry capacity....	0,00666	bushels.
"	*Warsaw*	......,, ...	0,00708	"

Acre = 4840 square yards. Bushel = 2150,42 cubic inches. Cubic foot = 1728 cubic inches.
Gallon = 231 cubic inches. Mile = 1760 yards. Pound = 7000 grains. Yard = 36 inches.

NAME.	LOCALITY.	CHARACTER.	VALUE.
Lachter; *miners'*	*Prussia*	length........	2,28833 yards.
" "	*Saxony*..........	...,,..........	2,16400 "
Lachsa	*Sooloo Islands*....	weight........	66,666667 pounds.
Lädi......................	*Graubündten*	dry capacity ...	37,45896 bushels.
Lägel ; *for steel*	*Prussia*..........	weight........	103,115550 pounds.
" "	*Styria*..........	....,,..........	154,331590 "
Läp ; *old measure*..........	*Breslau*..........	....,,..........	21,452091 "
Lana	*Russia*..........	....,, ...	0,075220 "
Landfass..................	*Berne*	liquid capacity	264,97053 gallons.
Landhufe..................	*Pomerania*	superficial......	48,5659 acres.
Lappe.....................	*Ancona*..........	dry capacity ...	1,01479 bushels.
Last ; *shipping; heavy articles*	*N. Europe ; mean*	weight........	4500.—— pounds.
" " *for grain*....	...,,........,,..	dry capacity...	95.—— bushels.
" " *light articles*.	....,,........,,..	solid...........	120.—— cub. feet.
" *commercial*	*Amsterdam*......	weight........	85,245696 pounds.
" "	*Bremen*..........	....,,..........	329,718 "
" *for wool*	*England*	....,,..........	4368.—— "
" *commercial*..........	*Lübec*..........	....,,..........	96,930940 "
"	*Belgium*........	dry capacity....	85,13400 bushels.
"	*Bremen*..........	.....,,..........	84,07789 "
"	*Brunswic*........	.....,,..........	88,25558 "
"	*Cracow*	....,,..........	102,24593 "
"	*Denmark*........	....,,..........	86,83663 "
" *for dry malt*..........	*England*	....,,..........	82,52120 "
" *for barley*	*Finland*	....,,..........	126,28210 "
" *for oats*..........	...,,..........	....,,..........	140,31344 "
" *for rye*..........	...,,..........	....,,..........	112,25076 "
"	*Hamburg*........	....,,..........	89,81627 "
"	*Hanover*	....,,..........	84,73671 "
"	*Holland*........	....,,..........	85,13400 "
"	*Lübec*..........	....,,..........	91,00825 "
" *for oats*..........	...,,..........	....,,..........	106,89993 "
"	*Poland*..........	....,,..........	108,97152 "
"	*Portugal*........	....,,..........	92,06500 "
"	*Prussia*	....,,..........	112,29175 "
"	*Russia*	....,,..........	95,23280 "
"	*S. Gall*..........	....,,..........	2,06565 "
" *tillage*..........	*Lübec*..........	superficial	30,2028 acres.
" *woodland*..........	...,,..........	....,,..........	40,2703 "
Lathach..................	*Ancient Hebrews*	dry capacity ...	5,51150 bushels.
Latte.....................	*Angoulême*......	length........	4,54667 yards.
"	*Bordeaux*........	...,,..........	2,73103 "

Acre = 4840 square yards.   Bushel = 2150,42 cubic inches.   Cubic foot = 1728 cubic inches.
Gallon = 231 cubic inches   Mile = 1760 yards.   Pound = 7000 grains.   Yard = 36 inches.

NAME.	LOCALITY.	CHARACTER.	VALUE.	
Lawek....................	*Poland*.........	length.........	1,7	inches.
League	*England*	itinerary......	3.——	miles.
" *marine*.............	...,,.............	......,,...........	3,4284	"
Legger ; *for arrack*	*Amsterdam*......	liquid capacity	153,75160	gallons.
" "	*Batavia*.........	......,,.........	160.——	"
Legoa....................	*Brazil*.........	itinerary......	3,8365	miles.
"	*Portugal*........	....,,...........	3,8365	"
" *marine*.............	....,,........	....,,...........	3,4521	"
Legua ; *before* 1568	*Spain*...........	....,,...........	2,5943	"
" *of* 1718............	...,,........	....,,...........	3,9461	"
" *since* 1766..........	...,,.........	....,,...........	4,1508	"
" *common*..........	...,,........	....,,...........	3,4245	"
" *marine.*	...,,........	....,,...........	3,4590	"
Lehen ; *miners'*.............	*Prussia*	superficial......	0,0531	acres.
" "	*Saxony*	....,,...........	0,0474	"
Leib ; *for cheese*	*Appenzell*	weight.........	54,446429	pounds.
Lepton	*Ancient Greeks*..	....,,...........	0,18	grains.
Leuca, or Leuga............	*Ancient Gauls*...	itinerary......	1,3788	miles.
Leung....................	*China*..........	weight........	0,083333	pounds.
Li ; *new measure*	...,,.........	itinerary......	0,3458	miles.
" *old measure*............	...,,.........	....,,...........	0,3594	"
Libbra....................	*Barletta*........	weight........	1,865286	pounds.
" *peso grosso*..........	*Belluno*.........	....,,...........	1,139150	"
" *peso sottile*	...,,.........	....,,...........	0,664103	"
"	*Bergamo*........	....,,...........	1,797500	"
" *Italian lb. since* 1803.	...,,.........	....,,...........	2,204737	"
"	*Bologna*........	....,,...........	0,798406	"
" *apothecaries'*........	...,,.........	....,,...........	0,748257	"
"	*Brescia*.........	....,,...........	0,707757	"
" *new Italian*	...,,.........	....,,...........	2,204737	"
"	*Capua*	....,,...........	0,625286	"
"	*Corfu*..........	....,,...........	0,900419	"
"	*Cremona*........	....,,...........	0,681300	"
"	*Ferrara*.........	....,,...........	0,762571	"
"	*Florence*........	....,,...........	0,748513	"
"	*Forli*..........	....,,...........	0,726286	"
"	*Gaëta*	....,,...........	0,650429	"
" *peso grosso*	*Genoa*.........	....,,...........	0,769063	"
" *peso scarso*..........	...,,.........	....,,...........	0,700209	"
" *apothecaries'*	...,,.........	....,,...........	0,698903	"
" *of Venice*............	*Ionian Isles*......	....,,...........	1,051857	"
" *for gold, etc*........	...,,.........	....,,...........	0,701243	"

Acre = 4840 square yards.   Bushel = 2150,42 cubic inches.   Cubic foot = 1728 cubic inches.
    Gallon = 231 cubic inches.   Mile = 1760 yards.   Pound = 7000 grains.   Yard = 36 inches.

NAME.	LOCALITY.	CHARACTER.	VALUE.
Libbra; *new standard*......	*Ionian Isles*......	weight........	1.—— pounds.
" *new lb. of 1803*	*Italy*............	....,,...........	2,204747 "
"	*Leghorn*........	....,,........	0,748643 "
" *della commissione*....	*Lucca*...........	....,,........	0,751857 "
" *della grascia*	...,,........	....,,........	0,738629 "
"	*Messina*........	....,,........	0,707229 "
" *peso grosso*..........	*Milan*..........	....,,........	1,682058 "
" *peso sottile; apoth. etc.*	...,,........	....,,........	0,720882 "
" *new Italian lb*.......	...,,........	....,,........	2,204747 "
"	*Modena*........	....,,........	0,704414 "
"	*Naples*........	....,,........	0,707220 "
" *peso grosso*..........	*Padua*........	....,,........	1,072663 "
" *peso sottile*..........	...,,........	....,,........	0,747229 "
"	*Palermo*........	....,,........	0,700207 "
"	*Parma*........	....,,........	0,719715 "
" *for oil and honey*.....	*Patras*........	....,,........	6,755 "
"	*Placentia*........	....,,........	0,701143 "
"	*Ravenna*	....,,........	0,660514 "
"	*Reggio*........	....,,........	0,716571 "
"	*Roman States*....	....,,........	0,747560 "
" *peso grosso*..........	*Rovigo*..........	....,,........	1,052379 "
" *peso sottile*	...,,........	....,,........	0,664544 "
"	*Sardinia*	....,,........	0,896286 "
" *legat*............	*Sicily*........	....,,........	0,707229 "
" *Sicilian lb*..........	...,,........	....,,........	0,700156 "
"	*Sienna*........	....,,........	0,708943 "
"	*Sinigaglia*......	....,,........	0,743036 "
"	*Syracuse*........	....,,........	0,720571 "
" *peso grosso*..........	*Treviso*........	....,,........	1,139250 "
" *peso sottile*	...,,........	....,,........	0,747226 "
"	*Turin*	...,,........	0,813332 "
" *apothecaries'*........	...,,........	....,,........	0,677714 "
"	*Tuscany*........	....,,........	0,748643 "
" *peso grosso*..........	*Venice*	....,,........	1,052750 "
" *peso sottile; apoth. etc.*	...,,........	....,,........	0,665886 "
" *new standard*........	...,,........	....,,........	2,204747 "
" *peso grosso*..........	*Verona*........	....,,........	1,101986 "
" *peso sottile*	...,,........	....,,........	0,734657 "
" *peso grosso*..........	*Vicenza*........	....,,........	1,072663 "
" *peso sottile*	...,,........	....,,........	0,747229 "
Libra................	*Acapulco*........	....,,........	1,014286 "
"	*Ancient Romans*.	....,,........	0,721897 "

Acre = 4840 square yards. Bushel = 2150,42 cubic inches. Cubic foot = 1728 cubic inches.
Gallon = 231 cubic inches. Mile = 1760 yards. Pound = 7000 grains. Yard = 36 inches.

NAME.	LOCALITY.	CHARACTER.	VALUE.
Libra; *mayor*	*Alicant*	weight	1,177393 pounds.
" *menor; for spices*	...,,,	...,,,	0,784929 "
" *for chocolate*	...,,,	...,,,	1,046571 "
" *pensil*	*Aragon*	...,,,	0,771700 "
"	*Asturias*	...,,,	1,524146 "
"	*Balearic I.*	...,,,	0,882 "
"	*Barcelona*	...,,,	0,882 "
"	*Bilbao*	...,,,	1,078800 "
"	*Callao*	...,,,	1,014286 "
"	*Canary I.*	...,,,	1,014843 "
"	*Caraccas*	...,,,	1,014286 "
"	*Castille*	...,,,	1,016097 "
"	*Catalonia*	...,,,	0,882 "
" *gallega*	*Gallicia*	...,,,	1,270123 "
" *sutil*	...,,,	...,,,	1,016286 "
"	*Gibraltar*	...,,,	1,0175 "
" *English*	...,,,	...,,,	1.—— "
"	*Guatemala*	...,,,	1,014286 "
"	*Madeira*	...,,,	1,010929 "
"	*Madrid*	...,,,	1,016097 "
" *menor*	*Minorca*	...,,,	0,882 "
"	*Mexico*	...,,,	1,014286 "
"	*Montevideo*	...,,,	1,014286 "
"	*Saragossa*	...,,,	0,7717 "
"	*Seville*	...,,,	1,015337 "
" *apothecaries'*	*Spain*	...,,,	0,761500 "
" "	*Sweden*	...,,,	0,785590 "
"	*Tortosa*	...,,,	0,671714 "
" *menor*	*Valencia*	...,,,	0,784887 "
" *gruesa; for leather, fish*	...,,,	...,,,	1,177331 "
" *for bread*	...,,,	...,,,	2,354662 "
"	*Valparaiso*	...,,,	1,014286 "
"	*Vera Cruz*	...,,,	1,015337 "
" *for oil*	*Spain*	liquid capacity	0,13278 gallons.
Libreta	*Valencia*	weight	0,784887 pounds.
Lichas	*Ancient Greeks*	length	7,5858 inches.
Liespfund	*Berlin*	weight	17,020570 pounds.
" *old measure*	...,,,	...,,,	14,463075 "
"	*Bremen*	...,,,	15,386840 "
"	*Brunswic*	...,,,	14,418960 "
"	*Courland*	...,,,	18,431601 "
"	*Hamburg*	...,,,	14,948116 "

Acre = 4840 square yards. Bushel = 2150,42 cubic inches. Cubic foot = 1728 cubic inches.
Gallon = 231 cubic inches. Mile = 1760 yards. Pound = 7000 grains. Yard = 36 inches.

NAME.	LOCALITY.	CHARACTER.	VALUE.	
Liespfund ; *wagon freight*...	*Hamburg*........	weight........	17,086712	pounds
"	*Hanover*	....,,..........	15,102448	"
"	*Holstein*.........	....,,..........	14,948116	"
" *sea freight*	*Lübec*...........	....,,..........	14,962416	"
" *wagon freight*...	...,,.............	....,,..........	17,099904	"
"	*Mecklenburg*.....	....,,..........	15,686328	"
"	*Oldenburg*.......	....,,..........	15,477254	"
Lieue ; *old measure*........	*Brabant*........	itinerary......	3,4522	miles.
"	*Flanders*........	....,,..........	3,9005	"
" *de poste*...........	*France*..........	....,,..........	2,4222	"
" *marine*	...,,...........	....,,..........	3,4521	"
"	...,,...........	....,,..........	2,7617	"
"	...,,...........	....,,...•.....	3,1069	"
Ligne ; *de Paris*............	...,,...........	length........	0,0888	inches.
"	*Lausanne*.......	...,,..........	0,1181	"
"	*Nancy*........	...,,..........	0,1127	"
Ligula...................	*Ancient Romans.*	liquid capacity	0,00297	gallons.
"	...,,...........	dry capacity ...	0,00032	bushels.
Line...................	*England*........	length	0,1	inches.
" *artificers'*...........	...,,...........	...,,..........	0,0833	"
" *not used*.............	*United States*....	...,,..........	0,1	"
Linea.................	*Bologna*.........	...,,..........	0,1039	"
"	*Cagliari*........	...,,..........	0,0679	"
"	*Genoa*........	...,,..........	0,0681	"
"	*Madrid*........	...,,..........	0,0773	"
"	*Modena*........	...,,..........	0,1430	"
"	*Naples*........	...,,..........	0,0721	"
"	*Palermo*........	...,,..........	0,0647	"
"	*Rome*........	...,,..........	0,0814	"
"	*Turin*	...,,..........	0,0936	"
" *artificers'*...........	*Tuscany*	...,,..........	0,15	"
"	*Venice*.........	...,,..........	0,0942	"
Linha.................	*Portugal*........	...,,..........	0,0896	"
Linie...................	*Amsterdam*......	...,,..........	0,0921	"
"	*Baden*	...,,..........	0,1192	"
"	*Bavaria*........	...,,..........	0,0798	"
" *old measure*	*Berlin*...	...,,..........	0,0858	"
" *surveyors'*...........	...,,...........	...,,..........	0,1483	"
"	*Berne*........	...,,..........	0,0802	"
"	*Bohemia*........	...,,..........	0,0810	"
"	*Bremen*........	...,,..........	0,0791	"
"	*Brunswic*........	...,,..........	0,0780	"

Acre = 4840 square yards   Bushel = 2150,42 cubic inches.   Cubic foot = 1728 cubic inches.
Gallon = 231 cubic inches.   Mile = 1760 yards.   Pound = 7000 grains.   Yard = 36 inches.

NAME.	LOCALITY.	CHARACTER.	VALUE.	
Linie....................	Denmark........	length........	0,0858	inches.
"	Dresden..........	...,,,..........	0,0774	"
"	Gotha............	...,,,..........	0,0944	"
"	Hamburg........	...,,,..........	0,1036	"
"	Hanover.........	...,,,..........	0,0798	"
"	Hesse Darmstadt.	...,,,..........	0,0983	"
"	Lippe...........	...,,,..........	0,0792	"
"	Lübec...........	...,,,..........	0,0787	"
"	Nürnberg........	...,,,..........	0,0831	"
"	Oldenburg.......	...,,,..........	0,0802	"
"	S. Petersburg....	...,,,..........	0,0417	"
"	Sweden..........	...,,,..........	0,0810	"
"	Vienna..........	...,,,..........	0,0864	"
"	Weimar.........	...,,,..........	0,0774	"
" surveyors'..........	...,,,..........	...,,,..........	0,1110	"
"	Würtemberg.....	...,,,..........	0,1128	"
"	Zurich..........	...,,,..........	0,0824	"
Liniöw	Poland	...,,,..........	0,0787	"
Link; surveyors'...........	England.........	...,,,..........	7,92	"
" old measure.........	Scotland	...,,,..........	8,9280	"
Lippy..................	...,,,..........	dry capacity...	0,06386	bushels.
Lira....................	Ancona..........	weight........	0,729357	pounds.
" for gold and silver......	Malta...........	...,,,..........	0,698057	"
" for oil.................	Zante	liquid capacity	1,99015	gallons.
Liretta..................	Bergamo........	weight........	0,719	pounds.
Lispund.................	Denmark........	...,,,..........	17,615849	"
"	Norway.........	...,,,..........	17,615849	"
" viktualie-wigt.......	Sweden.........	...,,,..........	18,745680	"
" metall-wigt.........	...,,,..........	...,,,..........	14,996544	"
Liter	Abyssinia........	...,,,..........	0,687880	"
Litre	France..........	liquid capacity	0,26418	gallons.
"	...,,,..........	dry capacity...	0,02838	bushels.
Litron; de Paris...........	...,,,..........	...,,,..........	0,02307	"
Livre..................	Aix-en-Provence.	weight........	0,836	pounds.
" old measure	Amiens..........	...,,,..........	1,017286	"
"	Antwerp	...,,,..........	1,036668	"
"	Arles...........	...,,,..........	0,862671	"
"	Avignon.........	...,,,..........	0,901143	"
" apothecaries'; since 1811	Belgium.........	...,,,..........	0,826776	"
"	Besançon........	...,,,..........	1,064943	"
" old measure..........	Bordeaux........	...,,,..........	1,09	"
" new measure..........	...,,,..........	...,,,..........	1,102369	"

Acre = 4840 square yards. Bushel = 2150,42 cubic inches. Cubic foot = 1728 cubic inches. Gallon = 231 cubic inches. Mile = 1760 yards. Pound = 7000 grains. Yard = 36 inches.

NAME.	LOCALITY.	CHARACTER.	VALUE.
Livre....................	Bourbon I.	weight........	1,079219 pounds.
"	Bourges.........	...,,.........	1,032571 "
" commercial...........	Brussels.........	...,,.........	1,031143 "
" for gold and silver.....	...,,..........	...,,.........	1,084740 "
" metrical...............	...,,..........	...,,.........	2,204737 "
"	Cambrai.........	...,,.........	1,036286 "
"	Carpentras	...,,.........	0,881895 "
" metrical..............	France ; till 1840.	...,,.........	1,102369 "
" poids de marc..........	...,,....bef. 1800	...,,.........	1,079219 "
" for silk.............	...,,..........	...,,.........	1,011768 "
" de Charlemagne or esterlin	...,,...about 800	...,,.........	0,809464 "
" apothecaries'; old meas..	...,,..........	...,,.........	0,809514 "
" " new meas..	...,,... since 1837	...,,.........	1,102369 "
" current...............	Geneva	...,,.........	1,011816 "
"	...,,..........	...,,.........	1,214189 "
" old measure	Grenoble........	...,,.........	0,920186 "
" for cast-iron...........	...,,..........	...,,.........	1,218357 "
" of Savoy..............	...,,..........	...,,.........	1,216757 "
"	Guadeloupe......	...,,.........	1,079219 "
"	Haïti...........	...,,.........	1,079219 "
"	Lausanne........	...,,.........	1,102369 "
"	Liège...........	...,,.........	1,029871 "
" jewellers'..............	...,,..........	...,,.........	1,084913 "
" old measure...........	Limoges........	...,,.........	1,062514 "
"	Louvain	...,,.........	1,034614 "
" commercial...........	Lyons	...,,.........	0,944317 "
" for silk.............	...,,..........	...,,.........	1,011768 "
" poids de marc..........	...,,..........	...,,.........	1,079219 "
" commercial...........	Marseilles.......	...,,.........	0,899349 "
" "	Mons...........	...,,.........	1,026457 "
" jewellers'.............	...,,..........	...,,.........	1,034264 "
" old measure...........	Montpellier......	...,,.........	0,887259 "
"	Namur..........	...,,.........	1,023729 "
" old measure...........	Nancy..........	...,,.........	1,004714 "
" "	Nantes.........	...,,.........	1,090071 "
" commercial...........	Neufchâtel......	...,,.........	1,146710 "
" for gold, silver, etc.....	...,,..........	...,,.........	1,079219 "
" wholesale.............	Rouen	...,,.........	1,122378 "
" of Alsace ; old measure.	Strasburg	...,,.........	1,037711 "
" old measure	Toulouse	...,,.........	0,899430 "
" "	Tours...........	...,,.........	1,043857 "
" "	Troyes..........	...,,.........	1,146464 "

Acre = 4840 square yards. Bushel = 2150,42 cubic inches. Cubic foot = 1728 cubic inches. Gallon = 231 cubic inches. Mile = 1760 yards. Pound = 7000 grains. Yard = 36 inches.

NAME.	LOCALITY.	CHARACTER.	VALUE.	
Livre; *for oil*	*Marseilles*	liquid capacity	0,35214	gallons.
" "	*Tournay*	...,,.......	0,12569	"
Load *of hay*	*England*	weight	2016.——	pounds.
" *of straw*	...,,...	...,,......	1296.——	"
" *of timber*	...,,...	solid	50.——	cub. feet.
Löcher	*Brunswic*	dry capacity...	0,05528	bushels.
Lod	*Denmark*	weight	0,034403	pounds.
"	*Sweden*	...,,......	0,029290	"
Lof	*Riga*	...,,......	92,158007	"
" *minimum*	*Russia; Reval*...	dry capacity...	1,11894	bushels.
" *maximum*	...,,...*Riga* ..	...,,......	1,93793	"
" *mean of 5*	...,,...	...,,......	1,85450	"
Löffel; *for milk*	*Graubündten*	liquid capacity	0,08779	gallons.
Log	*Ancient Hebrews*	...,,......	0,14252	"
Lokiec	*Cracow*	length	0,64475	yards.
" *since* 1819	*Poland*	...,,......	0,62994	"
Lood; *old measure*	*Amsterdam*	weight	0,033996	pounds.
" *new measure*	...,,...	...,,......	0,022047	"
Looper	*Friesland*	dry capacity...	2,30032	bushels.
Lot	*Dunkirk*	liquid capacity	0,59739	gallons.
Loot	*Antwerp*	weight	0,032398	pounds.
Loth	*Aarau*	...,,......	0,032836	"
"	*Aix-la-Chapelle*..	...,,......	0,032178	"
"	*Appenzell*	...,,......	0,032224	"
"	*Augsburg*	...,,......	0,032527	"
"	*Bavaria*	...,,......	0,033071	"
"	*Berlin*	...,,......	0,032224	"
"	*Berne*	...,,......	0,035835	"
"	*Bremen*	...,,......	0,034346	"
"	*Brunswic*	...,,......	0,033206	"
"	*Cologne*	...,,......	0,032207	"
"	*Cracow*	...,,......	0,027896	"
"	*Dresden*	...,,......	0,032165	"
"	*Frankfort*	...,,......	0,034815	"
"	*Hamburg*	...,,......	0,033317	"
"	*Hanover*	...,,......	0,033733	"
"	*Hesse Cassel*	...,,......	0,033360	"
"	...,,...	...,,......	0,032229	"
"	*Hesse Darmstadt.*	...,,......	0,034449	"
"	...,,...	...,,......	0,032237	"
"	*Königsberg*	...,,......	0,032279	"
"	*Leipsic*	...,,......	0,032206	"

Acre = 4840 square yards.   Bushel = 2150,42 cubic inches.   Cubic foot = 1728 cubic inches.   Gallon = 231 cubic inches.   Mile = 1760 yards.   Pound = 7000 grains.   Yard = 36 inches.

NAME.	LOCALITY.	CHARACTER.	VALUE.
Loth	Lübec	weight	0,033398 pounds.
"	Mecklenburg	" ,,	0,033349 "
"	Nürnberg	" ,,	0,035135 "
" for gold and silver	" ,,	" ,,	0,032590 "
"	Prague	" ,,	0,035438 "
"	Rostock	" ,,	0,035014 "
"	S. Gall	" ,,	0,032285 "
"	S. Petersburg	" ,,	0,028178 "
"	Schaffhausen	" ,,	0,031692 "
"	Solothurn	" ,,	0,035722 "
"	Vienna	" ,,	0,038679 "
Lui	China	" ,,	2,43 grains.
Luong	An-nam	" ,,	0,086095 pounds.
Lutow ; old measure	Warsaw	" ,,	0,026026 "
" since 1819	" ,,	" ,,	0,027940 "
Ly	An-nam	" ,,	0,60 grains.
" commercial	" ,,	length	0,0256 inches.
" builders'	" ,,	" ,,	0,0192 "
"	" ,,	itinerary	0,2762 miles.
Lyspond ; old measure	Amsterdam	weight	16,337101 pounds.
Maat ; for salt	Amsterdam	dry capacity	1,74525 bushels.
" for grain	Rotterdam	" ,,	0,05931 "
"	Amsterdam	superficial	1,6728 acres.
Maatje ; legal	Holland	liquid capacity	0,02642 gallons.
" "	" ,,	dry capacity	0,00284 bushels.
Mace	Amboyna	weight	28,49 grains.
"	Borneo	" ,,	38,39 "
" mean of 11	Hindostan	" ,,	15,90 "
"	Japan	" ,,	56,88 "
"	Malacca	" ,,	44,83 "
" mean of 5	Sumatra	" ,,	38,88 "
"	Sooloo Islands	" ,,	58,33 "
Macūca ; for grain	Aleppo	" ,,	1256,7 pounds.
Madēga	Gondar	dry capacity	0,01146 bushels.
"	Massouah	" ,,	0,01389 "
Mäss	Aarau	" ,,	0,38056 "
"	Aix-la-Chapelle	" ,,	1,11123 "
"	Baireuth	" ,,	0,87943 "
" average	Bavaria	" ,,	0,46525 "
" " for oats	" ,,	" ,,	0,62534 "
"	Berne	" ,,	0,39760 "

Acre = 4840 square yards. Bushel = 2150,42 cubic inches. Cubic foot = 1728 cubic inches.
Gallon = 231 cubic inches. Mile = 1760 yards. Pound = 7000 grains. Yard = 36 inches.

NAME.	LOCALITY.	CHARACTER.	VALUE.	
Mäss	Fribourg	dry capacity ...	0,45311	bushels.
" for salt	Glaris	......,,........	2,61333	"
"	Gruyères........	......,,........	0,76554	"
"	Hesse Cassel....	......,,........	0,51421	"
" for coal..............	Hesse Darmstadt.	......,,........	17,73625	"
"	Ratisbon	......,,........	4,16107	"
" for oats.............	...,,....	......,,........	7,28180	"
" for salt.............	Schweitz........	......,,........	2,61333	"
"	Solothurn........	......,,........	0,37584	"
" for salt.............	Uri and Zurich..	......,,........	2,61333	"
Mässchen; legal...........	Berlin...........	......,,........	0,02438	"
" old measure.....	...,,....	......,,........	0,02290	"
" legal...........	Breslau........	......,,........	0,02438	"
"	Dresden.........	......,,........	0,04766	"
"	Frankfort	......,,........	0,01272	"
"	Gotha...........	......,,........	0,07744	"
" mean of 11......	Hesse Cassel....	......,,........	0,08931	"
"	Hesse Darmstadt.	......,,........	0,01419	"
"	Leipsic..........	......,,........	0,04766	"
"	Mannheim.......	......,,........	0,02463	"
"	Mentz	......,,........	0,01212	"
"	Nassau..........	......,,........	0,01212	"
" barley..........	Tréves or Trier ..	......,,........	0,05253	"
" oats	...,,....	......,,........	0,07311	"
" wheat..........	...,,....	......,,........	0,04730	"
"	Weimar.........	......,,........	0,13016	"
Mässel; old measure	Augsburg.... ...	......,,........	0,01139	"
" legal..............	Baden	......,,........	0,04257	"
" old measure	Breslau........	......,,........	0,03281	"
"	Prague	......,,........	0,18937	"
" for flour..........	Ratisbon	......,,........	0,18914	"
" for salt	...,,....	......,,........	0,37827	"
"	Würzburg	......,,........	0,03834	"
" for oats..........	...,,....	......,,........	0,05926	"
Mässlein..................	Augsburg........	......,,........	0,06572	"
"	Baden	......,,........	0,04257	"
" legal.............	Bavaria.........	......,,........	0,06572	"
"	Carlsruhe	......,,........	0,04257	"
"	Graubündten	......,,........	0,05311	"
"	Munich	......,,........	0,06572	"
"	Würtemberg.....	......,,........	0,03930	"
Mässli..................	Aarau.........	......,,........	0,03994	"

Acre = 4840 square yards. Bushel = 2150,42 cubic inches. Cubic foot = 1728 cubic inches.
Gallon = 231 cubic inches. Mile = 1760 yards. Pound = 7000 grains. Yard = 36 inches.

NAME.	LOCALITY.	CHARACTER.	VALUE.	
Mässli....................	Berne..........	dry capacity ...	0,19882	bushels.
" mean	Glaris and Schw.	.....,,,.........	0,03689	"
" "	S. Gall and Uri.	.....,,,.........	0,03689	"
" old measure..........	S. Gall........	.....,,,.........	0,93448	"
" mean	Zug and Zurich..	.....,,,.........	0,03991	"
Maille ; jewellers'...........	France..........	weight........	11,8	grains.
Main ; old measure..........	Antwerp........	.....,,,.........	28,35	"
Malaborong ; for prec. stones	Borneo..........	.....,,,.........	2,13	"
Mallal....................	Barcelona.......	.....,,,.........	3,98116	gallons.
Malter....................	Aarau..........	dry capacity ...	10,22460	bushels.
"	Aix-la-Chapelle..	.....,,,.........	4,20700	"
" for barley and oats...	.....,,,.........	.....,,,.........	6,31127	"
"	Baden	.....,,,.........	4,25674	"
" before 1816..........	Berlin	.....,,,.........	18,63768	"
"	Breslau..........	.....,,,.........	18,71643	"
"	Coblentz	.....,,,.........	4,54190	"
" old measure..........	Cologne.........	.....,,,.........	4,07341	"
" "	Dantzic.........	.....,,,.........	23,39397	"
"	Dresden.........	.....,,,.........	35,38200	"
"	Frankfort	.....,,,.........	3,25626	"
"	Gotha..........	.....,,,.........	4,95619	"
"	Hanover	.....,,,.........	5,30559	"
" mean of 13..........	Hesse Cassel.....	.....,,,.........	6,34362	"
" legal..............	Hesse Darmstadt.	.....,,,.........	3,63238	"
" old meas ; mean of 11.	.....,,,.........	.....,,,.........	5,92674	"
"	Leipsic.........	.....,,,.........	36,58520	"
"	Lucerne.........	.....,,,.........	15,77982	"
"	Mannheim......	.....,,,.........	2,92253	"
" barley and oats......	.....,,,.........	.....,,,.........	3,54629	"
" wheat.............	.....,,,.........	.....,,,.........	3,15225	"
"	Mentz..........	.....,,,.........	3,10398	"
"	Nassau.........	.....,,,.........	3,10398	"
"	Nürnberg.......	.....,,,.........	9,02818	"
" legal..	Prussia.........	.....,,,.........	18,71643	"
"	S. Gall	.....,,,.........	4,68805	"
" mean...............	Schweitz and Uri	.....,,,.........	9,44164	"
" "	Zug.....	.....,,,.........	10,21608	"
" "	Zurich.........	.....,,,.........	9,44164	"
" for lime...........	.....,,,.........	.....,,,.........	9,19674	"
"	Gotha..........	solid..........	36,065	cub. feet.
Mana....................	Mangalore......	weight........	23,244	pounds.
Mandel...................	Vienna....	.....,,,.........	0,90	grains.

Acre = 4840 square yards. Bushel = 2150,42 cubic inches. Cubic foot = 1728 cubic inches.
Gallon = 231 cubic inches. Mile = 1760 yards. Pound = 7000 grains. Yard = 36 inches.

NAME.	LOCALITY.	CHARACTER.	VALUE.
Maneh....................	*Ancient Hebrews.*	weight........	1,925166 pounds.
Mangal; *for pearls*........	*Madras*.........	...,,........	6.—— grains.
Manneswerk..............	*Zurich*..........	superficial.....	0,7182 acres.
Mannïkeh.................	*Masulipatan*.....	dry capacity...	0,06714 bushels.
Maon....................	*Bet-el-faki*......	weight........	2,039063 pounds.
"	*Bengal*.........	...,,.........	74,661217 "
"	*Bombay*.........	...,,.........	27,9984 "
"	*Calcutta*........	...,,.........	82,119838 "
"	*Calicut*.........	...,,.........	24,125 "
"	*Jidda*..........	...,,.........	1,830078 "
"	*Madras*.........	...,,.........	24,998568 "
"	...,,.........	liquid capacity	3,72323 gallons.
"	*Mysore*.........	weight........	24,274286 pounds.
"	*Pondichery*.....	...,,.........	25,901930 "
Maõney..................	*Madras*........	superficial......	0,0551 acres.
Mapp....................	*Anjar; Bombay*..	dry capacity...	0,22062 bushels.
Marc; *for gold and silver*....	*Belgium*........	weight........	0,542364 pounds.
"	*France; bef.* 1792	...,,.........	0,539609 "
"	...,,...1812 *to* '40	...,,.........	0,551184 "
"	...,,...*in* 800....	...,,.........	0,539643 "
"	*Geneva*.........	...,,.........	0,540601 "
" *for gold and silver*.....	*Neufchâtel*......	...,,.........	0,539609 "
" *commercial*........	...,,.........	...,,.........	0,573355 "
" *for gold and silver*....	*Solothurn*.......	...,,.........	0,539609 "
"	*Vaud; since* 1822	...,,.........	0,551184 "
Marcal; *for grain; mean*...	*Mysore*.........	...,,.........	25,375 "
"	*Madras*.........	dry capacity...	0,34884 bushels.
" *maximum*........	*Masulipatan*.....	...,,.........	0,40297 "
" *minimum*.........	*Pondichery*.....	...,,.........	0,10397 "
" *mean*..............	*E. Indies*.......	...,,.........	0,30971 "
Marco; *commercial*.........	*Aragon*........	weight........	0,514467 pounds.
" *for gold and silver*..	*Balearic I*......	...,,.........	0,507641 "
" " *old meas.*	*Bergamo*........	...,,.........	0,518113 "
" "	*Brazil*.........	...,,.........	0,505987 "
" "	*Catalonia*.......	...,,.........	0,592248 "
" "	*Chili*..........	...,,.........	0,507090 "
" "	*Dalmatia*.......	...,,.........	0,489086 "
" " *old meas.*	*Ferrara*........	...,,.........	0,518113 "
" "	*Illyria*.........	...,,.........	0,526107 "
" " *of Vienna*	...,,.........	...,,..	0,618870 "
"	*Ionian Isles*......	...,,.........	0,701243 "
"	*Italy; since* 1803.	...,,.........	2,204737 "

Acre = 4840 square yards. Bushel = 2150,42 cubic inches. Cubic foot = 1728 cubic inches.
Gallon = 231 cubic inches. Mile = 1760 yards. Pound = 7000 grains. Yard = 36 inches.

NAME.	LOCALITY.	CHARACTER.	VALUE.
Marco ; *for gold and silver*..	*Mantua*........	weight.........	0,518113 pounds.
" "	*Milan*.........	...,,..........	0,518113 "
" *commercial*.........	*Navarre*........	...,,..........	0,539369 "
" *for gold and silver*...	*Padua*.........	...,,..........	0,525830 "
" "	*Parma & Placent.*	...,,..........	0,525830 "
" "	*Peru*...........	...,,..........	0,507090 "
" "	*Portugal*.......	...,,..........	0,505930 "
" *for gold and silver*...	*Roman States*....	...,,..........	0,747560 "
" "	*Sardinia*........	...,,..........	0,542144 "
" "	*Spain*...........	...,,..........	0,507641 "
" *commercial*.........	...,,..........	...,,..........	0,508049 "
" "	*Tyrol*...........	...,,..........	0,618870 "
" "	*Valencia*........	...,,..........	0,508229 "
" "	*Venice*..........	...,,..........	0,525830 "
" "	*Verona*..........	...,,..........	0,525830 "
Margel....................	*Hamburg*........	liquid capacity	0,31966 gallons.
Mark ; *commercial*.........	*Aix-la-Chapelle*..	weight........	0,514852 pounds.
" *for gold and silver*...	...,,..........	...,,..........	0,515590 "
" "	*Antwerp*........	...,,..........	0,518290 "
" "	*Appenzell*.......	...,,..........	0,515306 "
" "	*Augsburg*........	...,,..........	0,520430 "
" "	*Austria, generally*	...,,..........	0,618870 "
" "	*Baden*..........	...,,..........	0,515115 "
" "	*Basel*..........	...,,..........	0,515306 "
" "	*Bavaria*.........	...,,..........	0,515306 "
" "	*Berne*..........	...,,..........	0,539609 "
" *commercial*.........	*Bremen*.........	...,,..........	0,549530 "
" *for gold and silver*...	...,,..........	...,,..........	0,515306 "
" "	*Brunswic*.......	...,,..........	0,515300 "
" "	*Cologne*.........	...,,..........	0,515306 "
" "	*Cracow*.........	...,,..........	0,447465 "
" *commercial*.........	*Denmark*........	...,,..........	0,518995 "
" *for gold and silver*...	...,,..........	...,,..........	0,515306 "
" *commercial*.........	*Frankfort*.......	...,,..........	0,557037 "
" *for gold and silver*...	...,,..........	...,,..........	0,515776 "
" "	*Friburg*.........	...,,..........	0,539609 "
" "	*Glaris*..........	...,,..........	0,517892 "
" *commercial*.........	*Hamburg*........	...,,,....	0,533943 "
" *for gold and silver*...	...,,..........	...,,..........	0,515306 "
" *commercial*.........	*Hanover*........	...,,..........	0,539722 "
" *for gold and silver*...	...,,..........	...,,..........	0,515306 "
" "	*Hesse C. and D.*	...,,..........	0,515306 "

Acre = 4840 square yards.   Bushel = 2150,42 cubic inches.   Cubic foot = 1728 cubic inches.
Gallon = 231 cubic inches.   Mile = 1760 yards.   Pound = 7000 grains.   Yard = 36 inches.

NAME.	LOCALITY.	CHARACTER.	VALUE.	
Mark ; *commercial*	*Holland*	weight	0,543937	pounds.
" *for gold and silver*	...,,....*old mea.*	....,,..........	0,542370	"
" " ...	...,,....*new..,,.*	....,,..........	2,204737	"
" " ...	*Holstein*	....,,..........	0,515306	"
" " ...	*Königsberg; o. m.*	....,,..........	0,516470	"
" " ...	*Lübec*	....,,..........	0,515306	"
" " ...	*Mecklenburg*	....,,..........	0,515306	"
" " ...,,	*Nassau*	....,,..........	0,515814	"
" *commercial*	*Nürnberg*	....,,..........	0,523857	"
" *for gold and silver* ...	....,,..........	....,,..........	0,515590	"
" " ...	*Oldenburg*	....,,..........	0,515306	"
" " ...	*Poland*	....,,..........	0,515306	"
" *jewellers'*	...,,...*Warsaw* ..	....,,..........	0,444714	"
" *for gold and silver* ...	*Prague; old meas.*	....,,..........	0,559397	"
" " ...	*Prussia ; gener'y.*	....,,..........	0,515590	"
" " ...	*Ratisbon*	....,,..........	0,542694	"
" " ...	*Riga ; old meas.* .	....,,..........	0,461	"
" " ...	*Saxony*	....,,..........	0,515306	"
" " ...	*Schweitz*	....,,..........	0,517892	"
" *commercial ; old meas.*	*Silesia*	....,,..........	0,451033	"
" *for gold and silver* ...	....,,..........	....,,..........	0,430806	"
" " ...	*Sweden*	....,,..........	0,468642	"
" " ...	*Vienna*	....,,..........	0,618870	"
" " ...	*Wilna ; old meas.*	....,,..........	0,428429	"
" " ...	*Würtemberg*	....,,..........	0,515306	"
" " ...	*Zurich*	....,,..........	0,517892	"
Marschrüthe	*Hamburg*	length	4,38641	yards.
Mascais	*Tauris*	weight	33,33	grains.
Mass	*Aarau*	liquid capacity	0,38042	gallons.
"	*Aix-la-Chapelle.*.	....,,.......	0,35136	"
"	*Appenzell*	....,,.......	0,34586	"
" *for wine ; old measure.*.	*Augsburg*	....,,.......	0,37724	"
" *for beer* " ..	....,,.......	....,,.......	0,24489	"
" *legal*	*Austria*	....,,.......	0,37381	"
" "	*Baden*	....,,.......	0,39627	"
" "	*Bavaria*	....,,.......	0,28241	"
"	*Basel*	....,,.......	0,37569	"
"	*Berne*	....,,.......	0,44144	"
" *of Moravia*	*Bohemia*	....,,.......	0,28241	"
"	*Brunswic*	....,,.......	0,494	"
" *old measure*	*Carlsruhe*	....,,.......	0,60893	"
" *for beer*	*Coblentz*	....,,.......	0,45438	"

Acre = 4840 square yards. Bushel = 2150,42 cubic inches. Cubic foot = 1728 cubic inches. Gallon = 231 cubic inches. Mile = 1760 yards. Pound = 7000 grains. Yard = 36 inches.

NAME.	LOCALITY.	CHARACTER.	VALUE.
Mass; *for oil*	*Coblentz*	liquid capacity	0,33683 gallons.
" *for wine*	..,,..	.....,,.......	0,37223 "
"	*Cologne*	.....,,.......	0,35110 "
" *alt-mass*	*Frankfort*	.....,,.......	0,47367 "
" *neu-mass*	..,,..	.....,,.......	0,42104 "
"	*Friburg*	.....,,.......	0,41265 "
"	*Glaris*	....,,......	0,47 "
"	*Gotha*	.....,,.......	0,24030 "
" *for oil*	..,,..	....,,..	0,13209 "
"	*Graubündten*	...,,....	0,35099 "
" *for wine*	*Hesse Cassel*	.....,,.......	0,52423 "
" *for beer*	..,,..	.....,,.......	0,57667 "
" *for wine*	*Hesse Darmstadt*	.....,,..	0,45932 "
" *for beer*	..,,..	.....,,.......	0,51673 "
" *old measure*	*Lausanne*	...,,..	0,26312 "
"	*Lucerne*	...,,..	0,45653 "
" *eich-mass*	*Mannheim*	.....,,.......	0,52677 "
" *wirths-mass*	..,,..	....,,..	0,44752 "
" *for wine*	*Mentz*	.....,,.......	0,44778 "
" *for beer and oil*	..,,..	.....,,.......	0,49824 "
"	*Moravia*	.....,,.......	0,28241 "
"	*Neufchâtel*	.....,,.......	0,503 "
" *schenk-mass; old meas.*	*Nürnberg*	.....,,.......	0,28505 "
" *visir-mass; old measure*	..,,..	.....,,.......	0,30302 "
"	*S. Gall*	.....,,.......	0,34665 "
" *for oil*	..,,..	.....,,.......	0,35844 "
"	*Solothurn*	.....,,.......	0,42115 "
"	*Strasburg*	.....,,.......	0,50748 "
"	*Thurgau*	.....,,.......	0,42190 "
"	*Tyrol*	.....,,.......	0,21372 "
"	*Uri*	.....,,.......	0,47949 "
"	*Vaud*	.....,,.......	0,35664 "
" *old measure*	*Vienna*	.....,,.......	0,38306 "
"	*Weimar*	.....,,.......	0,24196 "
" *hell-eichmass*	*Würtemberg*	.....,,.......	0,48529 "
" *schenk-mass*	..,,..	.....,,.......	0,44116 "
" *trüb-eichmass*	..,,..	.....,,.......	0,50652 "
" *lauter-mass*	*Zurich*	.....,,.......	0,48212 "
" *schenk-mass*	..,,..	.....,,.......	0,43379 "
" *for oil*	..,,..	.....,,.......	0,36325 "
"	*Altona*	dry capacity...	0,04677 bushels.
"	*Hamburg*	.....,,.......	0,04669 "

Acre = 4840 square yards. Bushel = 2150,42 cubic inches. Cubic foot = 1728 cubic inches.
Gallon = 231 cubic inches. Mile = 1760 yards. Pound = 7000 grains. Yard = 36 inches.

NAME.	LOCALITY.	CHARACTER.	VALUE.	
Mass; *for wheat and rye*	Nürnberg........	dry capacity ...	0,03529	bushels.
" *for barley and oats*....	....,,........	....,,........	0,03260	"
"	Weimar.........	....,,........	0,02952	"
" *for lime*	Würtemberg.....	....,,........	0,05213	,,
" *in mining*...........	Prussia.........	superficial	0,2124	acres.
" "	Saxony	....,,........	0,1896	"
Massel....................	Austria.........	dry capacity...	0,12003	bushels.
"	Bavaria.........	....,,........	0,13148	"
Masskänne	....,,......	liquid capacity	0,28241	gallons.
Mastello	Ferrara........	....,,........	14,64017	"
"	Padua.........	....,,........	18,83589	"
"	Rome.........	....,,........	21,693	"
"	Rovigo......	....,,........	27,68585	"
"	Venice........	....,,........	17,11873	"
"	Vicenza........	....,,........	30,08987	"
Matăro; *for oil*...........	Tripoli in Africa.	....,,........	6,163	"
Mau....................	An-nam	superficial.....	1,3201	acres.
Maund	Anjar; *prov*.....	weight........	26,229	pounds.
" *mean of 3*	Aurengabad; *prov*	....,,........	75,866667	"
"	Bassora.........	....,,........	116.——	"
" *for indigo, spices, etc.*	....,,......	....,,........	23.——	"
" *mean of 6*..........	Bengal; *prov*.....	....,,........	85,541833	"
"	Bet-el faki......	....,,........	2,039063	"
"	Bombay.........	....,,........	28.——	"
"	Bushire........	....,,........	7,683	"
" *bazar*............	Calcutta........	....,,........	82,133333	"
" *English factory*.....	....,,......	....,,........	74,666667	"
"	Calicut........	....,,........	34,7770	"
" *mean of 4.*.........	Calpee; *prov*....	....,,........	81,151750	"
" " 4..........	Carnatic..,,......	....,,........	25.——	"
" " 2..........	Deccan...,,.....	....,,........	79,78	"
"	Doab....,,.....	....,,........	24,686	"
"	Gambroon.......	....,,........	6,75	"
"	Goa	....,,........	24,75	"
" *mean of 32.*.........	Gujerat, *prov* ...	....,,........	39,739656	"
"	Jidda.........	....,,........	1,830078	"
"	Madras	....,,........	25.——	"
"	Mahratta; *dist*..	....,,........	26,249	"
" *mean of 9*	Malabar; *coast*..	....,,........	30,130111	"
" " 2	Malda; *prov*....	....,,........	100,45	"
" " 9..........	Malwah .,,......	....,,........	37,352222	"
" *for cotton; mean of 2.*	...,,............	....,,........	86,4745	"

Acre = 4840 square yards.   Bushel = 2150,42 cubic inches.   Cubic foot = 1728 cubic inches.
Gallon = 231 cubic inches.   Mile = 1760 yards.   Pound = 7000 grains.   Yard = 36 inches.

NAME.	LOCALITY.	CHARACTER.	VALUE.	
Maund	Masulipatan	weight	25.——	pounds.
" pucka	"	"	80.——	"
"	Mocha	"	3.——	"
"	Muscat	"	8,75	"
" mean of 5	Mysore; prov	"	25,8686	"
"	Orissa	"	75,625	"
"	Pondichery	"	25,9	"
"	Seringapatam	"	24,274	"
"	Sindh	"	74,666667	"
"	Sumatra	"	77.——	"
" for oil	Baroach; Gujerat	liquid capacity	5,51861	gallons.
" for sesame	"	dry capacity	0,59281	bushels.
"	Calcutta	"	1,44	"
" for oil	Madras	liquid capacity	3,24675	gallons.
Maunee; mean of 15	Malwah; prov	weight	456,2093	pounds.
Mauney	Madras	superficial	0,0551	acres.
Media-cana	Barcelona	length	0,84867	yards.
"	Majorca	"	0,85522	"
Media-tabla; for gold	Guinea	weight	20,03	grains.
"	Nigritia	"	30,86	"
Medïda	Rio Janeiro	liquid capacity	0,72828	gallons.
Medïmnos	Ancient Greeks	dry capacity	1,46973	bushels.
Medïo	Alicant	"	0,07282	"
"	Cadiz	"	0,06460	"
"	Valencia	"	0,06002	"
"	"	liquid capacity	0,38913	gallons.
Meile	Austria	itinerary	4,7141	miles.
" marine	"	"	1,1507	"
"	Baden	"	5,5234	"
"	Bavaria	"	4,6143	"
" of Anspach	"	"	5,3652	"
"	Belgium	"	3,4528	"
"	Bohemia	"	4,2938	"
"	"	"	5,7547	"
"	Brunswic	"	6,7520	"
"	Hamburg	"	4,6803	"
"	Hanover	"	6,3779	"
"	Holstein	"	4,6806	"
"	Hungary	"	5,1925	"
"	Lithuania	"	4,9958	"
"	Livonia	"	4,0622	"
" marine	Lübec	"	1,1520	"

Acre = 4840 square yards.   Bushel = 2150,42 cubic inches.   Cubic foot = 1728 cubic inches. Gallon = 231 cubic inches.   Mile = 1760 yards.   Pound = 7000 grains.   Yard = 36 inches.

NAME.	LOCALITY.	CHARACTER.	VALUE.	
Meile....................	Mecklenburg.....	itinerary.......	4,6806	miles.
"	Oldenburg.......	...,,..	6,1346	"
" since 1819.............	Poland..........	...,,...........	5,3031	"
" geographical..........	...,,...	...,,.........	4,6038	"
" since 1816.............	Prussia.........	...,,...........	4,68	"
" geographical..........	...,,...	...,,...........	4,6038	"
" polizei-meile..........	Saxony........	...,,........	5,6324	"
" post-meile.............	...,,...	...,,........	4,2220	"
"	Silesia.........	...,,.......	4,0260	"
"	Weimar.........	...,,.......	4,2292	"
"	Würtemberg.....	...,,........	4,6028	"
Meio.:....................	Azores..........	dry capacity....	0,17027	bushels.
"	Lisbon..........	....,,....... ..	0,19183	"
"	Madeira........	....,,........	0,2	"
"	Oporto.........	....,,........	0,24206	"
"	Rio Janeiro....	....,,........	0,19183	"
Mencăudée.............	Valenciennes....	....,,........	1,41890	"
"	Cambray.......	superficial......	0,8760	acres.
Mencault.................	Saint Quentin...	dry capacity...	0,07379	bushels.
Mengel...................	Amsterdam......	liquid capacity	0,32032	gallons.
" for beer.............	...,,...	....,,........	0,32454	"
"	Bremen........	....,,........	0,05319	"
" for beer.............	...,,...	....,,........	0,06227	"
"	Hamburg.......	....,,........	0,31966	"
Menu ; old meas. ; mean of 5	Languedoc......	length........	1,2287	inches.
" " mean of 3	Provence........	....,,........	1,2174	"
Mequîa.................	Lisbon.........	dry capacity....	0,02406	bushels.
Messklafter...............	Würtemberg.....	solid..........	119,583	cub. feet.
Mesure.................	Beaune.........	dry capacity...	0,41503	bushels.
"	Besançon.......	....,,........	0,66404	"
" for milk.............	Louvain........	liquid capacity	0,14530	gallons.
"	Arras..........	superficial.....	1,06	acres.
"	Burgundy.......	....,,........	0,1440	"
"	Saint Omer.....	....,,........	0,9760	"
Mesurée; old measure.......	Foix..........	....,,........	0,1557	"
Meta....................	Milan..........	dry capacity...	0,03243	bushels.
Metĭcal ; for pearls..........	Aleppo..........	weight........	73,85	grains.
"	Algiers.........	....,,........	72,06	"
"	Constantinople...	....,,........	74,25	"
"	Damascus.......	....,,........	69,21	"
" jewellers'..........	Tripoli in Africa.	...,,........	73,62	"
" for gold-dust......	......,,...	....,,........	63.—	"

Acre = 4840 square yards. Bushel = 2150,42 cubic inches. Cubic foot = 1728 cubic inches.
Gallon = 231 cubic inches. Mile = 1760 yards. Pound = 7000 grains. Yard = 36 inches.

NAME.	LOCALITY.	CHARACTER.	VALUE.	
Metĭcal....................	Tunis..........	weight.........	59,70	grains.
Metre	France..........	length........	1,09363	yards.
Metre cube or Stère........	...,,..........	solid..........	35,317	cub. feet.
Metrètes.	Ancient Greeks..	liquid capacity	10,26150	gallons.
Mettar ; for oil............	Tunis...........	.....,,........	5,12426	"
" for wine...........	..,,...........	.....,,........	2,56213	"
Metze ; old measure	Augsburg........	dry capacity ...	0,72909	bushels.
" legal..............	Bavaria.........	.....,,........	0,05167	"
" for wheat; mean of 19	...,,....old meas.	.....,,........	0,64294	"
" for oats; mean of 19..	...,,.......,,....	.....,,........	0,95454	"
" legal..............	Berlin..........	.....,,........	0,09748	"
" before 1816.........	...,,..........	.....,,........	0,09707	"
" old measure........	Breslau.........	.....,,........	0,13128	"
"	Buda and Pesth.	.....,,........	2,27066	"
" for wheat..........	Coburg..........	.....,,........	0,15776	"
" for oats	...,,...........	.....,,........	0,19580	"
" old measure	Dantzic.........	.....,,........	0,09138	"
"	Dresden.........	.....,,........	0,18428	"
"	Frankfort	.....,,........	0,40703	"
"	Gotha...........	.....,,........	0,30976	"
"	Hanover	.....,,........	0,29476	"
" standard	Hesse Cassel.....	.....,,........	0,28509	"
" maximum	.....,,....Hanau	.....,,........	0,43316	"
" mean of 23.........	.....,,........	.....,,........	0,28750	"
" mean of 4	Hesse Darmstadt.	.....,,........	0,48208	"
" old measure........	Königsberg	.....,,........	0,08627	"
"	Leipsic.........	.....,,........	0,18428	"
"	Linz...........	.....,,........	3,63083	"
"	Lippe...,,.......	.....,,........	0,20949	"
" for flour...........	.....,,........	.....,,........	0,05237	"
"	Nürnberg........	.....,,........	0,56426	"
" for barley and oats..	...,,...........	.....,,........	0,52175	"
" of Moravia	Prague	.....,,........	2,00343	"
" old measure	Ratisbon........	.....,,........	0,52014	"
" for salt	...,,...........	.....,,........	1,51311	"
"	Rostock.........	.....,,........	0,06399	"
"	Ulm............	.....,,........	0,27169	"
"	Vienna....	.....,,........	1,74512	"
"	Weimar.........	.....,,........	0,13650	"
Metze....................	Vienna..........	superficial	0,4739	acres.
Meuke....................	Antwerp	dry capacity ...	0,54627	bushels.
"	Mechlin.........	.....,,........	0,61368	"

Acre = 4840 square yards. Bushel = 2150,42 cubic inches. Cubic foot = 1728 cubic inches.
Gallon = 231 cubic inches. Mile = 1760 yards. Pound = 7000 grains. Yard = 36 inches.

NAME.	LOCALITY.	CHARACTER.	VALUE.	
Meytĕrée..................	*Bourg-en-Bresse.*	superficial......	0,9774	acres.
Mezzaruōla.............'......	*Genoa*	liquid capacity	39,21722	gallons.
Mezzĕtta..................	*Naples* and *Sicily*	dry capacity...	0,78352	bushels.
"	*Tuscany*	.....,,.......	0,02161	"
"	....,,...........	liquid capacity	0,15053	gallons.
"	*Verona*	weight.........	40,18	grains.
Mezzīno..................	*Corsica*	dry capacity....	2,12835	bushels.
Miam..................	*Malacca*	weight.........	44,83	grains.
"	*Singapore*........	.....,,.........	52.——	"
Migliăjo	*Leghorn*........	.....,,.........	748,6	pounds.
"	*Rome*...........	.....,,.........	747,56	"
"	*Venice*	superficial	0,7467	acres.
Miglio ; *since* 1803..........	*Austr. Lombardy.*	itinerary.......	0,6214	miles.
" *d' Italia*............	*Milan*	.....,,.........	1,1536	"
"	*Naples*..........	.....,,.........	1,1593	"
"	*Rome*...........	.....,,.........	0,9252	"
"	*Turin*...........	.....,,.........	1,5744	"
"	*Tuscany*	.....,,.........	1,0276	"
"	*Venice*	.....,,.........	1,1397	"
Miil	*Denmark*........	.....,,.........	4,68	"
Mijl ; *old measure*..........	*Holland*.........	.....,,.........	3,6394	"
" *marine*.............	....,,........	.....,,.........	3,4521	"
" *legal ; Netherlandic* ...	....,,........	.....,,.........	0,6214	"
Mil..................	*Sweden*.........	.....,,.........	6,6235	"
" *of Norway*.....	....,,........	.....,,.........	6,9216	"
Mile ; *legal*..............	*Great Britain*....	.....,,.........	1.——	"
" *marine*.............	....,,........	.....,,.........	1,1428	"
"	*Ireland*.........	.....,,.........	1,2727	"
"	*Scotland*	.....,,.........	1,1273	"
"	*United States*....	.....,,.........	1.——	"
" *of land*	*England* and *U. S.*	superficial......	640.——	acres.
Milha..................	*Portugal*........	itinerary.......	1,2788	miles.
" *marine*..............	....,,........	.....,,.........	1,1507	"
Milla..	*Spain*...........	.....,,.........	0,8648	"
" *marine*	....,,........	.....,,.........	1,1530	"
Mille ; *old measure*	*France* and *Belg.*	.....,,.........	1,2111	"
" *marine*..............	......,,........	.....,,.........	1,1507	"
" *metrical*..........	......,,........	.....,,.........	0,6214	"
Millerolle ; *for oil*	*Marseilles*.......	liquid capacity	15,74618	gallons.
"	*Tunis*...........	.....,,.........	16,99457	"
Milliărium..................	*Ancient Romans.*	itinerary.......	0,9192	miles.
Millier ; *old measure*........	*France*..........	weight........	1079,219	pounds.

Acre = 4840 square yards. Bushel = 2150,42 cubic inches. Cubic foot = 1728 cubic inches.
Gallon = 231 cubic inches. Mile = 1760 yards. Pound = 7000 grains. Yard = 36 inches.

NAME.	LOCALITY.	CHARACTER.	VALUE.	
Millier; metrique.........	France.........	weight.........	2204,844	pounds.
" for vineyards.......	Sardinia	superficial......	0,4255	acres.
Milligramme	France and Belg.	weight.........	0,015	grains.
Milligrämmow............	Poland.........	......,,..........	0,015	"
Millimètre	France and Belg.	length.........	0,0394	inches.
Miltre....................	Corfu..........	liquid capacity	0,18756	gallons.
Mina or Mna..............	Ancient Œgina..	weight.........	1,604304	pounds.
"	Ancient Attica...	......,,..........	0,962582	"
" old measure.........	Milan..........	liquid capacity	3,32653	gallons.
" since 1803...........	......,,..........	......,,........	2,64178	"
"	Florence and Leg.	dry capacity....	0,34577	bushels.
"	Genoa	......,,.........	3,42570	"
" since 1803...........	Milan	......,,.........	0,28378	"
"	Parma.........	......,,.........	0,66688	"
"	Pisa..........	......,,.........	0,34577	"
"	Placentia.......	......,,.........	0,49961	"
"	Turin..........	......,,.........	0,65297	"
Mine................	Dieppe.........	......,,.........	2,95321	"
"	Orleans.........	......,,.........	0,92288	"
" old measure..........	Paris	......,,.........	2,21491	"
" for oats.............	......,,.........	......,,.........	4,42982	"
" for salt.............	......,,.........	......,,.........	2,95321	"
" for charcoal..........	......,,.........	......,,.........	5,90642	"
"	Rouen	......,,.........	2,58406	"
"	Beauvais........	superficial	0,6307	acres.
Minée................	Angers.........	......,,.........	0,9774	"
Minĕlla................	Verona	dry capacity...	1,08498	bushels.
Minkel	Coblentz	......,,....	0,04209	"
Minot; old measure........	Paris	......,,.........	1,10746	"
"	Lower Canada..	......,,.........	1,11111	"
Minūto................	Naples.........	length.........	0,1730	inches.
"	Rome..........	......,,.........	0,1465	"
Miro; for oil..............	Venice.........	liquid capacity	4,02555	gallons.
Miscal	Bagdad	weight.........	72.——	grains.
"	Cairo..........	......,,.........	69,27	"
"	Calicut.........	......,,.........	66,7	"
"	Gambroon.......	......,,.........	71,75	"
"	Mocha.........	......,,.........	72.——	"
"	Smyrna........	......,,.........	74,36	"
Misūra	Corfu..........	dry capacity ...	0,59476	bushels.
"	Naples.........	......,,.........	0,06530	"
"	Ionian Isles......	superficial.....	0,2988	acres.

Acre = 4840 square yards. Bushel = 2150,42 cubic inches. Cubic foot = 1728 cubic inches.
Gallon = 231 cubic inches. Mile = 1760 yards. Pound = 7000 grains. Yard = 36 inches.

NAME.	LOCALITY.	CHARACTER.	VALUE.
Misurĕlla ; *for oil*	*Naples*	liquid capacity	0,02786 gallons.
Mitadĕlla	*Barcelona*	,,	0,24531 "
Mite; *disused*	*England*	weight	0,05 grains.
Mitja-canna	*Barcelona*	length	0,84867 yards.
Mitjëra	*Catalonia*	liquid capacity	1,96248 gallons.
Mitre	*Tunis*	,,	2,61455 "
Mocha	*Abyssinia*	weight	0,068571 pounds.
Modĭllo	*Sicily*	dry capacity	0,12152 bushels.
Modĭo	*Florence*	,,	5,53239 "
Modĭus	*Ancient Romans.*	,,	0,24496 "
Moggĭo	*Corfu* and *Paxos*	,,	4,77968 "
"	*Ferrara*	,,	17,76122 "
"	*Florence* and *Leg.*	,,	16,59035 "
"	*Ithaca*	,,	5.—— "
"	*Milan*	,,	4,15 "
"	*Padua*	,,	9,86987 "
"	*Venice*	,,	9,08104 "
" *for oil*	*Mantua*	liquid capacity	29,33377 gallons.
"	*Ionian Isles*	superficial	2,3995 acres.
"	*Naples*	,,	0,8584 "
" *mean*	*Piedmont*	,,	0,7881 "
Moio	*Lisbon*	dry capacity	23,02020 bushels.
Mole-vat	*Louvain*	,,	0,42567 "
Molster-vat	*Brussels*	,,	0,06919 "
Molt	*Oldenburg*	,,	7,76506 "
Mondĭno ; *for salt*	*Genoa*	,,	27,40265 "
Monkelzer	*Persia*	length	0,78359 yards.
Moo ; *for gold and silver*	*Pegu*	weight	2,375 grains.
Moon "	*Sindh*	,,	0,10 "
Moorah ; *carpentry*	*Trichinopoly*	length	0,94613 yards.
" *stone-cutting*	,,	,,	0,91713 "
Moosa	*Cyprus*	weight	112.—— pounds.
Morah ; *mean*	*Hindostan*	dry capacity	1,34639 bushels.
Morgen ; *old measure*	*Aix-la-Chapelle.*	superficial	0,7441 acres.
"	*Amsterdam*	,,	2,0076 "
" *Rhenish*	,,	,,	2,1031 "
"	*Antwerp*	,,	3,2248 "
"	*Baden*	,,	0,8896 "
" *legal; since* 1809	*Bavaria*	,,	0,8416 "
" " 1816	*Berlin*	,,	0,6309 "
" *old measure*	,,	,,	1,3655 "
" *of Silesia*	*Breslau*	,,	1,3825 "

Acre = 4840 square yards. Bushel = 2150,42 cubic inches. Cubic foot = 1728 cubic inches.
Gallon = 231 cubic inches. Mile = 1760 yards. Pound = 7000 grains. Yard = 36 inches.

NAME.	LOCALITY.	CHARACTER.	VALUE.	
Morgen..................	Brunswic.......	superficial......	0,6208	acres.
" old measure.........	Cologne.........	.....,,.........	0,7850	"
" "	Dantzic.........	.....,,.........	1,3722	"
"	Dresden.........	.....,,.........	0,3682	"
" tillage	Frankfort	.....,,.........	0,5004	"
" woodland...........	.....,,.........	.....,,.........	0.8045	"
"	Hamburg........	.....,,.........	2,3852	"
"	Hanover........	.....,,.........	0,6472	"
"	H. Cassel; Hanau	.....,,.........	0,5035	"
"	Hesse Darmstadt.	.....,,.........	0,6178	"
"	Leyden..........	.....,,.........	2,0022	"
"	Lippe..........	.....,,.........	0,6363	"
"	Lithuania.......	.....,,.........	1,7593	"
"	Nassau.........	.....,,.........	0,6178	"
" old measure, tillage ..	Nürnberg	.....,,.........	0,1677	"
" " woodland	...,,...........	.....,,.........	0,9341	"
"	Oldenburg......	.....,,.........	3,0904	"
"	Pomerania......	.....,,.........	1,5727	"
"	Würtemberg....	.....,,.........	0,7789	"
Morgow..................	Poland	.....,,.........	1,3829	"
Mötte	Marburg........	dry capacity ...	2,94506	bushels.
Motúreau.................	Nice...........	.....,,.........	0,07095	"
"	...,,...........	superficial	0,0193	acres.
Moule	Lausanne	solid...........	119,194	cub. feet.
Mouwer ; old mea., mean of 5	Holland........	dry capacity ...	3,88120	bushels.
Moyo.....................	Castille........	liquid capacity	67,93808	gallons.
"	Gallicia........	.....,,.........	42,46123	"
Muce.....................	French W. Indies	.....,,.........	0,03117	"
Mud.....................	Morocco........	dry capacity....	5,18372	bushels.
Mudde	Amsterdam......	.....,,.........	3,15725	"
" legal..............	Belgium........	.....,,.........	2,83782	"
" "	Holland........	.....,,.........	2,83782	"
" minimum...........	...,,...Deventer.	.....,,.........	2,30032	"
" maximum...........	...,,...Amersfort	.....,,.........	5,17011	"
" mean of 15........	...,,...........	.....,,.........	3,59218	"
Müdde ; old measure.......	Augsburg........	liquid capacity	14,92156	gallons.
Mudi.....................	Mangalore	dry capacity....	1,30188	bushels.
Mühlmassel..............	Vienna..........	.....,,.........	0,10907	"
Muid....................	Brussels........	.....,,.........	8,30199	"
"	Neufchâtel	.....,,.........	10,37578	"
"	Paris..........	.....,,.........	53,15789	"
" for oats...........	...,,...........	.....,,.........	106,31578	"

Acre = 4840 square yards. Bushel = 2150,42 cubic inches. Cubic foot = 1728 cubic inches.
Gallon = 231 cubic inches. Mile = 1760 yards. Pound = 7000 grains. Yard = 36 inches.

NAME.	LOCALITY.	CHARACTER.	VALUE.	
Muïd ; *for plaster*	*Paris*	dry capacity	26,57900	bushels.
" *for salt*	" ,,	,,	70,87779	"
" *for charcoal*	" ,,	,,	118,12864	"
" *for salt*	*Rochelle*	,,	34,05360	"
"	*Tremblade*	,,	68,10720	"
"	*Valais*	,,	0,11409	"
"	*Vaud*	,,	0,38310	"
"	*Bayonne*	liquid capacity	73,73088	gallons.
"	*Montpellier*	,,	160,73117	"
"	*Neufchâtel*	,,	96,58876	"
" *old meas. ; fined wine*	*Paris*	,,	70,85779	"
" ,, *on the lees*	" ,,	,,	73,81023	"
Munjändee ; *mean of 4*	*Travancore*	weight	3,90	grains.
Mutchkin	*Scotland*	liquid capacity	0,11191	gallons.
Muth ; *for lime*	*Munich*	dry capacity	25,24024	bushels.
" *for grain*	*Vienna*	,,	52,35360	"
Müthel ; *for lime*	" ,,	,,	4,37304	"
Mutsje	*Amsterdam*	liquid capacity	0,08008	gallons.
Mütt	*Aarau*	dry capacity	2,55615	bushels.
" *for barley and rye*	*Aix-la-Chapelle*	,,	6,66736	"
"	*Appenzell*	,,	2,59280	"
"	*Berne*	,,	4,77129	"
"	*Lucerne*	,,	3,94495	"
"	*S. Gall*	,,	2,344	"
"	*Schaffhausen*	,,	2,56573	"
"	*Solothurn*	,,	4,51	"
"	*Zurich*	,,	2,33042	"
Myriagramme	*France* and *Belg.*	weight	22,047370	pounds.
Myriamètre	" ,,	itinerary	6,2138	miles.
" carré	" ,,	superficial	24711,43	acres.
Mystron	*Ancient Greeks*	liquid capacity	0,00297	gallons.
"	" ,,	dry capacity	0,00032	bushels.
Nail	*England*	length	2,25	inches.
Nanki ; *for gold and silver*	*Madagascar*	weight	10.——	grains.
Nelli[9]	*Sumatra*	,,	29,333333	pounds.
Nello ; *for gold and silver*	*Pondichery*	,,	0,37	grains.
Nely	*Bengal*	,,	0,28	"
Nen	*An-nam*	,,	0,860950	pounds.
Ngu	" ,,	length	2,66442	yards.
Niou	*Siam*	,,	0,7882	inches.
Nonagëssis	*Ancient Romans*	weight	64,970743	pounds.

Acre = 4840 square yards. Bushel = 2150,42 cubic inches. Cubic foot = 1728 cubic inches.
Gallon = 231 cubic inches. Mile = 1760 yards. Pound = 7000 grains. Yard = 36 inches.

NAME.	LOCALITY.	CHARACTER.	VALUE.	
Nonŭncium...............	Ancient Romans..	weight........	0,541423	pounds.
Nonŭssis...............	....,,.......	....,,......	6,497074	"
Nössel.................	Brunswic........	liquid capacity.	0,12350	gallons.
"	Dresden.........	....,,.......	0,12371	"
" for beer...........	Erfurt...........	....,,.......	0,13512	"
" for wine...........	...,,...........	....,,.......	0,11153	"
"	Gotha...........	....,,.......	0,12015	"
"	Hamburg........	....,,.......	0,11954	"
"	Hanover	....,,.......	0,12839	"
"	Holstein........	....,,.......	0,11954	"
"	Leipsic.........	....,,.......	0,15904	"
" old measure........	Quedlinburg.....	....,,.......	0,11333	"
" for oil............	Weimar........	....,,.......	0,13498	"
"	...,,..........	....,,.......	0,12098	"
"	Gotha..........	dry capacity ...	0,01291	bushels.
"	Weimar........	....,,........	0,14757	"
Nowtăuk	Masulipatan.....	weight........	0,078125	pounds.
Nuggah................	Bellary..........	....,,.......	315,98	"
Nusfiah................	Mocha..........	liquid capacity	0,24992	gallons.
"	Tripoli in Africa.	dry capacity...	1,00552	bushels.
Obole ; esterlin..........	France; A. D. 800	weight........	11,80	grains.
Obŏlo.................	Roman States....	....,,.......	9,08	"
Obŏlos	Ancient Œgina..	....,,.......	18,717	"
"	...,,....Attica ..	....,,.......	11,230	"
"	...,,....Eubœa ..	....,,.......	15,597	"
Obŏlus................	...,,......Romans.	....,,.......	8,773	"
Occa.................	Bucharest	....,,.......	2,828571	pounds.
"	...,,..........	liquid capacity	0,39	gallons.
"	...,,..........	dry capacity ...	0,04191	bushels.
Occha................	Moldavia........	weight........	2,866158	pounds.
Ochăva ; commercial.......	Spain..........	....,,.......	56,44	grains.
Ochavĭllo..............	Castille.........	dry capacity ...	0,00208	bushels.
Ochăvo...............	...,,..........	....,,.......	0,00833	"
Octăva	Cadiz	length........	4,1094	inches.
Octogĕssis	Ancient Romans..	weight........	57,751771	pounds.
Octŭssis..............	...,,..........	....,,.......	5,775177	"
Oder.................	Majorca.........	....,,.......	100,217784	"
Ohm.................	Baden	liquid capacity.	39,62670	gallons.
"	Basel..........	....,,.......	13,44589	"
"	Berlin..........	....,,.......	49,81965	"
"	Bremen.........	....,,.......	38,29651	"

Acre = 4840 square yards. Bushel = 2150,42 cubic inches. Cubic foot = 1728 cubic inches. Gallon = 231 cubic inches. Mile = 1760 yards. Pound = 7000 grains. Yard = 36 inches.

NAME.	LOCALITY.	CHARACTER.	VALUE.	
Ohm..................	*Brunswic........*	liquid capacity	39,52016	gallons.
"	*Cologne........*	.........,,.........	36,51486	"
"	*Frankfort......*	.........,,.........	37,89104	"
"	*Hesse Cassel.....*	.........,,.........	46,13328	"
"	*Hesse Darmstadt.*	.........,,.........	41,33857	"
"	*Lippe..........*	.........,,.........	39,26490	"
"	*Lucerne........*	.........,,.........	13,69618	"
" *large*............	*Mannheim......*	.........,,.........	42,14168	"
" *small*............	....,,.........	.........,,.........	25,28500	"
"	*Mecklenburg.....*	.........,,.........	38,27410	"
"	*Strasburg........*	.........,,.........	12,17749	"
Oïphi..................	*Ancient Egypt...*	.........,,.........	0,28504	"
"	....,,.........	dry capacity...	0,03062	bushels.
Oka..................	*Alexandria......*	weight.........	2,705653	pounds.
"	*Cairo.........*	....,,.........	2,777143	"
"	*Candia.........*	....,,.........	2,649212	"
"	*Cyprus.........*	....,,.........	2,797143	"
"	*Constantinople...*	....,,.........	2,828571	"
"	*Greece.........*	....,,.........	3,371429	"
"	*Hungary........*	....,,.........	2,778023	"
"	....,,.........	dry capacity...	0,04684	bushels.
"	*Patras.........*	weight.........	2,643429	pounds.
"	*Smyrna........*	....,,.........	2,812488	"
" *retail*............	....,,.........	....,,.........	2,813918	"
"	*Tripoli in Syria..*	....,,.........	2,670476	"
Oke..................	*Aleppo.........*	....,,.........	2,813489	"
"	*Bagdad.........*	....,,.........	2,742857	"
"	*Ionian Isles......*	....,,.........	2,699800	"
"	*Ragusa.........*	....,,.........	2,952833	"
"	*Tripoli in Africa.*	....,,.........	2,742857	"
"	*Candia.........*	liquid capacity	0,34581	gallons.
Okshoofd............	*Amsterdam......*	.........,,.........	61,50060	"
Olla.................	*Gallicia........*	.........,,.........	2,65383	"
Ollock..............	*Madras.........*	dry capacity...	0,00545	bushels.
Omer.................	*Ancient Hebrews.*	.........,,.........	0,11023	"
Onça.................	*Portugal........*	weight.........	0,063241	pounds.
Once................	*Brussels.........*	liquid capacity	0,00559	gallons.
" *esterlin*............	*France ; A.D.*800	weight........	0,067470	pounds.
" *poids de marc*........	....,,.........	....,, ...	0,067451	"
" *for gold and silver*......	....,,....1812 *to* '40	....,,.........	0,068893	"
" *apothecaries'; old measure*	....,,.........	....,,.........	0,067451	"
" " *new measure*	....,,.........	....,,.........	0,070551	"

Acre = 4840 square yards. Bushel = 2150,42 cubic inches. Cubic foot = 1728 cubic inches.
Gallon = 231 cubic inches. Mile = 1760 yards. Pound = 7000 grains. Yard = 36 inches.

NAME.	LOCALITY.	CHARACTER.	VALUE.
Once.....................	*Geneva*	weight.........	0,067451 pounds.
"	*Lausanne*........	....,,..........	0,068898 "
"	*Neufchâtel*	....,,..........	0,071669 "
Oncïa..	*Bologna*.........	....,,..........	0,066534 "
" *apothecaries'*	....,,.........	....,,..........	0,062356 "
"	*Cagliari*	....,,..........	0,073305 "
"	*Florence*........	....,,..........	0,062376 "
"	*Genoa*	....,,..........	0,064089 "
"	..,,.............	....,,..........	0,058351 "
"	*Lucca*..........	....,,..........	0,068379 "
" *for gold and silver*.....	*Malta*..........	....,,..........	0,054533 "
"	..,,.............	....,,..........	0,058174 "
"	*Milan*	....,,..........	0,060074 "
"	..,,.............	....,,..........	0,064804 "
"	*Modena*.........	....,,..........	0,058701 "
"	*Naples*	....,,..........	0,058935 "
"	*Palermo*.........	....,,..........	0,058350 "
"	*Parma*..........	....,,..........	0,059976 "
" *for gold and silver*.....	*Ragusa*.	....,,..........	0,060195 "
"	*Rome*	....,,..........	0,062297 "
" *for gold and silver*.....	..,,.............	....,,..........	0,064768 "
"	*Turin*..........	....,,..........	0,067778 "
" *apothecaries'*.........	..,,.............	....,,..........	0,056461 "
"	*Venice*.........	....,,..........	0,087729 "
"	..,,.............	....,,..........	0,055490 "
" *metrical*.............	*Venit. Lombardy*.	....,,..........	0,220474 "
"	*Carrara*........	length	0,8 inches.
"	*Malta*..........	....,,..........	0,8560 "
"	*Milan*	....,,..........	1,9242 "
"	*Naples* and *Nice*.	..,,..........	0,8651 "
"	*Parma*..........	....,,..........	1,7831 "
"	*Rome*	....,,..........	0,7330 "
"	*Turin*..........	....,,..........	1,6855 . "
Onza.....................	*Canary I*........	....,,..........	0,7992 "
"	*Valencia*........	....,,..........	0,9920 "
"	*Canary I*.......	weight.........	0,063320 pounds.
"	*Castille*.........	....,,..........	0,063506 "
Onz.....................	*Amsterdam*......	....,,..........	0,067992 "
" *Troy*..................	....,,...........	....,,..........	0,067796 "
" *Netherlandic; legal*......	....,,...........	....,,..........	0,220474 "
Ootan ; *for camphor*.........	*Sumatra*	....,,.........	4.——— "
Ora.....................	*England ; in* 1000	....,,..........	0,064286 "

Acre = 4840 square yards. Bushel = 2150,42 cubic inches. Cubic foot = 1728 cubic inches.
Gallon = 231 cubic inches. Mile = 1760 yards. Pound = 7000 grains. Yard = 36 inches.

NAME.	LOCALITY.	CHARACTER.	VALUE.	
Orbah....................	*Tripoli in Africa.*	dry capacity...	0,19040	bushels.
Orcïo ; *for oil*..............	*Florence*	liquid capacity	8,83147	gallons.
Orgūia ; *Olympic*...........	*Ancient Greeks.*.	length.........	2,02287	yards.
" *Philetairic*	.....,,.........	..,,..........	2,31552	"
" *Pythic*............	.....,,.........	..,,..........	1,62050	"
Orlong	*Malacca*	superficial......	1,3223	acres.
Orna ; *old measure*	*Trieste*..........	liquid capacity	17,34769	gallons.
"	..,,.............	....,,.........	14,95248	"
Ort.....................	*Bremen*	weight........	15,03	grains.
" *commercial*..............	*Denmark* and *N'y*	...,,.........	15,05	"
" *gold and silver*	.....,,.........	..,,..........	14,19	"
"	*Lippe*..........	liquid capacity	0,09089	gallons.
"	*Lübec*..........	....,,.........	0,06188	"
"	*Luneburg*.......	....,,.........	0,06419	"
" *for wine*	*Oldenburg*	...,,.........	0,09702	"
" *for beer*..............	...,,.........	....,,.........	0,09042	"
"	*Osnabrück*	...,,.........	0,08057	"
" *legal*.................	*Rostock*.........	...,,.........	0,05977	"
"	*Sweden*.........	....,,.........	0,02157	"
"	..,,.............	dry capacity ...	0,00232	bushels.
Oertchen...................	*Hanover*	weight........	14,76	grains.
"	*Holstein*.........	...,,.........	14,60	"
Orthodōron	*Ancient Greeks.*.	length.........	8,3443	inches.
Oertlein	*Revel*	weight........	12,99	grains.
"	*Riga*	...,,.........	12,73	"
Osmin ; *legal*..............	*S. Petersburg*....	dry capacity...	2,876	bushels.
"	*Lithuania*.......	....,,.........	1,59882	"
Osmūschka...............	*Russia*..........	liquid capacity	0,40605	gallons.
Ocssel	*Berlin*	...,,.........	0,15122	"
"	*Bremen*	...,,.........	0,10625	"
"	*Lübec* and *Rost'k*	....,,.........	0,11954	"
Ottávo...................	*Bologna*	weight........	0,008317	pounds.
"	*Florence*.........	...,,.........	0,38	grains.
"	*Turin*...........	...,,.........	0,008471	pounds.
"	*Genoa*	dry capacity ...	0,42821	bushels.
Ottïngar..................	*Finland*.........	liquid capacity	4,14759	gallons.
Ottïngkar.................	*Denmark* and *N'y*	dry capacity....	0,06170	bushels.
Ounce ; *Tower*	*England, in* 1500	weight........	0,064286	pounds.
" *imperial*............	..,,..*since* 1825	...,,.........	0,0625	"
" *apothecaries'*........	..,,..and *U. S.*	...,,.........	0,068571	"
" *avoirdupois ; old m.*.	..,,......,,....	...,,.........	0,0625	"
" *Troy*	..,,......,,....	...,,.........	0,068571	"

Acre = 4840 square yards. Bushel = 2150,42 cubic inches. Cubic foot = 1728 cubic inches. Gallon = 231 cubic inches. Mile = 1760 yards. Pound = 7000 grains. Yard = 36 inches.

NAME.	LOCALITY.	CHARACTER.	VALUE.	
Ounce; *Troy*	*Scotland*	weight	0,068490	pounds.
" *old Tron*	..,,	..,,	0,089319	"
" *Glasgow Tron*	..,,	..,,	0,087889	"
Outâva ; *for topazes*	*Brazil*	..,,	0,008167	"
"	*Lisbon*	..,,	0,007905	"
"	..,,	dry capacity	0,04796	bushels.
Ouvrée *or* Œuvre ; *mean of 7*	*France*	superficial	0,1071	acres.
"	*Geneva*	..,,	0,0944	"
" *for vineyards*	*Neufchâtel*	..,,	0,0870	"
Oxehoved	*Copenhagen*	liquid capacity	59,28942	gallons.
Oxhoft ; *new measure*	*Berlin*	..,,	54,43914	"
"	*Brunswic*	..,,	59,28024	"
"	*Courland*	..,,	62,49131	"
"	*Dresden*	..,,	53,43	"
"	*Erfurt*	..,,	56,21708	"
" *of Thuringia*	..,,	..,,	53,38773	"
"	*Hamburg*	..,,	57,22098	"
"	*Hanover*	..,,	62,15928	"
" *for brandy*	*Leipsic*	..,,	60,11529	"
" *for wine*	..,,	..,,	53,43581	"
"	*Lippe*	..,,	58,89732	"
"	*Lübec*	..,,	59,36076	"
"	*Oldenburg*	..,,	60,49676	"
"	*Rostock*	..,,	57,38221	"
" *old measure*	*Warsaw*	..,,	59,84080	"
Oxhufwud	*Sweden*	..,,	62,19804	"
Oxybaphon	*Ancient Greeks*	..,,	0,01782	"
"	..,,	dry capacity	0,00191	bushels.
Pace	*England* and *U.S.*	itinerary	60.——	inches.
" *military*	*United States*	..,,	54.——	"
Pacho	*Casal*	dry capacity	6,91543	bushels.
Pachys metrios	*Babylon*	length	0,50572	yards.
"	*Ancient Greeks*	..,,	0,50572	"
" *Philetairic*	..,,	..,,	0,57888	"
Pack ; *of wool*	*England*	weight	240.——	pounds.
Packen	*S. Petersburg*	..,,	1082,0292	"
Pägel	*Denmark*	liquid capacity	0,06380	gallons.
"	*Rostock*	..,,	0,05979	"
"	*Stralsund*	..,,	0,06419	"
Pagliâzza	*Cephalonia*	..,,	1,99015	"
Pagôda; *gold etc.; mean of 13*	*East Indies*	weight	53,514	grains.

Acre = 4840 square yards. Bushel = 2150,42 cubic inches. Cubic foot = 1728 cubic inches.
Gallon = 231 cubic inches. Mile = 1760 yards. Pound = 7000 grains. Yard = 36 inches.

NAME.	LOCALITY.	CHARACTER.	VALUE.	
Pagŏda; *maximum*	E.Indies; Madura	weight	56,01	grains.
" *minimum*	...,, ...Madras	....,,	52,56	"
Pahaw; *for precious stones*	Borneo	....,,	0,021943	pounds.
Pakha	Sumatra	dry capacity	0,01561	bushels.
"	...,,	liquid capacity	0,14535	gallons.
Palāista	Ancient Greeks	length	3,0343	inches.
Paletz	S. Petersburg	....,,	0,5	"
Palgat; *mean*	E. Indies	....,,	1.——	"
Pallie	Calcutta	dry capacity	0,11689	bushels.
Palm; *ship-building*	Altona	length	3,7592	inches.
" "	Amsterdam	....,,	3,7148	"
" *Netherlandic; legal*	...,,	....,,	3,9370	"
" *ship-building*	Bergen	....,,	3,4895	"
"	England and U.S.	....,,	3.——	"
" *ship-building*	Hamburg	....,,	3,7598	"
"	Masulipatan	....,,	3,1875	"
Palme; *legal*	Belgium	....,,	3,9370	"
"	Montpellier	....,,	8,7073	"
Palmïpes	Ancient Romans	....,,	0,40444	yards.
Palmo	Alicant	....,,	8,9080	inches.
"	Aragon	....,,	7,5888	"
"	Bahia	....,,	8,5592	"
"	Cagliari	....,,	9,7783	"
" *marble-work*	Carrara	....,,	9,5919	"
" *mayor*	Castille	....,,	8,2188	"
" *menor*	....,,	....,,	2,7396	"
"	Florence and Leg	....,,	11,4884	"
"	Genoa	....,,	9,8070	"
" *da craveira*	Lisbon	....,,	8,6616	"
Palmo; *commercial*	...,,	....,,	8,9750	"
" *da Junta; shipping*	...,,	....,,	7,8822	"
"	Majorca	....,,	7,6970	"
"	Malta	....,,	10,2758	"
"	Messina	....,,	10,4	"
"	Naples	....,,	10,3810	"
"	Nice	....,,	10,4181	"
"	Palermo	....,,	9,3128	"
"	Pisa	....,,	11,4844	"
"	Rio Janeiro	....,,	8,5592	"
" *commercial*	Rome	....,,	9,8034	"
" *clothiers'*	...,,	....,,	8,3470	"
"	Sardinia	....,,	10,3348	"

Acre = 4840 square yards. Bushel = 2150,42 cubic inches. Cubic foot = 1728 cubic inches.
Gallon = 231 cubic inches. Mile = 1760 yards. Pound = 7000 grains. Yard = 36 inches.

NAME.	LOCALITY.	CHARACTER.	VALUE.	
Palmo	Sicily	length	9,5297	inches.
"	Valencia	..,,..	8,9270	"
" menor	..,,..	..,,..	2,9760	"
"	Venice	..,,..	13,6775	"
" since 1803	Venit. Lombardy	..,,..	3,9370	"
Palmus	Ancient Romans	..,,..	2,9120	"
Paloon	Calicut	weight	0,241250	pounds.
Pan; minimum	France; Foix	length	8,6303	inches.
" of Dauphiny; maximum	..,,..Arles....	..,,..	10,0750	"
" mean of 31	..,,..	..,,..	9,5526	"
"	Piedmont	..,,..	9,8427	"
Panal	Marseilles	dry capacity	0,56756	bushels.
Panier; for coal	Mons	..,,..	2,68172	"
Panōro	Florence	superficial	0,0697	acres.
Pao; for grain; minimum	E. Indies; Bombay	weight	0,492857	pounds.
" " maximum	..,,....Bengal	..,,..	0,816114	"
" " mean of 8	..,,..	..,,..	0,629104	"
Para	Bombay	dry capacity	3,333333	bushels.
"	Madras	..,,..	1,74419	"
Parasang; [uncertain]	Ancient Persians	itinerary	4,1468	miles.
"	Persia & Turkey	..,,..	3,11	"
Pas	Bordeaux	length	0,97537	yards.
"	France, generally	..,,..	0,88814	"
" geometrical	..,,..	..,,..	1,77628	"
"	French W. Indies	..,,..	1,24340	"
"	Ypres	..,,..	0,74887	"
Paso; geometrical	Spain	..,,..	1,5456	"
Passëtto	Florence	..,,..	1,27662	"
Passo	..,,..	..,,..	1,79843	"
"	Ionian Isles	..,,..	1,9	"
"	Lisbon	..,,..	1,80450	"
" geometrical	Oporto	..,,..	1,79273	"
" or Pertica	Naples	..,,..	2,16269	"
"	Rome	..,,..	1,62897	"
"	Venice	..,,..	1,89965	"
" geometrical	..,,..	..,,..	1,51972	"
Passus	Ancient Romans	..,,..	1,61777	"
Paueen	Calpee	length	0,625	inches.
Paume; farriers'	Brussels	..,,..	3,9371	"
" "	France	..,,..	3,1969	"
Pause or Pose	Neufchâtel	superficial	0,6677	acres.
Payak	S. Petersburg	dry capacity	1,438	bushels.

Acre = 4840 square yards. Bushel = 2150,42 cubic inches. Cubic foot = 1728 cubic inches.
Gallon = 231 cubic inches. Mile = 1760 yards. Pound = 7000 grains. Yard = 36 inches.

NAME.	LOCALITY.	CHARACTER.	VALUE.
Pé..........................	Portugal........	length.........	0,36090 yards.
" architectural.............	...,,...........	...,,...........	0,37030 "
Peck; imperial.............	England........	dry capacity...	0,25788 bushels.
" old measure..........	...,,...........	....,,...........	0,25 "
" of Linlithgow; wheat.	Scotland	....,,...........	0,25545 "
" " for barley.	...,,...........	....,,...........	0,37264 "
"	United States....	....,,...........	0,25 "
Pecul.....................	Borneo and C'bes	weight.........	135,635421 pounds.
"	Cambodia.......	...,,...........	133,333333 "
"	China and Sum'a	...,,...........	133,333333 "
"	Japan...........	...,,...........	130.—— "
"	Java............	...,,...........	132.—— "
"	Malacca	...,,...........	135.—— "
" of China	...,,...........	...,,...........	125.—— "
" of Manilla............	Philippine I......	...,,...........	139,449615 · "
"	Siam...........	...,,...........	135.—— "
"	Tonquin	...,,...........	132.—— "
Pello......................	Rome	liquid capacity	21,6930 gallons.
Penge......................	Denmark........	weight.........	15,05 grains.
Penning...................	Amsterdam......	...,,...........	59,493 "
Pennyweight	England and U.S.	...,,...........	24.—— "
Perch, or Pole.............	...,,.....,,....	length	5,5 yards.
" of land...............	...,,.....,,....	superficial	0,00625 acres.
" of masonry	...,,.....,,....	solid...........	25.—— cub. feet.
" or Pole.............	Ireland..........	length.........	7.—— yards.
Perche ; legal ; old measure..	France...........	...,,...........	7,81561 "
" of Burgundy........	...,,	...,,...........	3,44101 "
" of Paris	...,,........	...,,...........	6,39460 "
" usual.............	...,,........	...,,...........	7,10509 "
" tillage	Neufchâtel	...,,...........	5,02456 "
" vineyards'	...,,........	...,,...........	5,13147 "
Pertïca	Ancona..........	...,,...........	4,47920 "
"	Bologna.........	...,,...........	4,15689 "
"	Florence	...,,...........	3,19122 "
"	Parma...........	...,,...........	3,55734 "
"	Pisa............	...,,...........	3,19011 "
"	Ancient Romans..	...,,...........	3,23555 "
"	Turin...........	...,,...........	6,74246 "
"	Venice	...,,...........	2,27958 "
"	Bergamo........	superficial	0,1636 acres.
"	Cremona	...,,...........	0,1970 "
"	Milan...........	...,,...........	0,1617 "

Acre = 4840 square yards. Bushel = 2150,42 cubic inches. Cubic foot = 1728 cubic inches.
Gallon = 231 cubic inches. Mile = 1760 yards. Pound = 7000 grains. Yard = 36 inches.

NAME.	LOCALITY.	CHARACTER.	VALUE.
Pertĭca	Placentia	superficial	0,1885 acres.
"	Ancient Romans	,,	0,0022 "
Pes	,,	length	0,32355 yards.
Pesinălo	Udino	dry capacity	0,25966 bushels.
Peso	Damascus	weight	45,94 grains.
Petrĭcon	Barcelona	liquid capacity	0,06133 gallons.
Pezza	Rome	superficial	0,6523 acres.
Pfennig	Aix-la-Chapelle	weight	14,08 grains.
"	Augsburg	,,	14,23 "
" legal; since 1810	Baden	,,	7,72 "
" commercial	Berne	,,	15,68 "
" for gold and silver	,,	,,	14,76 "
"	Brunswic	,,	14,07 "
"	Dresden	,,	14,07 "
" commercial	Frankfort	,,	15,23 "
" for gold and silver	,,	,,	14,10 "
"	Hamburg	,,	14,60 "
" legal	Hesse Darmstadt	,,	15,07 "
"	Holstein	,,	14,60 "
"	Leipsic	,,	14,08 "
"	Lübec	,,	14,61 "
"	Luneburg	,,	14,74 "
" old measure	Mecklenburg	,,	15,33 "
" commercial	Nürnberg	,,	15,37 "
" for gold and silver	,,	,,	14,38 "
"	Oldenburg	,,	14,60 "
" old measure	Prague	,,	15,51 "
" legal; since 1816	Prussia	,,	14,10 "
" old measure	Ratisbon	,,	17,09 "
"	Vienna	,,	16,88 "
Pfiff	,,	liquid capacity	0,0445 gallons.
Pflug	Denmark	superficial	43,6 acres.
Pfund	Aarau	weight	1,050747 pounds.
"	Aix-la-Chapelle	,,	1,029703 "
"	Appenzell	,,	1,288977 "
" for spices; etc.	,,	,,	1,025549 "
" old measure	Augsburg	,,	1,041943 "
" legal	Austria	,,	1,234677 "
" apothecary	Austria, generally	,,	0,926 "
"	Baden	,,	1,102369 "
" apothecary	,,	,,	0,788811 "
"	Basel	,,	1,079232 "

Acre = 4840 square yards.　Bushel = 2150,42 cubic inches.　Cubic foot = 1728 cubic inches.
Gallon = 231 cubic inches.　Mile = 1760 yards.　Pound = 7000 grains.　Yard = 36 inches.

NAME.	LOCALITY.	CHARACTER.	VALUE.
Pfund; *apothecary*..........	*Basel* and *Friburg*	weight........	0,809470 pounds.
"	*Bavaria*.........	...,,,..........	1,234655 "
" *apothecary*	...,,,.........	...,,,..........	0,793705 "
" *since 1816*..........	*Berlin*	...,,,..........	1,031180 "
" *before 1816*..........	...,,,.........	...,,,......:.....	1,032895 "
" *apothecary*	...,,,.........	...,,,..........	0,773384 "
" " *old measure*	...,,,.........	...,,,..........	0,788341 "
"	*Berne*.........	...,,,..........	1,146710 "
" *apothecary*	...,,,.........	...,,,..........	0,786077 "
"	*Bremen*.........	...,,,..........	1,099062 "
" *old measure*..........	*Breslau*.........	...,,,..........	0,902067 "
"	*Brunswic*	...,,,..........	1,0306 "
"	*Bohemia*	...,,,..........	1,134 "
"	*Coburg* ...:.....	...,,,..........	1,293078 "
"	*Cologne*.........	...,,,..........	1,030611 "
"	*Dresden*.........	...,,,..........	1,029265 "
"	*Frankfort*	...,,,..........	1,114073 "
" *for gold and silver*....	...,,,..........	...,,,..........	1,031552 "
" *apothecary*	...,,,.........	...,,,..........	0,788895 "
"	*Friburg*.........	...,,,..........	1,165887 "
" *apothecary*	*Germany, gen'y*..	...,,,..........	0,788974 "
"	*Gotha*.........	...,,,..........	1,030510 "
"	*Hamburg*........	...,,,..........	1,067886 "
"	*Hanover*.........	...,,,..........	1,079444 "
" *apothecary*	...,,,.........	...,,,..........	0,785654 "
" *old measure*..........	*Heidelberg*	...,,,..........	1,112382 "
"	*Hesse Cassel*.....	...,,,..........	1,067534 "
" *for gold and silver*....	.....,,,.........	...,,,..........	1,031310 "
" *since 1821*	*Hesse Darmstadt*.	...,,,..........	1,102369 "
"	*Holstein*.........	...,,,..........	1,067975 "
" *old measure*..........	*Königsberg*	...,,,..........	1,032940 "
"	*Leipsic*	...,,,..........	1,030598 "
"	*Lippe*..........	...,,,..........	1,030516 "
"	*Lübec*	...,,,..........	1,068744 "
" *old measure*..........	*Luneburg*	...,,,..........	1,073 "
"	*Mecklenburg*.....	...,,,..........	1,067154 "
" *old measure*..........	*Munich*.........	...,,,..........	1,237240 "
"	*Nürnberg*........	...,,,..........	1,124321 "
" *for gold and silver* ...	.....,,,.........	...,,,..........	1,052 "
" *apothecary*	...,,,.........	...,,,..........	0,788974 "
"	*Oldenburg*.......	...,,,..........	1,059083 "
" *old measure*..........	*Prague*..........	...,,,..........	1,134296 "

Acre = 4840 square yards.　Bushel = 2150,42 cubic inches.　Cubic foot = 1728 cubic inches. Gallon = 231 cubic inches.　Mile = 1760 yards.　Pound = 7000 grains.　Yard = 36 inches.

NAME.	LOCALITY.	CHARACTER.	VALUE.	
Pfund ; *legal*	*Prussia*	weight	1,031180	pounds.
" *old measure*	*Ratisbon*	...,,...	1,253	"
" ...,,...	*Rostock*	...,,...	1,120452	"
" ...,,...	*S. Gall*	...,,...	1,291414	"
" *for gold and silver*	...,,...	...,,...	1,033131	"
" ...,,...	*Schaffhausen*	...,,...	1,267684	"
" *for gold and silver*	...,,...	...,,...	1,014190	"
" ...,,...	*Solothurn*	...,,...	1,143110	"
" ...,,...	*Vienna*	...,,...	1,234677	"
" ...,,...	*Weimar*	...,,...	1,030598	"
" ...,,...	*Würtemberg*	...,,...	1,031114	"
" *apothecary*	...,,...	...,,...	0,788518	"
" ...,,...	*Zurich*	...,,...	1,165142	"
" *for gold and silver*	...,,...	...,,...	1,035682	"
Pfundschwer	*Bremen*	...,,...	329,57	"
" ...,,...	*Hanover*	...,,...	362,71	"
" ...,,...	*Nürnberg*	...,,...	337,33	"
" ...,,...	*Oldenburg*	...,,...	320,41	"
" ...,,...	*Osnabrück*	...,,...	326,82	"
Phan	*An-nam*	...,,...	6,03	grains.
Pibe	*Denmark*	liquid capacity	122,49933	gallons.
" *old measure*	...,,...	...,,...	118,62876	"
Pic	*Abyssinia*	length	0,74990	yards.
"	*Aleppo*	...,,...	0,73961	"
" *for muslins*	*Alexandria*	...,,...	0,68593	"
" *for cloths*	...,,...	...,,...	0,61244	"
" Stambuli	...,,...	...,,...	0,73272	"
" *Turkish*	*Algiers*	...,,...	0,69227	"
" *Arabic*	...,,...	...,,...	0,52494	"
"	*Cairo*	...,,...	0,74039	"
" *geometrical*	...,,...	...,,...	0,84372	"
"	*Candia*	...,,...	0,69694	"
" *for silks*	*Constantinople*	...,,...	0,73173	"
" Stambuli	...,,...	...,,...	0,70854	"
"	*Damascus*	...,,...	0,63704	"
"	*Jerusalem*	...,,...	0,75019	"
"	*Misitra*	...,,...	0,50018	"
"	*Morocco*	...,,...	0,72289	"
" *for cottons and woollens*	*Patras*	...,,...	0,75019	"
" *for silks*	...,,...	...,,...	0,69472	"
"	*Rhodes*	...,,...	0,82669	"
"	*Smyrna*	...,,...	0,73022	"

Acre = 4840 square yards.   Bushel = 2150,42 cubic inches.   Cubic foot = 1728 cubic inches.
Gallon = 231 cubic inches.   Mile = 1760 yards.   Pound = 7000 grains.   Yard = 36 inches.

NAME.	LOCALITY.	CHARACTER.	VALUE.	
Pic......................	*Tripoli in Africa.*	length........	0,60423	yards.
' *for ribbons*............	......,,......	......,,........	0,52861	"
" *for cloth*.............	*Tunis*..........	......,,........	0,73591	"
" *for linen*............	...,,.......	......,,........	0,51729	"
" *for silk*.............	...,,.........	......,,........	0,68975	"
Pice...................	*Bombay*........	weight........	0,023332	pounds.
"	*Calcutta*........	......,,........	0,94	grains.
"	*Deccan*..........	......,,........	0,023855	pounds.
"	*Malwah*..........	......,,........	0,039510	"
"	*Sindh*..........	......,,........	0,029167	"
" *old measure*	*Surat*...........	......,,........	0,031250	"
" *actual* "	...,,.......	......,,........	0,022321	"
Picötin.................	*Barcelona*.......	dry capacity ...	0,04198	bushels.
" *old measure ; for wheat*	*Brussels*........	......,,......	0,08647	"
" " *for oats*..	...,,..........	......,,........	0,09129	"
"	*Lyons*	......,,........	0,06080	"
"	*Marseilles*......	......,,........	0,07195	"
"	*Namur*..........	......,,........	0,05383	"
"	*Paris*	......,,........	0,09192	"
Pie.....................	*Aragon*..........	length	0,28106	yards.
"	*Canary I*.......	...,,........	0,30906	"
"	*Castille*.........	...,,........	0,30440	"
"	*Curaçao*.........	...,,........	0,30903	"
"	*Havana* and *Mex.*	...,,............	0,30914	"
"	*Valencia*	...,,........	0,33067	"
Pié.....................	*Bassano*	...,,........	0,39086	"
"	*Bologna*	...,,........	0,41569	"
"	*Brescia*.........	...,,........	0,51511	"
" *surveyors'*...........	*Carrara*	...,,........	0,32078	"
"	*Casal*..........	...,,........	0,52933	"
"	*Cremona*	...,,........	0,52524	"
"	*Ferrara*.........	...,,........	0,44167	"
" *architects'*...........	*Florence*........	...,,........	0,59950	"
" liprando..............	*Genoa*	...,,........	0,56186	"
"	...,,........	...,,........	0,32458	"
"	*Ionian Isles*.....	...,,........	0,36364	"
"	*Lodi*..........	...,,........	0,49797	"
"	*Lucca*..........	...,,........	0,64514	"
"	*Malta*..........	...,,........	0,31019	"
"	*Mantua*.........	...,,........	0,51058	"
"	*Milan*..........	...,,........	0,47593	"
" *architects'*...........	...,,........	...,,........	0,43362	"

Acre = 4840 square yards. Bushel = 2150,42 cubic inches. Cubic foot = 1728 cubic inches.
Gallon = 231 cubic inches. Mile = 1760 yards. Pound = 7000 grains. Yard = 36 inches.

NAME.	LOCALITY.	CHARACTER.	VALUE.	
Pié......................	Modena........	length........	0,57202	yards.
"	Padua..........	...,,...........	0,38735	"
" surveyors'.............	Parma.........	...,,...........	0,59567	"
"	Placentia.......	...,,...........	0,51390	"
"	Ravenna........	...,,...........	0,63933	"
"	Reggio..........	...,,...........	0,58061	"
"	Rome..........	...,,...........	0,32578	"
"	Sardinia........	...,,...........	0,52356	"
"	Turin..........	...,,...........	0,37458	"
" liprando...............	...,,..........	...,,...........	0,56187	"
"	Urbino..........	...,,...........	0,44792	"
"	Venice.........	...,,...........	0,38031	"
" mean	Venit. Lombardy.	...,,...........	0,37992	"
"	Verona.........	...,,...........	0,37503	"
"	Vicenza........	...,,...........	0,39086	"
Pied; old measure.........	Aix-en-Provence	...,,...........	0,27183	"
" " ......,,....	Alsace.........	...,,...........	0,32294	"
" "	Avignon........	...,,...........	0,27108	"
" "	Bordeaux.......	...,,...........	0,39014	"
" "	Brussels........	...,,...........	0,30156	"
" "	Burgundy.......	...,,...........	0,36222	"
" "	Dauphiny.......	...,,...........	0,37294	"
" du Roi; till 1812.....	France, generally	...,,...........	0,35526	"
" metrique; 1812 to '40.	......,,.......	...,,...........	0,36454	"
" old measure..........	Franche-Comté...	...,,...........	0,39097	"
"	Geneva.........	...,,...........	0,53360	"
" old measure..........	Guienne.........	...,,...........	0,37889	"
" "	Hainault........	...,,...........	0,32090	"
" of S. Hubert; builders'	Liége..........	...,,...........	0,32330	"
" of S. Lambert; land..	...,,..........	...,,..........	0,32010	"
" old measure..........	Lorraine........	...,,...........	0,31307	"
" "	Lyons..........	...,,...........	0,37456	"
" "	Normandy......	...,,...........	0,32564	"
" "	Rouen.........	...,,...........	0,29356	"
Ping......................	China..........	dry capacity...	17,41864	bushels.
Pinga....................	Malacca........	weight........	0,534405	pounds.
Pint....................	Amsterdam......	liquid capacity	0,16016	gallons.
" imperial...............	England........	...,,.........	0,15008	"
" old measure; for beer....	...,,...........	...,,........	0,15260	"
" "	Scotland........	...,,.........	0,44764	"
" '......................	United States....	...,,.........	0,125	"
" imperial...............	England........	dry capacity...	0,01612	bushels.

Acre = 4840 square yards. Bushel = 2150,42 cubic inches. Cubic foot = 1728 cubic inches. Gallon = 231 cubic inches. Mile = 1760 yards. Pound = 7000 grains. Yard = 36 inches.

NAME.	LOCALITY.	CHARACTER.	VALUE.	
Pint; *Winchester*	*England* and *U.S.*	dry capacity	0,01556	bushels.
Pinta	*Bergamo*	liquid capacity	0,36507	gallons.
"	*Brescia*	...,,.	0,35420	"
"	*Genoa*	...,,.	0,39217	"
" old measure	*Milan*	...,,.	0,41582	"
" new measure	" and *Sard'a*	...,,.	0,26418	"
"	*Turin*	...,,.	0,41340	"
" new measure	*Venice*	...,,.	0,26418	" "
" "	*Milan* and *Venice*	dry capacity	0,02838	bushels.
Pinte	*Antwerp*	liquid capacity	0,18149	gallons.
" for wine	*Brussels*	...,,.	0,17890	"
" for beer	...,,.	...,,.	0,17175	"
"	*French W. Indies*	...,,.	0,25	"
"	*Liége*	...,,.	0,16903	"
"	*Lille*	...,,.	0,13209	"
"	*Mechlin*	...,,.	0,18136	"
" old legal measure	*Paris*	...,,.	0,24603	"
" actual	...,,.	...,,.	0,25138	"
"	*Antwerp*	dry capacity	0,01892	bushels.
"	*Mechlin*	...,,.	0,01948	"
Pinte	*Bohemia*	liquid capacity	0,50442	gallons.
" or Pintchen	*Cologne*	...,,.	0,08777	"
"	*Strasburg*	...,,.	0,25370	"
Pio	*Brescia*	superficial	0,7790	acres.
Pipa	*Alicant*	liquid capacity	121,522	gallons.
" for rum	*Bahia*	...,,.	134,88650	"
" for molasses	...,,.	...,,.	187,34183	"
"	*Barcelona*	...,,.	125,6	"
" for wine	*Cadiz*	...,,.	115,10235	"
" for oil	...,,.	...,,.	112,8542	"
"	*Canary I.*	...,,.	120.——	"
"	*Gibraltar*	...,,.	126.——	"
"	*Lisbon*	...,,.	113,61298	"
" London guage	...,,.	...,,.	135.——	"
"	*Madeira*	...,,.	110.——	"
" mean	*Malaga*	...,,.	106,576	"
"	*Naples*	...,,.	162,0294	"
" London guage	*Oporto*	...,,.	138.——	"
"	*Palermo*	...,,.	113,23728	"
"	*Rio Janeiro*	...,,.	132,0890	"
" for wine	*Spain, generally*	...,,.	115,10208	"
" for oil	...,,.	...,,.	114,48929	"

Acre = 4840 square yards. Bushel = 2150,42 cubic inches. Cubic foot = 1728 cubic inches.
Gallon = 231 cubic inches. Mile = 1760 yards. Pound = 7000 grains. Yard = 36 inches.

NAME.	LOCALITY.	CHARACTER.	VALUE.	
Pipa....................	*Sweden, generally*	liquid capacity	124,39608	gallons.
"	*Valencia*	........,,........	127,38928	"
" *for coal*..............	*Lisbon*..........	dry capacity ...	127.——	bushels.
Pipe....................	*Anjou*	liquid capacity	134,70172	gallons.
" or Piece ; *for brandy*....	*Bordeaux*.......	........,,........	99,59511	"
" *for brandy*............	*Cognac*..........	........,,........	152,78206	"
" *old measure ; for wine*...	*England*	........,,........	126.——	"
" " *for ale*....	....,,.........	........,,........	117,19488	"
" *for brandy*............	*Montpellier*.....	........,,........ ;	164,84707	"
"	*Nantes*	........,,........	126,80544	"
" or Muid	*Roussillon*	........,,........	124,63918	"
Pipĕ.............	*Dantzic*.........	........,,........	108,89412	"
"	*Hamb.* and *Holst.*	........,,........	114,44196	"
"	*Königsberg*	........,,........	81,67327	"
Piquet ; *old measure*	*Amiens*..........	dry capacity...	0,23411	bushels.
Piso.......................	*Guinea*..........	weight.........	0,017669	pounds.
Plank.....................	*Lübec* and *Rost'k*	liquid capacity	0,11954	gallons.
Plethron ; *Olympic*	*Ancient Greeks.*.	itinerary.......	0,0192	miles.
" ....,,........	superficial......	0,2348	acres.
Po.......................	*China*..........	length.......	1,67484	yards.
Pognoux ; *old measure*......	*Liege*	dry capacity....	0,05446	bushels.
Poinçon....................	*France*..........	liquid capacity	53,14205	gallons.
Point.....................	....,,..*generally*..	length.........	0,0074	inches.
"	*Toulouse*........	....,,...........	0,0172	"
Pole, *or Perch*	*England*	....,,........	5,50	yards.
" *Cheshire*...........	....,,...........	....,,........	8.——	"
" *forest*	....,,...........	....,,........	7.——	"
" *woodland*...........	....,,...........	....,,........	6.——	"
" *old measure*	*Ireland*	....,,........	7.——	"
Polkörzow	*Cracow*..........	dry capacity ...	1,70410	bushels.
"	*Warsaw*	........,,......	1,81619	"
Pollam	*Arcot*...........	weight.........	0,075536	pounds.
"	*Calicut*.........	....,,........	0,255714	"
"	*Madras*..........	....,,........	0,078120	"
" or Paloin	*Pondichery*......	....,,........	0,080947	"
"	*Seringapatam* ...	....,,........	0,075857	"
" *mean of 4*	*Travancore*......	....,,........	0,154510	"
Pollegăda..................	*Portugal*........	length.........	1,0827	inches.
Polönic....................	*Trieste*..........	dry capacity ...	0,86177	bushels.
Pond *of Brabant*............	*Amsterdam*......	weight.........	1,037080	pounds.
" *Troy*...................	....,,.........	....,, ...	1,084740	"
" *former*	....,,.........	....,,..........	1,087875	"

Acre = 4840 square yards. Bushel = 2150,42 cubic inches. Cubic foot = 1728 cubic inches.
Gallon = 231 cubic inches. Mile = 1760 yards. Pound = 7000 grains. Yard = 36 inches.

NAME.	LOCALITY.	CHARACTER.	VALUE.	
Pond ; *Netherlandic ; actual.*	*Amsterdam*	weight.........	2,204737	pounds.
" *apothecary ; old meas.*	....,,..........	....,,..........	0,813826	"
" " *new* "	....,,..........	....,,..........	0,826776	"
Pondo....................	*Ancient Romans.*	....,,..........	0,72897	"
Ponto	*Portugal........*	length	0,0090	inches.
Porrōne..................	*Catalonia. ......*	liquid capacity	0,24532	gallons.
Port.	*Vannes.........*	superficial	0,0667	acres.
Pose.....................	*Geneva ....*	....,,..........	0,6672	"
"	*Lausanne.......*	....,,..........	1,1115	"
" *old measure..........*	....,,..........	....,,..........	0,8497	"
Posson " *Paris ......*	*France, generally.*	liquid capacity	0,03075	gallons.
Pot..................	*Antwerp ....*	....,,..........	0,36298	"
" *old measure..........*	*Bordeaux.......*	....,,..........	0,57169	"
" *for wine ....*	*Brussels........*	....,,..........	0,35780	"
" *for beer ....*	....,,..........	....,,..........	0,34350	"
"	*French W. Indies*	....,,..........	0,5	"
"	*Geneva ....*	....,,..........	0,24890	"
"	*Liége ....*	....,,..........	0,33806	"
"	*Lille ....*	....,,..........	0,52836	"
"	*Lyons ....*	....,,..........	0,24603	"
"	*Marseilles......*	....,,..........	0,26244	"
" *for wine...............*	*Montpellier.....*	....,,..........	0,27778	"
" *for oil ....*	....,,..........	....,,..........	0,30692	"
"	*Nantes.........*	....,,..........	0,52836	"
"	*Neufchâtel .....*	....,,..........	0,50307	"
"	*Paris ....*	....,,..........	0,49206	"
" *for brandy ....*	*Rouen ....*	....,,..........	0,42917	"
"	*Vaud ....*	....,,..........	0,35664	"
Pote	*Lisbon* and *Rio..*	....,,..........	2,18475	"
Pott.....................	*Basel..........*	....,,..........	0,10505	"
"	*Luneburg.......*	....,,..........	0,25678	"
"	*Mecklenburg....*	....,,..........	0,23921	"
Potte	*Denmark* and *N'y*	....,,..........	0,25520	"
Pottle ; *legal ....*	*England ....*	....,,..........	0,60030	"
" *old measure..........*	....,,..........	....,,.."	0,5	"
" *legal.............*	....,,..........	dry capacity...	0,06447	bushels.
" *old measure..........*	....,,..........	....,,..........	0,06250	"
Pouce	*France..........*	length	1,0658	inches.
"	*Lorraine........*	....,,..........	1,1271	"
Poueur ; *for vineyards; mean*	*Dauphiny ....*	superficial.....	0,2891	acres.
Pound ; *Tower* or *old sterling*	*England bef.* 1526	weight.........	0,777778	pounds.
" *imperial............*	....,,. *.since* 1825	....,,..........	1.———	"

Acre = 4840 square yards. Bushel = 2150,42 cubic inches. Cubic foot = 1728 cubic inches.
Gallon = 231 cubic inches. Mile = 1760 yards. Pound = 7000 grains. Yard = 36 inches.

NAME.	LOCALITY.	CHARACTER.	VALUE.	
Pound; *Troy*	*England* and *U.S.*	weight.........	0,822857	pounds.
" *apothecary*.........	.....,,.......,,.....	.....,,........:	0,822857	"
" *Troy*..............	*Scotland*	.....,,..........	1,088778	"
" *old Tron*..........	.....,,............	.....,,..........	1,429111	"
" *Glasgow Tron*.....	.....,,............	.....,,..........	1,406222	"
" *mint* or *Troy*	*United States*....	.....,,..........	0,822857	"
" *avoirdupois*.........	.....,,......	.....,,..........	1.——	"
Pous; *Macedonian*	*Ancient Greeks* ..	length	0,38592	yards.
" *Olympic*.............	.....,,............	.....,,..........	0,33714	"
" *Philetairic*..........	.....,,............	.....,,..........	0,38592	"
" *Pythian*.............	.....,,............	.....,,..........	0,27008	"
" *Sicilian*	.....,,...,.	.....,,..........	0,24333	"
Powe; *precious stones & metals*	*Bangalore*.......	weight.........	0,150943	pounds.
Precikow; *geometrical; o. m.*	*Poland*..........	length.	0,48855	yards.
" " *since* 1819	.....,,............	.....,,..........	0,47245	"
Pretow; *since* 1819	.....,,............	.....,,..........	4,72450	"
Prime; *old measure*........	*France*..........	weight.........	0,034	grains.
Provēnda................	*Ancona*	dry capacity....	0,25370	bushels.
Pud; *legal*................	*Russia*..........	weight.........	36,06764	pounds.
Puddälum................	*Masulipatan*.....	.....,,..........	1,5	"
Puddy...................	*Arcot*...........	dry capacity ...	0,06045	bushels.
"	*Madras*	.....,,..........	0,04360	"
Pugon...................	*Ancient Greeks* ..	length	13,6548	inches.
Pugma...................	.....,,............	.....,,..........	15,1720	"
Pulgāda.................	*Aragon*........	.....,,..........	0,8432	"
" *legal for Spain*......	*Castille*.........	.....,,..........	0,9132	"
"	*Valencia*	.....,,..........	0,9920	"
Pullah; *minimum*	*E. Indies; Bellary*	weight.........	138,23701	pounds.
" *maximum*	.....,,. *Secund'rbd*	.....,,..........	252,464434	"
" *mean of* 8..........	.....,,............	.....,,..........	228,631227	"
Puncheon; *old measure*.....	*England*	liquid capacity	84.——	gallons.
" *for rum*.........	*Jamaica*.........	.....,,..........	102,02290	"
Pund....................	*Denmark*........	weight.........	1,100885	pounds.
" *for gold and silver*....	.....,,............	.....,,..........	1,038000	"
"	*Sweden*.........	.....,,..........	0,937284	"
Punko; *for gold and silver*..	*Calcutta*........	.....,,..........	0,14	grains.
Punkt; *legal*..............	*Austria*.........	length	0,0072	inches.
" *since* 1810.........	*Baden*..........	.....,,..........	0,0118	"
" " 1809.........	*Bavaria*.........	.....,,..........	0,0067	"
" *actual*..............	.....,,...*Rhenish*..	.....,,..........	0,0076	"
"	*Cracow*	.....,,..........	0,0081	"
"	*Dresden*........	.....,,..........	0,0065	"

Acre = 4840 square yards. Bushel = 2150,42 cubic inches. Cubic foot = 1728 cubic inches.
Gallon = 231 cubic inches. Mile = 1760 yards. Pound = 7000 grains. Yard = 36 inches.

NAME.	LOCALITY.	CHARACTER.	VALUE.	
Punkt..................................	*Gotha*...........	length	0,0094	inches.
"	*Lübec*...............	....,,.............	0,0066	"
" *since* 1819	*Poland*...........	....,,.............	0,0065	"
"	*Sweden*..........	....,,.............	0,0117	"
"	*Würtemberg*......	...,,.............	0,0113	"
Punt......................................	*Mons* and *Namur*	...,,.............	0,0116	"
" or Punto................	*Canton*...........	....,,.............	1,2188	"
Punto......................................	*Genoa* and *Turin*	...,,.............	0,1405	"
"	*Milan*	...,,.............	0,1604	"
"	*Parma*............	...,,.............	0,1486	"
" *legal*..................	*Spain*............	...,,.............	0,0065	"
" *for gold and silver*	*Manilla*.........	weight.........	0,537	pounds.
Pussäree................................	*Calcutta*........	....,,.............	10,266137	"
"	*Seringapatam*....	...,,.............	3,034159	"
Pye..	*Malwah*..........	....,,.............	1,8965	"
Quadragëssis	*Ancient Romans* .	....,,.............	28,875886	"
Quadrans	....,,............	....,,.............	0,180474	" .
Quadrāntal............................	....,,............	liquid capacity	6,8410	gallons.
Quadrāto..................................	*Tuscany*	superficial......	0,8413	acres.
Quadrŭssis...............................	*Ancient Romans*..	weight.........	2,887589	pounds.
Quan......................................	*An-nam*..........	....,,.............	688,760	"
Quärtlein.................................	*Graubündten*	liquid capacity	0,08775	gallons.
"	*Hesse Cassel*.....	....,,.............	2,09692	"
Quärtli	*Uri*	....,,.............	0,23975	"
" *standard*...........	*Zürich*..........	....,,.............	0,21689	"
Quardeel; *for whale oil*; *mean*	*Amsterdam*......	....,,.............	98,14213	"
Quart; *old measure*.........	*Breslau*.........	....,,.............	0,18343	"
" *imperial*............	*England*	....,,.............	0,30017	"
"	*Marseilles*......	....,,.............	0,07045	"
" *old measure*.........	*Paris*	....,,.............	0,49207	"
" *actual; till* 1840.....	..,,..............	....,,.............	0,06604	"
" *legal*..............	*Prussia*	....,,.............	0,30244	"
"	*Scotland*........	....,,.............	0,89527	"
" *actual*.............	*Silesia*	....,,.............	0,18550	"
"	*United States*....	....,,.............	0,25	"
"	*England*	dry capacity...	0,03224	bushels.
" *Winchester; bef.* 1825	....,,............	....,,..........	0,03125	"
" *old measure*.........	*Paris*	....,,..........	0,09229	"
" *actual; till* 1840.....	..,,..............	....,,..........	0,00709	"
"	*Strasburg*	....,,..........	0,13416	"
"	*United States*....	....,,..........	0,03125	"

Acre = 4840 square yards. Bushel = 2150,42 cubic inches. Cubic foot = 1728 cubic inches.
Gallon = 231 cubic inches. Mile = 1760 yards. Pound = 7000 grains. Yard = 36 inches.

NAME.	LOCALITY.	CHARACTER.	VALUE.	
Quarta; *for oil*............	*Barcelona*......	liquid capacity	0,06789	gallons.
" *for wine*..........	*Majorca*........	.....,,.........	0,27581	"
"	*Ferrara*.........	dry capacity...	0,22201	bushels.
"	*Lisbon*..........	.....,,.........	0,09592	"
"	*Rome*...........	.....,,.........	2,08873	"
"	*Rovigo*..........	.....,,.........	0,23506	"
"	*Saragossa*.......	length.........	7,5888	inches.
"	*Spain, generally*..	...,,..........	8,2188	"
"	*Rome*..........	superficial......	1,1414	acres.
Quartal; *for oil*...........	*Montpellier*......	liquid capacity	2,44536	gallons.
Quartăna.................	*Sardinia*........	.....,,.........	1,10955	"
Quartăne.................	*Graubündten*....	dry capacity...	0,21244	bushels.
Quartărius...............	*Ancient Romans*	liquid capacity	0,03563	gallons.
"	.....,,........	dry capacity...	0,00383	bushels.
Quartăro	*Milan*..........	.....,,.........	0,12972	"
"	...,,..........	liquid capacity	1,66326	gallons.
" *mean*...........	*Sicily*..........	.....,,.........	1,36435	"
Quartarōlo...............	*Bologna*.......	.....,,.........	5,19045	"
"	.....,,........	dry capacity...	0,27130	bushels.
"	*Parma*.........	.....,,.........	0,09111	"
"	*Venice*.........	.....,,.........	0,14777	"
Quartaruōla.............	*Padua*.........	.....,,.........	0,20564	"
"	*Vicenza*........	.....,,.........	0,04799	"
Quartaut; *mean*..........	*Burgundy*.......	liquid capacity	26,85810	gallons.
" "	*Champagne*......	.....,,.........	23,87191	"
" *old measure*......	*Paris*	.....,,.........	17,71445	"
" *for salt*.........	*Nantes*..........	weight.........	43,168760	pounds.
Quarte...................	*Liége* and *Namur*	dry capacity...	0,21784	bushels.
" *for coal*..........	*Paris*	.....,,.........	0,09229	"
"	*Montpellier*......	superficial	0,0875	acres.
Quarteel; *for whale oil*......	*Hamb'g* and *Holst*	liquid capacity	61,20741	gallons.
Quartel; *old measure*	*Augsburg*........	.....,,.........	0,09431	"
" *legal*..............	*Bavaria*........	.....,,.........	0,07060	"
"	*Ratisbon*........	.....,,.........	0,05503	"
Quarter; *disused*............	*England*	weight.........	28.——	pounds.
" *imperial*..........	.....,,..........	dry capacity ...	8,25212	bushels.
" *Winchester*.......	....,,.. and *U. S.*	.....,,.........	8.——	"
"	*Sweden*	liquid capacity	0,08635	gallons.
Quartĕra	*Barcelona*.......	dry capacity...	2,01484	bushels.
"	*Majorca*........	.....,,.........	2,04237	"
"	*Minorca*........	.....,,.........	2,15673	"
"	*Barcelona*.......	liquid capacity	0,98125	gallons.

Acre = 4840 square yards. Bushel = 2150,42 cubic inches. Cubic foot = 1728 cubic inches. Gallon = 231 cubic inches. Mile = 1760 yards. Pound = 7000 grains. Yard = 36 inches.

NAME.	LOCALITY.	CHARACTER.	VALUE.	
Quartĕrée..................	Agen.............	superficial......	1,8006	acres.
"	Aix-en-Provence	.....,,...........	0,5861	"
"	Cahors...........	.....,,...........	1,2615	"
"	Marseilles.......	.....,,...........	0,5065	"
Quartern; old measure......	England........	liquid capacity	0,5	gallons.
" legal	....,,..............	.....,,...........	0,6003	"
Quartĕron ; old measure.....	France	weight.........	0,269805	pounds.
"	Friburg.........	.....,,...........	0,113286	"
"	Geneva..........	liquid capacity	0,403	gallons.
" old measure	Lausanne.......	.....,,..........	0,52651	"
" for oil..........	Marseilles.......	.....,,..........	0,09841	"
"	Friburg.........	dry capacity ...	0,22662	bushels.
"	Vaud............	.....,,..........	0,38310	"
Quarterōne ; for oil	Genoa	liquid capacity	0,26698	gallons.
Quartès ; for wine.........	Majorca	.....,,..........	1,10274	"
Quarticīno..............	Bologna........	dry capacity ...	0,06974	bushels.
Quartier..............	Altona..........	liquid capacity	0,23911	gallons.
"	Bremen...........	.....,,..........	0,21250	"
"	Brunswic	.....,,..........	0,247	"
"	Dresden.........	.....,,..........	0,03093	"
"	Hamburg	.....,,..........	0,23842	"
"	Hanover	.....,,..........	0,25899	"
"	Leipsic..........	.....,,..........	0,03226	"
"	Lübec...........	.....,,..........	0,24734	"
"	Oldenburg.......	.....,,..........	0,25206	"
"	Rostock	.....,,..........	0,23908	"
" mean	Belgium........	dry capacity ...	0,38310	bushels.
"	Morlaix.........	.....,, ...	2,34119	"
"	Nice...........	.....,,..........	0,28378	"
"	Angers..........	superficial	0,4072	acres.
"	Rochelle.........	.....,,..........	2,5240	"
Quartiĕra..............	Sardinia........	liquid capacity	1,32089	gallons.
"	Treviso.........	dry capacity ...	0,15409	bushels.
Quartĭerchen	Breslau	liquid capacity	0,04586	gallons.
Quartière ; mean..........	France	dry capacity....	2,89456	bushels.
Quartiĕre..............	Turin...........	.....,,..........	0,32648	"
Quartīlho..............	Lisbon..........	liquid capacity	0,09104	gallons.
"	Rio.............	.....,,..........	0,18207	"
Quartīllo	Aragon..........	weight.........	0,016068	pounds
"	Catalonia	liquid capacity	0,24531	gallons.
"	Gallicia.........	.....,,..........	0,15611	"
"	Spain..........	superficial......	0,0331	acres.

Acre = 4840 square yards.   Bushel = 2150,42 cubic inches.   Cubic foot = 1728 cubic inches.
Gallon = 231 cubic inches.   Mile = 1760 yards.   Pound = 7000 grains.   Yard = 36 inches.

NAME.	LOCALITY.	CHARACTER.	VALUE.
Quartin....................	*Majorca*	liquid capacity	7,16781 gallons.
Quartinillo; *for brandy*.....	....,,............	....,,.........	1,79195 "
Quartino..................	*Turin*...........	....,,.........	0,10335 "
"	*Ferrara*.........	dry capacity...	0,11101 bushels.
"	*Milan*	....,,.........	0,00811 "
Quarto	*Azores*..........	....,,.........	0,08499 "
"	*Bergamo*.......	....,,.........	0,39160 "
"	*Brescia*.........	....,,.........	0,34525 "
"	*Florence* and *Pisa*	....,,.........	0,17288 "
"	*Genoa*	....,,.........	0,42821 "
"	*Rio Janeiro*	....,,.........	0,09592 "
"	*Treviso*.........	....,,.........	0,61636 "
"	*Venice*..........	....,,.........	0,59108 "
"	*Verona*..........	....,,.........	0,27125 "
" *for oil*	*Genoa*	liquid capacity	4,27086 gallons.
" "	*Naples*..........	....,,.........	0,16716 "
Quartúccio; *mean of 5*	*Ionian Isles*......	....,,.........	0,13877 "
"	*Palermo*.........	....,,.........	0,07212 "
"	*Rome*	....,,.........	0,03390 "
"	*Sardinia*........	....,,.........	0,27739 "
"	*Tuscany*	....,,.........	0,07523 "
"	*Rome*	dry capacity....	0,09494 bushels.
"	*Tuscany*	....,,.........	0,01080 "
Quartúzzo.................	*Venice*..........	liquid capacity	0,17832 gallons.
Quattrino.................	*Tuscany*	length.........	0,3829 inches.
Quent; *old measure*........	*Baireuth*	weight.........	0,008775 pounds.
"	*Cologne*.........	....,,.........	0,008051 "
"	*Nürnberg*........	....,,.........	0,008784 "
" *for gold and silver* ..	...,,............	....,,.........	0,008219 "
"	*Prague*..........	....,,.........	0,008861 "
"	*Trieste & Vienna*	....,,.........	0,009646 "
"	*Tyrol*	....,,.........	0,009691 "
"	*Zurich*..........	....,,.........	0,009102 "
Quentchen.................	*Baden*	....,,.........	0,008612 "
"	*Bavaria*.........	....,,.........	0,009646 "
"	*Bremen*.........	....,,.........	0,008586 "
"	*Breslau*.........	....,,.........	0,007047 "
"	*Brunswic*	....,,.........	0,008052 "
"	*Frankfort*.......	....,,.........	0,008704 "
"	*Glaris*	....,,.........	0,009105 "
"	*Hamburg*........	....,,.........	0,008343 "
"	*Hanover*	....,,.........	0,008433 "

Acre = 4840 square yards.   Bushel = 2150,42 cubic inches.   Cubic foot = 1728 cubic inches.
Gallon = 231 cubic inches.   Mile = 1760 yards.   Pound = 7000 grains.   Yard = 36 inches.

NAME.	LOCALITY.	CHARACTER.	VALUE.
Quentchen	Hesse Cassel	weight	0,008340 pounds.
"	Hesse Darmstadt	...,,.	0,008612 "
"	Holstein	...,,.	0,008344 "
"	Libau	...,,.	0,007199 "
"	Lübec	...,,.	0,008350 "
"	Mecklenberg	...,,.	0,008350 "
"	Oldenburg	...,,.	0,008274 "
"	Prussia	...,,.	0,008056 "
"	Würtemberg	...,,.	0,008055 "
Quentin	Aix-la-Chapelle	...,,.	0,008045 "
Queue	Burgundy	liquid capacity	106,28410 gallons.
"	Champagne	...,,.	94,47532 "
" for wine, refined ; o. m.	Paris	...,,.	106,28762 "
" " on the lees	...,,.	...,,.	110,71436 "
Quiba	Tunis	dry capacity	0,93744 bushels.
Quilāte ; for precious stones	Lisbon and Rio	weight	3,176 grains.
" for diamonds	Oporto	...,,.	3,074 "
"	Rio Janeiro	...,,.	3,075 "
Quincunx	Ancient Romans	...,,.	0,30079 pounds.
Quinquagĕssis	...,,.	...,,.	36,094857 "
Quinquĕssis	...,,.	...,,.	3,609486 "
Quintal	Aragon	...,,.	109,738476 "
"	Asturias	...,,.	152,281185 "
"	Bordeaux	...,,.	110,23685 "
"	Brazil	...,,.	130,060416 "
"	Buenos Ayres	...,,.	101,4178 "
"	Canary I.	...,,.	101,483944 "
"	Castille and Chili	...,,.	101,6097 "
" macho	...,,.	...,,.	152,41455 "
"	Catalonia	...,,.	87,282 "
" metrical	France	...,,.	220,4737 "
" old measure	...,,. generally	...,,.	107,9219 "
"	Gallicia	...,,.	127,012124 "
" Castillian	...,,.	...,,.	101,6163 "
"	Majorca	...,,.	89,95327 "
" barbaresco	...,,.	...,,.	92,794247 "
" old measure	Marseilles	...,,.	89,931222 "
"	Mexico and Peru	...,,.	101,6097 "
"	Minorca	...,,.	91,937533 "
"	Valencia	...,,.	109,728476 "
Quintāle	Modena	...,,.	75,005153 "
" peso grosso; old mea.	Venice	...,,.	105,275 "

Acre = 4840 square yards. Bushel = 2150,42 cubic inches. Cubic foot = 1728 cubic inches.
Gallon = 231 cubic inches. Mile = 1760 yards. Pound = 7000 grains. Yard = 36 inches.

NAME.	LOCALITY.	CHARACTER.	VALUE.	
Quintăle ; *peso-sottile*	*Venice*	weight	66,5886	pounds.
Quintin	*Brunswic*	....,,.........	0,008052	"
"	*Denmark*	....,,.........	0,008601	"
"	*Norway*	....,,.........	0,008594	"
"	*Sweden*	....,,.........	0,007323	"
Quintlein	*Berne*	....,,.........	0,008959	"
" *old measure*	*Ratisbon*	....,, ...	0,009789	"
Quinto	*Guinea*	....,,.........	0,008863	"
Quirăte	*Alexandria*	....,,.........	2,959	grains.
Quontar ; *khebir*	*Algiers*	....,,.........	203,167	pounds.
Racȳon ; *mean*	*Spain*	dry capacity ...	0,00813	bushels.
Rackay ; *for gold and silver* ..	*Sumatra*	weight	1,521	grains.
Raïk	*Calcutta*	dry capacity ...	0,02922	bushels.
Rasiëra	*Cagliari*	....,,.........	4,16569	"
Rasiëre ; *maximum ; Tournay*	*Belgium*	....,,.........	6,04054	"
" *minimum ; Tirlemont*	....,,......	....,,.........	0,85134	"
" *mean of* 39	....,,......	....,,.........	2,35537	"
" *maximum*	*France ; Dunkirk*	....,,.........	4,2567	"
" *minimum*	....,,...*Bavay* ..	....,,.........	1,4785	"
" *mean of* 11	....,,......	....,,.........	3,14144	"
"	*Douay*	superficial	1,1172	acres.
Raso	*Cagliari*	length	0,60073	yards.
"	*Chambéri*	....,,.........	0,62836	"
"	*Nice*	....,,.........	0,60033	"
"	*Turin*	....,,.........	0,65552	"
Ratel ; *mean*	*Persia*	weight	1,025	pounds.
Rautul ; *for pepper ; mean* ...	*Travancore*	....,,.........	0,999964	"
Raza ; *for salt*	*Oporto*	dry capacity ...	1,2509	bushels.
Raze ; *old measure ; mean* ..	*Brittany*	....,,.........	1,4189	"
Raziere ; *for grain*	*Antwerp*	....,,.........	2,25968	"
Real ; *for gold and silver*	*East Indies*	weight	0,060263	pounds.
" *old measure*	*Nancy*	dry capacity	5,53728	bushels.
Rebēb	*Alexandria*	....,,.........	4,45819	"
Reep *or* Reif	*Bremen*	solid	86,526	cub. feet.
Restière	*Sardinia*	dry capacity	4,16569	bushels.
Rezal ; *mean of* 12	*Alsace & Lorraine*	....,,.........	3,11625	"
Richtpfennig ; *gold and silver*	*Cologne*	weight	0,055	grains.
" "	*Vienna*	....,,.........	0,066	"
Rimpel	*Hungary*	liquid capacity	0,05505	gallons.
"	....,,.........	dry capacity	0,00592	bushels.
Ringit ; *for gold and silver* ...	*Sumatra*	weight	0,060762	pounds.

Acre = 4840 square yards.   Bushel = 2150,42 cubic inches.   Cubic foot = 1728 cubic inches.
Gallon = 231 cubic inches.   Mile = 1760 yards.   Pound = 7000 grains.   Yard = 36 inches.

NAME.	LOCALITY.	CHARACTER.	VALUE.	
Rittermäss.................	Solothurn........	dry capacity ...	0,51506	bushels.
Rob *or* Robi................	Algiers..........	length.........	0,08653	yards.
Rod.......................	England and U.S.	...,,..........	5,5	"
Rod *or* Rood	....,,......,,..	superficial.....	0,25	acres.
Rode	Denmark........	length.........	3,43205	yards.
Roed ; *old measure*.........	Amsterdam	...,,..........	4,02427	"
" *Rhenish*............	.....,,........	...,,..........	4,11889	"
" *legal*...............	Holland.........	...,,..........	10,93633	"
Roëneng...................	Siam...........	itinerary.......	2,3886	miles.
Rood	Scotland	superficial......	0,3177	acres.
Rope	England........	length.........	6,66667	yards.
Roquille ...,...............	French W. Indies	liquid capacity	0,0625	gallons.
" *old measure*	Paris...........	.........,,.....	0,00769	"
Rotl *or* Rottŏlo	Abyssinia.......	weight........	0,68788	pounds.
" *attari ; for spices*	Algiers..........	...,,..........	1,203963	"
" *feuddi ; gold and silver*	...,,..........	...,,..........	1,096714	"
" *gheddari ; for fruits*....	...,,..........	...,,..........	1,354458	"
" *khebir*................	...,,..........	...,,..........	2,03167	"
"	Bet-el-faki	...,,..........	1,019531	"
"	Cairo	...,,..........	0,950312	"
"	Guinea.........	...,,..........	0,953782	"
"	Jidda.........	...,,..........	0,366016	"
" *sottile*...............	Malta..........	...,,..........	1,745047	"
"	Morocco	...,,..........	1,189934	"
" *market*..............	...,,..........	...,,..........	1,701139	"
"	Tripoli in Africa.	...,,..........	1,112095	"
"	Tunis.........	...,,..........	1,091547	"
Rotŏlo....................	Aleppo.........	...,,..........	5,06428	"
" *for Persian silks*.....	...,,..........	...,,.........	4,78293	"
" *Damascene*...........	...,,..........	...,,..........	4,22023	"
" *Tripolitan*...........	...,,..........	...,,..........	4,923606	"
"	Damascus.......	...,,..........	3,9375	"
"	Genoa	...,,..........	1,15359	"
"	Majorca.........	...,,..........	0,92794	"
"	Naples.......	...,,..........	1,9645	"
"	Palermo........	...,,..........	1,925569	"
"	...,,..........	...,,..........	1,750518	"
"	Smyrna	...,,..........	1,26562	"
"	Tripoli in Syria .	...,,..........	4,0057	"
"	...,,..........	...,,..........	4,80686	"
Rottel.....................	Constantinople...	...,,..........	1,403	"
Roupell....................	Ragusa..........	dry capacity ...	0,70309	bushels.

Acre = 4840 square yards. Bushel = 2150,42 cubic inches. Cubic foot = 1728 cubic inches.
Gallon = 231 cubic inches. Mile = 1760 yards. Pound = 7000 grains. Yard = 36 inches.

NAME.	LOCALITY.	CHARACTER.	VALUE.
Rubbiatella...............	Rome.............	dry capacity ...	4,17763 bushels.
Rubbio	Ancona..........	.....,,.........	7,97422 "
"	Leghorn.........	.....,,.........	7,77671 "
"	Milan...........	.....,,.........	8,3 "
"	Rome	.....,,.........	8,35525 "
" for wine...........	Turin...........	liquid capacity	2,48037 gallons.
" peso scarso.........	Genoa	weight........	17,461517 pounds.
" peso grosso.........	....,,.........	....,,.........	19,225307 "
"	Mantua.........	....,,.........	17,395475 "
" for oil; old measure..	Milan..........	....,,.........	48,0588 "
" new measure	....,,.........	....,,.........	22,04737 "
"	Naples.........	....,,.........	18,387506 "
"	Nice...........	....,,.........	17,174901 "
"	Parma..........	....,,.........	17,990654 "
"	Placentia.......	....,,.........	17,527659 "
"	Turin..........	....,,.........	20,327675 "
" legal..............	Venit. Lombardy	....,,.........	22,04737 "
"	Rome...........	superficial......	4,5658 acres.
Rundlet or Runlet; for wine	England	liquid capacity	18.—— gallons.
Rupee or Rupia ; maximum..	E. Indies; Madras	weight........	0,025714 pounds.
" minimum............	....,,.. Calcutta	....,,.........	0,023333 "
" mean of 38..........	....,,.........	....,,.........	0,024965 "
Rupp....................	Graubündten	....,,.........	19,107721 "
Ruthe ; old measure	Aix-la-Chapelle ..	length	4,93410 yards.
"	Altona..........	....,,.........	3,43241 "
"	Baden	....,,.........	3,28090 "
"	Basel	....,,.........	3,33052 "
" legal..............	Bavaria.........	....,,.........	3,19187 "
"	Berne...........	....,,.........	3,20717 "
"	Bremen.........	....,,.........	5,06040 "
"	Brunswic.......	....,,.........	4,99328 "
" old measure	Coblentz	....,,.........	5,08528 "
"	Cologne........	....,,.........	5,03278 "
"	Dantzic.........	....,,.........	4,70621 "
"	Dresden........	....,,.........	4,95383 "
" surveyors'..........	....,,.........	....,,.........	3,09783 "
"	Frankfort	....,,.........	3,89074 "
"	Friburg.........	....,,.........	3,20717 "
" tillage.............	Gotha..........	....,,.........	4,40368 "
" woodland..........	....,,.........	....,,.........	5,03278 "
" geestruthe.........	Hamburg.......	....,,.........	5,01304 "
" marschruthe........	....,,.........	....,,.........	4,38641 "

Acre = 4840 square yards.   Bushel = 2150,42 cubic inches.   Cubic foot = 1728 cubic inches. Gallon = 231 cubic inches.   Mile = 1760 yards.   Pound = 7000 grains.   Yard = 36 inches.

NAME.	LOCALITY.	CHARACTER.	VALUE.
Ruthe	Hanover	length	5,10938 yards.
"	Hesse Cassel.....	...,,.........	4,36223 "
" old measure..........	Königsberg......	...,,.........	5,04759 "
"	Lausanne........	...,,.........	3,28090 "
"	Leipsic..........	...,,.........	4,94595 "
" ,,...............	Lippe...........	...,,.........	5,06594 "
"	Lithuania........	...,,.........	5,32883 "
"	Lübec...........	...,,.........	5,03773 "
"	Mecklenburg....	...,,.........	5,09198 "
" since 1818	Nassau..........	...,,.........	5,46817 "
"	Nürnberg........	...,,.........	5,31580 "
"	...,,..........	...,,.........	3,98686 "
" old measure..........	Oldenburg.......	...,,.........	6,48341 "
" actual "	...,,.........	...,,.........	5,83507 "
" old "	Pomerania......	...,,.........	5,11172 "
" legal...............	Prussia.........	...,,.........	4,11889 "
"	Saxony..........	...,,.........	4,68835 "
"	Silesia	...,,.........	4,72378 "
"	Solothurn........	...,,.........	3,20718 "
" old measure..........	Stettin	...,,.........	4,98818 "
"	Strasburg........	...,,.........	3,16280 "
" builders'............	Vienna..........	...,,.........	3,45707 "
"	Weimar.........	...,,.........	5,93411 "
" legal...............	Würtemberg.....	...,,.........	3,13315 "
" old measure..........	...,,.........	...,,.........	5,01304 "
" "	...,,.........	...,,.........	5,14860 "
" Prussian...........	...,,.........	...,,.........	4,11889 "
"	Zurich..........	...,,.........	3,29598 "
Ruttee; gold, etc.; mean of 8..	East Indies......	weight.........	2,267 grains.
" for pearls...........	Bombay.........	...,,.........	3.—— "
" "	Calcutta	...,,.........	2,825 "
" for precious stones....	Delhi..........	...,,.........	1,25 "
" "	Sindh..........	...,,.........	16.—— "
" "	Surat	...,,.........	2,846 "
Saâ or Saha..............	Algiers..........	dry capacity...	1,36215 bushels.
Sabbath-day journey.......	Ancient Hebrews.	itinerary.......	0,5432 miles.
Sac....................	Brussels.........	dry capacity....	6,89665 bushels.
"	Courtray.......	...,,.......	3,58754 "
" maximum..............	France; Nantes .	...,,........	4,25670 "
" minimum.............	...,,...Aiguillon	...,,.......	2,01796 "
" mean of 35............	...,,........	...,,.......	2,77594 "

Acre = 4840 square yards.   Bushel = 2150,42 cubic inches.   Cubic foot = 1728 cubic inches.
Gallon = 231 cubic inches.   Mile = 1760 yards.   Pound = 7000 grains.   Yard = 36 inches.

NAME.	LOCALITY.	CHARACTER.	VALUE.	
Sac.....................	Ghent..........	dry capacity...	2,99780	bushels.
"	Geneva	.....,,.........	2,20403	"
"	Lausanne........	.....,,.........	3,83106	"
"	Neufchâtel	.....,,.........	3,45860	"
" for charcoal	Paris	.....,,........	5,90642	"
" for lime...............	...,,...........	.....,,.........	0,73830	"
" for wheat and flour	...,,...........	.....,,.........	5,99872	"
"	Vaud	.....,,.........	3,83103	"
Saccáto...................	Florence	superficial......	1,3236	acres.
Sacco...................	Belluno	dry capacity...	2,71861	bushels.
"	Bergamo........	.....,,.........	4,70129	"
"	Cremona........	.....,,.........	3,03645	"
"	Florence and Pisa	.....,,.........	2,07462	"
"	Leghorn........	.....,,.........	2,07462	"
" for charcoal	Lisbon..........	.....,,.........	1,47140	"
"	Lucca..........	.....,,.........	2,08720	"
"	Milan..........	.....,,.........	4,15104	"
"	Modena.........	.....,,.........	3,60401	"
"	Nice..........	.....,,.........	3,40536	"
"	Reggio	.....,,.........	3,38698	"
"	Rovigo.........	.....,,.........	2,82077	"
"	Treviso.........	.....,,.........	2,46321	"
"	Turin..........	.....,,.........	3,26350	"
"	Verona..........	.....,,.........	3,255	"
"	Vicenza.........	.....,,.........	3,07050	"
Sachine or Sagine	Russia..........	length	2,33410	yards.
Sack...................	Altona..........	dry capacity...	5,98776	bushels.
"	Basel..........	.....,,.........	3,87806	"
" coal miners'...........	Carinthia	.....,,.........	28,378	"
" for coal; old measure....	England	.....,,.........	3.——	"
" ...,,...new measure...	...,,..........	.....,,.........	3,09455	"
"	Friburg	.....,,.........	3,42488	"
" for charcoal............	Hamburg........	.....,,.........	5,98776	"
"	Strasburg........	.....,,.........	2,95322	"
" for wheat; millers'......	United States....	.....,,.........	2.——	"
" for salt...............	...,,.........	weight........	215.——	pounds.
" for wool	England	...,,.........	364.——	"
Saco....................	Grenada	dry capacity ...	2,75778	bushels.
Sadang..................	Pegu..........	length	0,60133	yards.
Sadon...................	Medoc	superficial	0,1965	acres.
Saga ; for gold and silver....	Malacca	weight........	4,33	grains.
Saggio or Sazio	Ragusa	.....,,.........	0,010033	pounds.

Acre = 4840 square yards.   Bushel = 2150,42 cubic inches.   Cubic foot = 1728 cubic inches.
Gallon = 231 cubic inches.   Mile = 1760 yards.   Pound = 7000 grains.   Yard = 36 inches.

NAME.	LOCALITY.	CHARACTER.	VALUE.	
Saggio ; *peso grosso*	*Venice*	weight	0,014622	pounds.
" *sottile*	...,, ...	....,, ...	0,009248	"
Saha *or* Zah	*Tunis*	dry capacity	0,07812	bushels.
Sahm ; *for charcoal*	*Austria*	....,, ...	6,981	"
Salma	*Calabria*	liquid capacity	80,49240	gallons.
" *mean*	*Naples*	......,, ...	40,27262	"
" *for oil* ; *mean*	....,, ...	......,, ...	42,16670	"
" *for wine* "	*Sicily*	......,, ...	22.——	"
"	*Barcelona*	dry capacity ...	8,18909	bushels.
" *rasa*	*Malta*	......,, ...	8,22038	"
" colma ; *(heaped)*	...,, ...	......,, ...	9,5	"
"	*Sicily*	......,, ...	7,8	"
" *grosso*	...,, ...	......,, ...	10.——	"
Salmée ; *old measure* ; *mean*.	*Languedoc*	superficial	1,6752	acres.
Saltus	*Ancient Romans*.	......,, ...	498,3475	"
Salup	*Sumatra*	weight	2.——	pounds.
Saö	*An-nam*	length	7,99325	yards.
"	...,, ...	superficial	0,0132	acres.
Sat	*Siam*	dry capacity	0,00837	bushels.
Satāro	*Bergamo*	......,, ...	0,58740	"
Satin ; *old measure*	*Brussels*	weight	0,016111	pounds.
Saum	*Tyrol*	....,, ...	441,829295	"
"	*Vienna*	....,, ...	339,535675	"
" *for steel*	...,, ...	....,, ...	308,669250	"
" *lauter-mass*	*Aarau*	liquid capacity	38,042	gallons.
" *trübes-mass*	...,, ...	......,, ...	41,08536	"
"	*Basel*	......,, ...	40,33767	"
"	*Berne*	......,, ...	44,14944	"
"	*Graubündten*	......,, ...	31,58910	"
"	*Lucerne*	......,, ...	45,65392	"
"	*S. Gall*	......,, ...	44,371	"
"	*Solothurn*	......,, ...	42,11473	"
" *lauter-mass*	*Zurich*	......,, ...	43,39124	"
" *trübes-mass*	...,, ...	......,, ...	46,299	"
Schachtruthe ; *for masonry* ..	*Prussia*	solid	157,226	cub. feet.
Schaf ; *old measure*	*Augsburg*	dry capacity	5,83270	bushels.
" *for wheat, etc.* ; *old m.*	*Ratisbon*	......,, ...	16,64427	"
" *for oats* "	....,, ...	......,, ...	29,12746	"
" *for lime* "	....,, ...	......,, ...	6,24174	"
Schatz ; *for vineyards*	*Strasburg*	superficial	0,0620	acres.
Scheffel	*Anhalt-Koethen*.	dry capacity ...	1,50289	bushels.
" *legal*	*Bavaria*	......,, ...	6,31002	"

Acre = 4840 square yards. Bushel = 2150,42 cubic inches. Cubic foot = 1728 cubic inches.
Gallon = 231 cubic inches. Mile = 1760 yards. Pound = 7000 grains. Yard = 36 inches.

NAME.	LOCALITY.	CHARACTER.	VALUE.	
Scheffel; *usual; for oats*	*Bavaria*	dry capacity...	7,36169	bushels.
" *old measure*	*Berlin*	...... ,, ...	1,55314	"
"	*Bremen*	...... ,, ...	2,10195	"
" *old measure*.......	*Breslau*..........	...... ,, ...	2,11416	"
" *for wheat*.........	*Brunswic*	...... ,, ...	8,66720	"
" *for oats*	.. ,, ...	...... ,, ...	10,40064	"
" *old measure*.......	*Dantzic*	...... ,, ...	1,46212	"
"	*Dresden*.........	...... ,, ...	2,94850	"
"	*Gotha*...........	...... ,, ...	2,47809	"
" *for coal*	.. ,, ...	...... ,, ...	1,14080	"
"	*Hamburg*........	...... ,, ...	2,98811	"
" *for oats and barley*.	.. ,, ...	...... ,, ...	4,48234	"
" *mean*.............	*Hesse Cassel*	...... ,, ...	2,3	"
"	*Leipsic*..........	...... ,, ...	2,94850	"
"	*Lippe*...........	...... ,, ...	1,25694	"
" *for oats*	.. ,, ...	...... ,, ...	1,46643	"
"	*Lübec*	...... ,, ...	1,00970	"
" *for oats*	.. ,, ...	...... ,, ...	1,12463	"
" *legal*.............	*Mecklenburg*.....	...... ,, ...	1,10360	"
" *old measure*	*Munster*.........	...... ,, ...	0,65936	"
" "	*Naumburg*	...... ,, ...	1,63856	"
"	*Oldenburg*.......	...... ,, ...	0,64710	"
" *old measure*.......	*Potsdam*	...... ,, ...	1,51085	"
" *legal*.............	*Prussia*	...... ,, ...	1,55970	"
"	*Silesia, Austrian*.	...... ,, ...	2,16723	"
"	.. ,, ... *Prussian*	...... ,, ...	2,11416	"
" *old measure*.......	*Stettin*	...... ,, ...	1,46573	"
"	*Weimar*.........	...... ,, ...	2,18413	"
"	*Würtemberg*	...... ,, ...	5,02919	"
" *for coal and lime*...	.. ,, ...	...... ,, ...	2,08621	"
"	*Hamburg*.	superficial......	1,0385	acres.
"	*Lippe*...........	...... ,, ...	0,4242	"
" *tillage*	*Lübec*...........	...... ,, ...	0,3146	"
" *woodland*.........	.. ,, ...	...... ,, ...	0,4195	"
"	*Oldenburg*.......	...... ,, ...	0,1717	"
"	*Rostock*.........	...... ,, ...	0,3931	"
Schenkkanne	*Leipsic*..........	liquid capacity	0,31807	gallons.
Schenkmass	*Augsburg*	...... ,, ...	0,34760	"
"	*S. Gall*.........	...... ,, ...	0,30313	"
"	*Weimar*	...... ,, ...	0,24205	"
Schepel; *old measure*.......	*Amsterdam*......	dry capacity...	0,78931	bushels.
" *legal*	*Holland*.........	...... ,, ...	0,28378	"

Acre = 4840 square yards.   Bushel = 2150,42 cubic inches.   Cubic foot = 1728 cubic inches. Gallon = 231 cubic inches.   Mile = 1760 yards.   Pound = 7000 grains.   Yard = 36 inches.

NAME.	LOCALITY.	CHARACTER.	VALUE.	
Schifflast	Berlin	weight	4124,72	pounds.
Schiffpfund	Aix-la-Chapelle	,,	308,911	"
"	Altona	,,	299,028479	"
" land carriage	,,	,,	341,77	"
" legal	Berlin	,,	340,4114	"
" old measure	,,	,,	289,2615	"
"	Bremen	,,	318,7274	"
"	Brunswic	,,	288,568	"
"	Dantzic	,,	340,28	"
"	Hamburg	,,	299,00819	"
" land carriage	,,	,,	341,72365	"
" for earths, metals, etc.	Königsberg	,,	340,8702	"
"	Lübec	,,	299,24832	"
" land carriage	,,	,,	341,99808	"
"	Mecklenburg	,,	313,72656	"
" land carriage	Nürnberg	,,	337,2963	"
"	Oldenburg	,,	309,54508	"
" old measure	Rostock	,,	299,05	"
" land carriage	,,	,,	341,77	"
" old measure	Stettin	,,	289,24	"
Schinck	Temeswar	dry capacity	3,02765	bushels.
Schippond	Amsterdam	weight	326,74202	pounds.
"	Antwerp	,,	310,974	"
Schnur; surveyors'	Königsberg	length	50,47586	yards.
Schoina; [uncertain]	Anc't Egyptians.	itinerary	4,1468	miles.
Schoppen	Aarau	liquid capacity	0,09514	gallons.
"	Baden	,,	0,09910	"
"	Basel	,,	0,09392	"
"	Frankfort	,,	0,11840	"
"	Friburg	,,	0,10316	"
"	Glaris	,,	0,11751	"
"	Hesse Cassel	,,	0,14417	"
"	Hesse Darmstadt.	,,	0,13209	"
"	Lucerne	,,	0,11413	"
"	Mannheim	,,	0,13169	"
"	Schaffhausen	,,	0,08682	"
Schott	Dantzic	weight	0,021483	pounds.
Schragen	Leipsic	solid	301,47	cub. feet.
Schreef; mean	Belgium	liquid capacity	1,44944	gallons.
Schritt	Germany, gen'y.	length	1,71620	yards.
Schrott; mean	,,	dry capacity	0,03122	bushels.
Schuh	Basel	length	0,33305	yards.

Acre = 4840 square yards.   Bushel = 2150,42 cubic inches.   Cubic foot = 1728 cubic inches.
Gallon = 231 cubic inches.   Mile = 1760 yards.   Pound = 7000 grains.   Yard = 36 inches.

NAME.	LOCALITY.	CHARACTER.	VALUE.	
Schuh....................	*Brunswic*	length.	0,31208	yards.
"	*Lindau ; Bavaria*	...,,............	0,33650	"
" *builders' and surveyors'*	.....,,.........	...,,..........	0,31578	"
" " "	*Lucerne*..........	...,,..........	0,31086	"
" *artizans'*	*Schaffhausen*	...,,..........	0,32578	"
" *city; old measure*......	*Strasburg*	...,,..........	0,31628	"
" *rural* "	....,,..........	...,,..........	0,32261	"
" *artizans' & surveyors'*	*Trèves* or *Trier*..	...,,..........	0,32125	"
" *carpenters'*..........	....,,..........	...,,..........	0,33367	"
" *stone-cutters'*........	*Zug*	...,,..........	0,29389	"
Scorzo	*Rome*	dry capacity ...	0,37978	bushels.
"	....,,..........	superficial	0,2854	acres.
Scriptŭlum *or* Scripŭlum ...	*Ancient Romans*..	weight	17,546	grains.
Scropŏlo ; *apothecaries'*......	*Bologna*..........	...,,..........	18,186	"
" *commercial*........	*Florence*	...,,..........	6,06	"
" *apothecaries'*......	*Genoa*	...,,..........	16,986	"
" "	*Milan*	...,,..........	17,514	"
" "	*Naples*..........	...,,..........	13,752	"
" "	*Rome*	...,,..........	17,896	"
" "	*Turin*...........	...,,..........	16,472	"
" "	*Tuscany*	...,,..........	18,196	"
" "	*Venice*..........	...,,..........	16,147	"
Scrupel " *old m.*	*Amsterdam*......	...,,..........	19,781	"
" " *since* 1817	....,,..........	...,,..........	20,096	"
" "	*Denmark & Holst.*	...,,..........	19,177	"
" "	*Germany, gener'y*	...,,..........	19,177	"
" " *legal*.....	*Holland*..........	...,,..........	20,096	"
" "	*Sweden*..........	...,,..........	19,024	"
" "	*Berlin*	length.	0,0716	inches.
" *old measure*	*Ulm*.............	...,,..........	0,0790	"
Scruple....................	*England* and *U.S.*	weight.........	20.——	grains.
Seah....................	*Ancient Hebrews.*	dry capacity....	0,36743	bushels.
Seam *of glass*	*England*	weight.........	120.——	pounds.
" *for malt ; old measure.*.	....,,..........	dry capacity ...	8.——	bushels.
Seau ; *old measure*	*Antwerp*	liquid capacity	79,2534	gallons.
Secchĭno....................	*Ferrara*	...,,..........	1,83002	"
Secchĭo....................	*Ionian Isles*......	...,,..........	3.——	"
"	*Venice*..........	...,,..........	2,85312	"
"	*Vicenza*..........	...,,..........	2,50749	"
Sechter....................	*Frankfort*	dry capacity ...	0,20352	bushels.
"	*Hanau*..........	...,,..........	0,21659	"
Seer ; *gold and sil. ; mean of* 43	*East Indies*	weight.........	0,596109	pounds.

Acre = 4840 square yards. Bushel = 2150,42 cubic inches. Cubic foot = 1728 cubic inches.
Gallon = 231 cubic inches. Mile = 1760 yards. Pound = 7000 grains. Yard = 36 inches.

NAME.	LOCALITY.	CHARACTER.	VALUE.
Seer; *commercial; mean of* 22	*East Indies*	weight	1,049423 pounds.
" *for grain; mean of* 183	....,,....	....,,....	2,127 "
Seidel	*Augsburg*	liquid capacity	0,15508 gallons.
"	*Nürnberg*	....,,....	0,15127 "
"	*Prague*	....,,....	0,13243 "
"	*Presburg*	....,,....	0,11007 "
"	*Ratisbon*	....,,....	0,11007 "
"	*Vienna*	....,,....	0,089 "
" *for coal*	*Munich*	dry capacity	4,23315 bushels.
"	*Prague*	....,,....	0,01578 "
"	*Presburg*	....,,....	0,01182 "
Seil; *vineyard*	*Bohemia*	length	41,57568 yards.
" *woodland*	....,,....	....,,....	27,28404 "
"	*Dantzic*	....,,....	47,06207 "
Selïbra *or* Semis	*Ancient Romans*	weight	0,360949 pounds.
Semōdius *or* Semi-modius	....,,....	dry capacity	0,12248 bushels.
Semūncia	....,,....	weight	0,030079 pounds.
Sen	*Siam*	length	42,0385 yards.
Septuagēssis	*Ancient Romans*	weight	50,53280 pounds.
Septunx	....,,....	....,,....	0,421107 "
Septus *or* Septūssis	....,,....	....,,....	5,05328 "
Seron	*Guinea*	....,,....	0,026504 "
Seroon; *for raisins; mean*	*Malaga*	....,,....	88,908488 "
Sescūncia	*Ancient Romans*	superficial	0,0779 acres.
Sester	*Trèves*	liquid capacity	1,36844 gallons.
"	*Baden*	dry capacity	0,42567 bushels.
"	*Basel*	....,,....	0,96951 "
"	..,,....	....,,....	0,48476 "
"	*Coblentz*	....,,....	0,14193 "
"	*Strasburg*	....,,....	0,52230 "
" *of Alsace*	....,,....	....,,....	0,53664 "
Sesti	*Siam*	....,,....	0,33462 "
Setërée; *maximum*	*France; Angers*	superficial	1,9547 acres.
" *minimum*	....,,*Montpellier*	....,,....	1,3501 "
" *mean of* 20	....,,....	....,,....	0,8441 "
"	*Nice*	....,,....	0,3815 "
Setïer	*Geneva*	liquid capacity	11,94719 gallons.
"	*Lausanne*	....,,....	10,69920 "
"	*Montpellier*	....,,....	8,92921 "
"	*Neufchâtel*	....,,....	8,04916 "
"	*Paris*	....,,....	1,96827 "
"	*Toulouse*	....,,....	9,22774 "

Acre = 4840 square yards.   Bushel = 2150,42 cubic inches.   Cubic foot = 1728 cubic inches.
Gallon = 231 cubic inches.   Mile = 1760 yards.   Pound = 7000 grains.   Yard = 36 inches.

NAME.	LOCALITY.	CHARACTER.	VALUE.	
Setier......................	Toulouse........	liquid capacity	12,30365	gallons.
"	Arles............	dry capacity ...	1,70268	bushels.
" maximum...........	Belgium; Florenne	.....,,.........	1,09085	"
" minimum	.....,,....Fleurus	.....,,.........	0,65894	"
" mean of 10..........	....,,..........	.....,,.........	0,85985	"
"	Calais	.....,,.........	4,79588	"
"	Montpellier......	.....,,.........	1,47566	"
" old measure	Nantes..........	.....,,.........	4,13411	"
"	Neufchâtel	.....,,.........	0,44128	"
"	Paris..........	.....,,.........	4,42982	"
" for oats.......	..,,.........	.....,,.........	8,85965	"
" for salt	..,,.........	.....,,.........	5,90648	"
" for charcoal	..,,..........	.....,,.........	11,81286	"
"	Rouen	.....,,.........	5,16480	"
"	Toulon	.....,,.........	2,21405	"
" of Vermandois........	La Fère, etc.....	superficial......	0,8480	acres.
Sexagessis	Ancient Romans.	weight..........	43,313829	pounds.
Sexis......................	.....,,.........	....,,.........	4,331383	"
Sextans....................	.....,,.........	....,,.........	0,120316	"
Sextarius................	.....,,.........	liquid capacity	0,14252	gallons.
"	.....,,.........	dry capacity ...	0,01531	bushels.
Sextingkar	Denmark........	.....,,.........	0,03185	"
"	Finland........	liquid capacity	2,07326	gallons.
Sextula...................	Ancient Romans.	weight..........	0,010027	pounds.
Shekel....................	Ancient Hebrews.	....,,.........	0,032086	"
Shik tsong................	China..........	.....,,.........	160.——	"
Shik shi..................	...,,..........	dry capacity ...	2,17733	bushels.
Shing shi.................	...,,..........	.....,,.........	0,02177	"
Shing tsong...............	...,,..........	liquid capacity	0,13175	gallons.
Shu......................	...,,..........	weight..........	0,243	grains.
Shye	Anjar...........	dry capacity....	0,88243	bushels.
Sicilicus	Ancient Romans.	weight..........	0,015040	pounds.
Sida	Mangalore	....,,.........	0,614	"
Sieb...................	Stettin	dry capacity....	0,51990	bushels.
Siebmass	Altenburg........	....,,.........	0,99759	"
Siliqua	Ancient Romans.	weight.........	2,924	grains.
"	Rome..........	....,,.........	3,03	"
Simmer...................	Rhenish Bavaria.	dry capacity....	0,35473	bushels.
"	Darmstadt.......	....,,.........	0,90809	"
" old measure........	...,,.........	....,,.........	0,79693	"
"	Frankfort.......	....,,.........	0,81407	"
"	Mannheim......	....,,.........	0,39403	"

Acre = 4840 square yards. Bushel = 2150,42 cubic inches. Cubic foot = 1728 cubic inches. Gallon = 231 cubic inches. Mile = 1760 yards. Pound = 7000 grains. Yard = 36 inches.

NAME.	LOCALITY.	CHARACTER.	VALUE.	
Simmer..................	*Mentz & Nassau*	dry capacity ...	0,77614	bushels.
"	*Nürnberg*	....,,........	9,02817	"
" *for oats and barley*..	....,,........	....,,........	16,69572	"
Simpŭlon................	*Ancient Greeks*..	liquid capacity	7,69613	gallons.
Simra.................	*Baireuth*	dry capacity....	14,07393	bushels.
"	*Bamberg*.......	....,,........	2,206	"
" *for oats and barley*....	....,,........	....,,........	2,7312	"
"	*Coburg*.........	....,,........	2,52419	"
" *for oats and barley*....	....,,........	....,,........	3,12357	"
Simri..................	*Carlsruhe*.......	....,,........	0,45519	"
"	*Stuttgard*.......	....,,........	0,62865	"
Sister.................	*Berg-op-Zoom* ...	....,,........	0,13117	"
"	*Lierre*..........	....,,........	7,89816	"
Sitarion...............	*Ancient Greeks*..	weight........	0,936	grains.
Skålpund..............	*Sweden*.........	....,,........	0,937284	pounds.
Skeppel...............	*Holstein*........	dry capacity...	0,49349	bushels.
Skeppund; *berg-wigt*......	*Sweden*.........	weight........	348,823363	pounds.
" *metall-wigt*......	....,,........	....,,........	299,93088	"
" *tachjern-wigt*....	....,,........	....,,........	453,470371	"
" *uppstadt-wigt*....	....,,........	....,,........	315,677251	"
" *viktualie-wigt*....	....,,........	....,,........	374,9136	"
Skieppe................	*Copenhagen*......	dry capacity ...	0,49349	bushels.
" *for coal and salt*.....	....,,........	....,,........	0,60315	"
" *mean of* 4..........	*Denmark*.......	....,,........	0,50484	"
Skiepper...............	....,,........	superficial......	0,6813	acres.
Skippund...............	....,,........	weight........	352,37	pounds.
" *duties'*............	*Elsinore*........	....,,........	352,75792	"
Skoyciec...............	*Cracow*........	....,,........	0,018644	"
" *since* 1819..........	*Poland*.........	....,,........	0,018627	"
Skrupŭlow............	....,,........	....,,........	16,298	grains.
" *apothecaries'*......	....,,........	....,,........	19,211	"
Soållee	*Culcutta*........	dry capacity...	2,3378	bushels.
Sok...................	*Siam*...........	length	0,52548	yards.
Soldo..................	*Florence*	....,,........	0,03188	"
Solive ; *for lumber ; old meas.*	*France*	solid..........	3,632	cub. feet.
Solläga ; *for grain*.........	*Bellary*	weight........	8,64	pounds.
Solotnik ; *for gold and silver.*	*Russia*..........	....,,........	65,75	grains.
Soma..................	*Ancona*.........	liquid capacity	18,49246	gallons.
" *for wine*............	*Florence*	....,,........	24,08459	"
" *for oil*.............	....,,........	....,,........	19,26768	"
" "	*Rome*..........	....,,........	43,3860	"
" *since* 1803...........	*Venit. Lombardy.*	....,,........	26,4178	"

Acre = 4840 square yards. Bushel = 2150,42 cubic inches. Cubic foot = 1728 cubic inches. Gallon = 231 cubic inches. Mile = 1760 yards. Pound = 7000 grains. Yard = 36 inches.

NAME.	LOCALITY.	CHARACTER.	VALUE.	
Soma......................	Bergamo........	dry capacity...	4,6692	bushels.
"	Brescia...........	......,,,........	4,143	"
" for rice; old measure...	Milan	......,,,........	6,22506	"
" since 1803.............	Venit. Lombardy.	......,,,........	2,8378	"
Somme; for lumber; old mea.	France..........	solid..........	29,056	cub. feet.
Sömmer..................	Coblentz	dry capacity...	0,56773	bushels.
" old measure	Cologne..........	......,,,........	0,50918	"
Sompay; for gold and silver	Siam............	weight........	14,11	grains.
Sompi....................	Madagascar....	......,,,.........	60.———	"
Sou; esterlin; old measure ..	France...........	......,,,.........	0,040473	"
" of the mint "	...,,,..........	......,,,.........	0,026982	"
Span	England and U.S.	length	9.———	inches.
"	Masulipatan.....	......,,,.........	6,375	"
Spann....................	Sweden........	dry capacity....	2,07856	bushels.
Spanne; miners'...........	Prussia..........	length	10,2975	inches.
" "	Saxony...........	......,,,.........	9,656	"
Spannland................	Sweden..........	superficial.....	0,6066	acres.
Spint....................	Altona..........	dry capacity...	0,18708	bushels.
"	Bremen...........	......,,,.........	0,13137	"
"	Hamburg........	......,,,.........	0,18675	"
"	Kiel	......,,,.........	0,07010	"
"	Mecklenburg....	......,,,.........	0,06898	"
Spithäma.................	Ancient Greeks..	length........	9,1029	inches.
"	Ancient Romans.	...,,,..........	8,7359	"
Stab......................	Frankfort	...,,,..........	1,31236	yards.
"	Friburg..........	...,,,..........	1,16975	"
"	Leipsic..........	...,,,..........	1,23646	"
" since 1823.............	S. Gall and Vaud	...,,,..........	1,31236	"
Stack of firewood...........	England	solid...........	108.———	cub. feet.
Stadïon; Delphic or Pythian	Ancient Greeks..	itinerary.......	0,0921	miles.
" Philetairic........	.....,,,.......	......,,,.......	0,1316	"
" Olympic..........	.....,,,.......	......,,,.......	0,1149	"
Stadïum	Ancient Romans.	......,,,.......	0,1149	"
Stajo	Bergamo	dry capacity...	0,58365	bushels.
" or Stara	Bologna..........	......,,,.......	1,11583	"
"	Corsica..........	......,,,.......	4,25670	"
"	Cremona........	......,,,.......	1,01215	"
"	Florence and Pisa	......,,,.......	0,69155	"
"	Leghorn.........	......,,,.......	0,69155	"
"	Lucca...........	......,,,.......	0,68448	"
"	Mantua..........	......,,,.......	0,98840	"
" or Staro	Milan...........	......,,,.......	0,51875	"

Acre = 4840 square yards. Bushel = 2150,42 cubic inches. Cubic foot = 1728 cubic inches.
Gallon = 231 cubic inches. Mile = 1760 yards. Pound = 7000 grains. Yard = 36 inches.

NAME.	LOCALITY.	CHARACTER.	VALUE.	
Stajo *or* Staro	*Modena*	dry capacity	1,99783	bushels.
"	*Nice*	...,,...	1,13512	"
"	*Padua*	...,,...	0,82249	"
"	*Palermo*	...,,...	0,06990	"
" *or* Staro	*Parma*	...,,...	1,33376	"
"	*Placentia*	...,,...	0,89322	"
"	*Ragusa*	...,,...	4,21851	"
"	*Reggio*	...,,...	1,69399	"
"	*Rome*	...,,...	0,69627	"
" *or* Staro	*Turin*	...,,...	1,08783	"
" "	*Venice*	...,,...	2,27026	"
"	*Vicenza*	...,,...	0,76763	"
" *old measure*	*Milan*	liquid capacity	6,65306	gallons.
" *or* Staro	*Naples*	...,,...	2,61633	"
Stajŏlo	*Florence*	superficial	0,1324	acres.
Stangiew	*Cracow*	liquid capacity	72,14172	gallons.
" *since* 1819	*Poland*	...,,...	52,83560	"
Stäng	*Sweden*	length	5,18104	yards.
Starëllo	*Cagliari*	dry capacity	1,38856	bushels.
"	*Milan*	...,,...	0,25938	"
"	*Rome*	...,,...	0,52220	"
"	*Cagliari*	superficial	0,9802	acres.
Starland	*Bolzano; Tyrol*	...,,...	0,2757	"
Staro	*Parma*	...,,...	0,1255	"
" *mean*	*Piedmont*	...,,...	0,09850	"
" *or* Star	*Bolzano*	dry capacity	1,08696	bushels.
"	*Ferrara*	...,,...	0,88606	"
"	*Patras*	...,,...	2,33041	"
" *or* Star	*Tyrol*	...,,...	0,86572	"
Stater	*Ancient Greeks*	weight	0,019252	pounds.
Stathmos	...,,...	itinerary	8,2936	miles.
Stechkanne ; *for whale oil*	*Bremen*	liquid capacity	5,12505	gallons.
" "	*Hamburg*	...,,...	5,11456	"
Stecken	*Frankfort*	solid	32,060	cub. feet.
"	*Hesse Darmstadt.*	...,,...	41,939	"
"	*Mentz*	...,,...	55,157	"
Steckan	*Amsterdam*	liquid capacity	5,12505	gallons.
" *for beer*	...,,...	...,,...	5,19268	"
" *for brandy*	...,,...	...,,...	4,95338	"
Steen	...,,...	weight	8,708711	pounds.
Stein ; *for flax*	*Altona*	...,,...	21,3595	"
" *for wool or feathers*	...,,...	...,,...	10,67975	"

Acre = 4840 square yards. Bushel = 2150,42 cubic inches. Cubic foot = 1728 cubic inches. Gallon = 231 cubic inches. Mile = 1760 yards. Pound = 7000 grains. Yard = 36 inches.

NAME.	LOCALITY.	CHARACTER.	VALUE.	
Stein	Antwerp	weight.........	8,29264	pounds.
"	Baden	....,,..........	11,023685	"
"	Berlin	....,,..........	22,685960	"
" for flax.............	Bremen..........	....,,..........	21,98124	"
"	Brunswic.......	....,,..........	20,612	"
" for sugar, rice, etc......	Dantzic	....,,..........	22,68596	"
" for flax.............	....,,......	....,,..........	34,02894	"
"	Dresden & Leipsic	....,,..........	22,64383	"
"	Frankfort	....,,..........	24,510606	"
" for flax.............	Hamburg.........	....,,..........	21,35772	"
" "	Hanover	....,,..........	21,58888	"
" for iron.............	Leipsic..........	....,,..........	22,67811	"
"	Lübec...........	....,,..........	21,37488	"
"	Munich	....,,..........	24,6931	"
" old measure...........	...,,...........	....,,..........	24,7448	"
"	Oldenburg.......	....,,..........	21,18166	"
"	Prague..........	....,,..........	22,68	"
" for flax	Rostock.........	....,,..........	24,649944	"
" old measure...........	...,,...........	...·,,..........	22,40904	"
"	Solothurn.......	....,,..........	11,4311	"
"	Vienna.........	....,,..........	24,694	"
Stekar....................	Russia..........	dry capacity...	0,52357	bushels.
Sten....................	Sweden	weight.........	29,993088	pounds.
Stère .... :....	France........	solid...........	35,3166	cub. feet.
Stiŏro	Florence	superficial	0,8363	acres.
Stochiăcah...............	Bolzano.........	....,,..........	2,2058	"
Stock ; for oats and barley...	Hamburg........	dry capacity...	89,6434	bushels.
Stof....................	Revel..	....,,..........	0,03107	"
"	Riga...........	....,,..........	0,03588	"
· "	Courland........	liquid capacity	0,34713	gallons.
" for wine ; old measure ...	Dantzic.........	....,,..........	0,45333	"
" for beer " ...,,......		....,,..........	0,60787	"
"	Narva	....,,..........	0,34053	"
"	Revel and Riga..	....,,..........	0,34369	"
Stone....................	England	weight.........	14.——	pounds.
" for glass	...,,........	....,,..........	5.——	"
" for meat and fish......	...,,........	....,,..........	8.——	"
" London weight.........	...,,....bef. 1304	....,,..........	12,5	"
" Tours "	...,,...........	....,,..........	12.——	"
" Troy.................	Scotland	....,,..........	17,420444	"
" old Tron.............	....,,........	....,,..........	22,865778	"
" Glasgow Tron	...,,........	....,,..........	22,499556	"

Acre = 4840 square yards.   Bushel = 2150,42 cubic inches.   Cubic foot = 1728 cubic inches.   Gallon = 231 cubic inches.   Mile = 1760 yards.   Pound = 7000 grains.   Yard = 36 inches.

NAME.	LOCALITY.	CHARACTER.	VALUE.	
Stoop...................	*Amsterdam......*	liquid capacity	0,64063	gallons.
"	*Antwerp........*	....,,........	0,75127	"
"	*Brussels........*	....,,........	0,71560	"
"	*Rotterdam......*	....,,........	0,77603	"
Stop	*Sweden........*	....,,........	0,34541	"
"	...,,........	dry capacity ...	0,03712	bushels.
Stopa...................	*Cracow.........*	length........	0,38981	yards.
" *since* 1819............	*Poland.........*	....,,........	0,31497	"
" *old measure*..........	...,,........	....,,........	0,32564	"
Stopello.................	*Naples.........*	dry capacity....	0,19590	bushels.
Stotz	*Glaris.........*	liquid capacity	0,11751	gallons.
" *lauter-mass*..........	*Zurich.........*	....,,........	0,12052	"
" *schenk-mass*.........	...,,........	....,,........	0,10847	"
Streep	*Holland........*	length........	0,03937	inches.
Strich ; *Rhenish*...........	*Germany, gener'y*	....,,........	0,0858	"
"	*Prague.........*	dry capacity....	2,65618	bushels.
"	*Ratisbon........*	....,,........	0,75675	"
"	*Bohemia........*	superficial.....	0,7107	acres.
Strike ; *for malt; old measure*	*England........*	dry capacity ...	2.——	bushels.
Stübchen	*Bremen........*	liquid capacity	0,85103	gallons.
" *for beer.*.........	...,,.........	....,,........	0,99636	"
"	*Brunswic......*	....,,........	0,988	"
"	*Denmark.......*	....,,........	0,9889	"
"	*Gotha.........*	....,,........	0,96120	"
"	*Hamburg......*	....,,........	0,95369	"
"	*Hanover.......*	....,,........	1,03599	"
"	*Holstein........*	....,,........	0,95644	"
"	*Lübec.........*	....,,........	0,98935	"
"	*Mecklenburg....*	....,,........	0,95685	"
Stückfass.................	*Frankfort.......*	....,,........	303,12832	"
"	*Heidelberg......*	....,,........	313,397	"
" *for Rhine-wine*....	*Nürnberg.......*	....,,........	290,43516	"
Stütz	*Carlsruhe.......*	....,,........	4,96367	"
"	*Neufchâtel.....*	....,,........	4,02458	"
"	*Solothurn.......*	....,,........	2,10574	"
Stykfad.................	*Denmark........*	....,,........	296,67189	"
Succäle.................	*Santa Maura...*	....,,........	0,85726	"
Sznur *or* Sznurow ; *surveying*	*Poland.........*	length........	47,245	yards.
Ta.......................	*An-nam........*	weight........	137,752	pounds.
Taakel ; *old measure*.......	*Holland........*	dry capacity...	0,23497	bushels.
Tac ; *builders'*.............	*An-nam........*	length........	1,9184	inches.

Acre = 4840 square yards. Bushel = 2150,42 cubic inches. Cubic foot = 1728 cubic inches.
Gallon = 231 cubic inches. Mile = 1760 yards. Pound = 7000 grains. Yard = 36 inches.

NAME.	LOCALITY.	CHARACTER.	VALUE.	
Tac; *mercers'*	*An-nam*	length	2,5578	inches.
Tael *or* Tale	*Amboyna*	weight	0,065109	pounds.
"	*Bantam; Java* ...	...,,.	0,151094	"
"	*Batavia* ...,,...	...,,.	0,084745	"
" *for gold and jewels*	*Borneo*	...,,.	0,087771	"
"	*China & Sooloo I.*	...,,.	0,083333	"
"	*Japan*	...,,.	0,081779	"
"	*Malacca*	...,,.	0,084375	"
" *mean of 3*	*Molucca I.*	...,,.	0,076941	"
"	*Siam*	...,,.	0,067627	"
"	*Singapore*	...,,.	0,083333	"
" *mean of 7*	*Sumatra*	...,,.	0,085871	"
Tagmatt	*Bolzano*	superficial	1,1029	acres.
Taim	*Constantinople* ...	weight	3,09	grains.
"	*Pegu*	length	5,4108	inches.
Talănton	*Anc. Babylonians*	weight	96,258295	pounds.
" Ptolemaïc	*Anc't Egyptians* .	...,,.	57,754977	"
" Xylic	" ,,..	...,,.	69,305973	"
" Œginetic	*Ancient Greeks* ..	...,,.	96,258295	"
" Attic; before Solon.	.....,,..	...,,.	80,215246	"
" " after...,,...	........,,..	...,,.	57,754977	"
" Eubœïc	......,,..	...,,.	80,215246	"
Talĕnto; *actual measure*	*Ionian Isles*	...,,.	100.——	"
Talie; *Brabanter*	*Antwerp*	length	1,7116	inches.
" *old measure*	*Brussels*	...,,.	1,7124	"
"	*Charleroi*	...,,.	1,6738	"
" *maximum*	*Halle; Belgium*..	...,,.	1,7963	"
"	*Gheel*	...,,.	1,6890	"
" *minimum*	*Louvain; Belgium*	...,,.	1,6733	"
"	*Wavre*	...,,.	1,6953	"
Tam	*China*	weight	133,333333	pounds.
Tampang; *for tin*	*Malacca*	...,,.	1,355925	"
Tank	*Bombay*	...,,.	68,056	grains.
" *for precious stones*	...,,.	...,,.	72.——	"
"	*Darwar*	...,,.	50.——	"
"	*Poonah*	...,,.	191,667	"
" *for precious stones*	*Surat*	...,,.	68,304	"
Taphach	*Ancient Hebrews.*	length	2,8680	inches.
Tarrie	*Algiers*	dry capacity ...	0,56295	bushels.
Tattämy	*Japan*	length	2,07845	yards.
Tau shi	*China*	dry capacity....	0,21773	bushels.
" tsong	...,,.	liquid capacity	1,31750	gallons.

Acre = 4840 square yards.　Bushel = 2150,42 cubic inches.　Cubic foot = 1728 cubic inches.
Gallon = 231 cubic inches.　Mile = 1760 yards.　Pound = 7000 grains.　Yard = 36 inches.

NAME.	LOCALITY.	CHARACTER.	VALUE.	
Tavŏla; *Lombardic*........	*Italy; mean of* 10	superficial	0,00851	acres.
" *Piedmontese*........	..,,........,,....7	....,,.........	0,00105	"
" *since* 1803.........	*Milan*	....,,.........	0,0247	"
" *old measure*	...,,.........	....,,.........	0,0067	"
"	*Modena*........	....,,.........	0,0097	"
"	*Turin*.........	....,,.........	0,0094	"
"	*Venice*.........	....,,.........	0,00107	"
Temen...................	*Tripoli in Africa*	dry capacity...	0,7617	bushels.
Tempoh...................	*Sumatra*	length.........	4,5	inches.
Terça...................	*Lisbon*.........	....,,.........	0,39843	yards.
Tercia	*Madrid*.........	....,,.........	0,30440	"
Termĭno.................	*Tripoli in Africa*	weight.........	0,008688	pounds.
Terŭncius	*Ancient Romans*.	....,,.........	0,180474	"
Tesa...................	*Turin*.........	length	1,87290	yards.
Tetarton.................	*Ancient Greeks* ..	liquid capacity	0,03563	gallons.
"	....,,.........	dry capacity....	0,00383	bushels.
Tetradrāchmon............	....,,.........	weight.........	0,038503	pounds.
Tetrobolon................	...,.,,.........	....,,.........	44,92	grains.
Thauen; *Rhenish vineyards*.	*Germany*........	superficial......	0,3156	acres.
Thermos	*Ancient Greeks* ..	weight.........	7,487	grains.
Thuoc; *builders'*...........	*China*..........	length.........	0,53288	yards.
" *mercers'*...........	...,,.........	....,,.........	0,71051	"
Tibĕro...................	*Tripoli in Africa*	dry capacity ...	0,05761	bushels.
Tica....................	*Borneo*.........	weight.........	6,40	grains.
Tical...................	*Pegu*..........	....,,.........	0,033333	pounds.
"	*Siam*...........	....,,.........	0,016907	"
Tierce	*England* and *U.S.*	liquid capacity	42.——	gallons.
Tierçon.................	*Bordeaux*........	....,,.........	39,83804	"
"	*Champagne*......	....,,.........	14,60112	"
" *old measure*	*Paris*...........	....,,.........	23,61926	"
Timbang; *for grain*.......	*Batavia*.........	weight.........	677,9625	pounds.
Tippree ......,,........	*Bombay*.........	....,,.........	0,35	"
To....................	*China*..........	itinerary.......	69,1797	miles.
Tod; *for wool*.............	*England*	weight.........	28.——	pounds.
Toende; *for beer*...........	*Denmark*........	liquid capacity	34,68114	gallons.
"	...,,.........	dry capacity...	3,94460	bushels.
"	....,,.........	superficial......	5,45	acres.
Toesa...................	*Spain*..........	length.........	1,85472	yards.
Toise; *le comte*.............	*Besançon*........	...,,.........	2,73783	"
" *de Roi*.............	....,,.........	...,,.........	2,13145	"
"	*Burgundy*.......	...,,.........	2,71658	"
"	*Dauphiny*	...,,.........	2,23769	"

Acre = 4840 square yards. Bushel = 2150,42 cubic inches. Cubic foot = 1728 cubic inches. Gallon = 231 cubic inches. Mile = 1760 yards. Pound = 7000 grains. Yard = 36 inches.

NAME.	LOCALITY.	CHARACTER.	VALUE.	
Toise; *episcopal*	*Dauphiny*	length	2,08212	yards.
" *of Peru; old standard*	*France*	..,,	2,13145	"
" *maximum; old meas..*	..,,...*Guingamp*	..,,	2,84204	"
" *minimum* "	..,,...*Lorraine* ..	..,,	1,87264	"
" *mean of 24*	..,,	...,,	2,31963	"
" *metrical; till 1840*...	..,,	...,,	2,18727	"
"	*Geneva*	..,,	2,84204	"
" *old measure*	*Guienne*	..,,	2,27334	"
"	*Liége*	..,,	1,83376	"
"	*Neufchâtel*	..,,	3,20717	"
"	*Vaud*	..,,	3,23090	"
Toise cube; *old measure*	*France*	solid	261,480	cub. feet.
" *usual*	..,,..1812—1840	..,,	282,533	"
" *earthwork, etc.*..	*Vaud*	..,,	954,232	"
Toise-toise-pied ; *old measure*	*France*	..,,	43,580	"
Toise-toise-pouce.....,, ...	..,,	..,,	3,632	"
Tola ; *for gold, etc. maximum*	*E.Indies ; Calcutta*	weight	0,032083	pounds.
" " *minimum*	..,,......*Bombay*	....,,	0,025571	"
" " *mean of 16*....	..,,	..,,	0,027148	"
" *for precious stones*	*Surat*	..,,	0,039031	"
Tomaun; *for rice*	*Bet-el-faki*	..,,	168.——	"
Tomin ; *for gold*	*Spain, etc.*	..,,	8,883	grains.
" *for silver*	...,,	..,,	9,254	"
Tomme	*Denmark*	length.	1,0297	inches.
Tomŏlo; *ordinary*	*Messina*	dry capacity	0,48612	bushels.
" *grosso*	..,,	...,,	0,60765	"
"	*Naples*	..,,	1,56460	"
Ton ; *for grain*	*Amsterdam*	..,,	3,94655	"
" *for lime*	..,,	..,,	3,03986	"
" *for beer*	..,,	liquid capacity	41,54144	gallons.
" "	*Antwerp*	..,,	41,26348	"
" *for gin; shipping*	..,,	..,,	237,76	"
" *shipping ; measurement*	*China* and *India.*	solid	50.——	cub. feet.
"	*England*	weight	2240.——	pounds.
"	*Maryland*	..,,	2000.——	"
" *for coal*	..,,	..,,	2240.——	"
" " *at the mines*....	..,,	..,,	2470.——	"
"	*U. States, gener'y*	..,,	2240.——	"
" *shipping ; measurement*	..,,	solid	40.——	cub. feet.
Tonelāda ; *shipping*	*Portugal*	weight	1755,8	pounds.
" "	..,,	liquid capacity	227,27	gallons.
" "	..,,	dry capacity	41,43	bushels.

Acre = 4840 square yards. Bushel = 2150,42 cubic inches. Cubic foot = 1728 cubic inches.
Gallon = 231 cubic inches. Mile = 1760 yards. Pound = 7000 grains. Yard = 36 inches.

NAME.	LOCALITY.	CHARACTER.	VALUE.	
Toneláda ; *shipping ; measur't*	Portugal........	solid..........	73,296	cub. feet.
"　　　"	Rio Janeiro.	liquid capacity	264,1780	gallons.
"　　　"	Spain...........	weight........	2032,2	pounds.
"　　　"	..,,...........	liquid capacity	255,78	gallons.
Tonne ; *for beer*	Berlin	.....,,.......	30,24838	"
"　　　"	Bremen.........	.....,,.......	43,83611	"
"　　　"	Brunswic	.....,,.......	30,27611	"
"　　" *old measure* .	Dantzic.........	.....,,.......	54,70863	"
"　　　"	Dresden........	.....,,.......	25,97134	"
"　　　"	Gotha..........	.....,,.......	23,0688	"
"　　　"	Hamburg	.....,,.......	45,77712	"
"　 *for whale oil*......	..,,...........	.....,,.......	30,51808	"
"　 *for beer*	Hanover	.....,,.......	41,26460	"
"　　　"	Holstein........	.....,,.......	30,60608	"
"　　　"	Leipsic.........	.....,,.......	23,85131	"
"　　　"	Oldenburg.......	.....,,.......	40,49740	"
"　　　"	Rostock	.....,,.......	30,61920	"
"　　　"	Hamburg & Holst.	dry capacity ...	3,94766	bushels.
"　　　"	Kiel	.....,,.......	3,36393	"
"　 *for wheat, etc*.......	Lübec..........	.....,,.......	4,03880	"
"　 *for oats*...........	..,,...........	.....,,.......	4,49852	"
"　　　"	Oldenburg.......	.....,,.......	5,17680	"
"　　　"	Stettin	.....,,.......	3,88235	"
"　 *shipping ; little used*.	Germany, gener'y	weight........	2190.——	pounds.
"　　　"	Hamburg........	.....,,.......	2135,77	"
"　　" *measurement*	....,,.........	solid	33,219	cub. feet.
Tonneau "　　"	Belgium.........	..,,.........	52,975	"
"　　" *old measure*	France	weight........	2158,43	pounds.
"　　" *metrical*....	..,,...........	..,,.........	2204,74	"
"　　"	..,,...........	dry capacity...	42,567	bushels.
"　　" *measurment*	..,,...........	solid..........	50,842	cub. feet.
Tonnelláta ; *shipping*	Leghorn.........	weight........	2240.—	pounds.
"　　　"	Rome	dry capacity ...	43,9859	bushels.
"　　　"	Tuscany	.....,,.......	41,439	"
"　　　"	Messina.........	liquid capacity	277,6839	gallons.
"　　　"	Syracuse........	.....,,.......	247.—	"
Toolam ; *max. Travancore*...	East Indies	weight........	19,9198	pounds.
"　 *min. Palamcotta*...	..,,..........	..,,.........	12,5	"
"　 *mean of 9*	..,,...........	..,,.........	17,297	"
Topf; *old measure*	Breslau..........	liquid capacity	0,73362	gallons.
Tornatūra.................	Bologna.........	superficial......	0,4827	acres.
"　 *since 1803*........	Venit. Lombardy.	.....,,..........	2,4711	"

Acre = 4840 square yards. Bushel = 2150,42 cubic inches. Cubic foot = 1728 cubic inches. Gallon = 231 cubic inches. Mile = 1760 yards. Pound = 7000 grains. Yard = 36 inches.

115

NAME.	LOCALITY.	CHARACTER.	VALUE.
Trabûcco	Sardinia	length	3,44494 yards.
"	Turin	...,,.	3,37123 "
Trait	France, till 1840	...,,.	0,03937 inches.
Trapēso	Malta	weight	12,73 grains.
"	Naples	...,,.	13,75 "
Tressis	Ancient Romans.	...,,.	2,165691 pounds.
Tricēssis	....,,.	...,,.	21,65691 "
Triens	....,,.	...,,.	0,240632 "
Trihemiŏbŏlon	Ancient Greeks	...,,.	16,845 grains.
Triŏbŏlon	....,,.	...,,.	33,69 "
" Eubœic	....,,.	...,,.	46,792 "
Tritos	....,,.	dry capacity	0,48991 bushels.
Troisken or Troyken	Holland	weight	2,966 grains.
Truss; of hay	England	...,,.	56.—— pounds.
" of new hay	....,,.	...,,.	60.—— "
" of straw	....,,.	...,,.	36.—— "
Tscharka	S. Petersburg	liquid capacity	0,32465 gallons.
Tschetwērik	....,,.	dry capacity	0,719 bushels.
Tschetwert	....,,.	....,,.	5,95205 "
Tschetwērtka	....,,.	....,,.	0,17975 "
Tsun	Canton	length	1,4763 inches.
"	Pekin	...,,.	1,3125 "
Tsut shi	China	dry capacity	0,000002 bushels.
Tub	Sumatra	....,,.	1,87360 "
"	....,,.	liquid capacity	17,44147 gallons.
Tucka; for pearls	Bombay	weight	0,218 grains.
Tum	Sweden	length	0,9714 inches.
Tun; for wine; old measure.	England	liquid capacity	252.—— gallons.
" for beer;	....,,.	....,,.	263,68831 "
Tung	Sumatra	length	4.—— yards.
Tunna	Sweden	liquid capacity	33,15962 gallons.
"	....,,.	dry capacity	4,15713 bushels.
Tunnland	....,,.	superficial	1,2132 acres.
Tussoo	Ahmednuggur	length	1.—— inches.
" builders'	Bombay	...,,.	2,3625 "
" mercers'	....,,.	...,,.	1,1250 "
"	Surat	...,,.	1,1611 "
" builders'	....,,.	...,,.	1.—— "
Ueba	Tripoli in Africa	dry capacity	3,04633 bushels.
Uncia	Ancient Romans	weight	0,060158 pounds.
"	....,,.	length	0,9707 inches.

Acre = 4840 square yards.   Bushel = 2150,42 cubic inches.   Cubic foot = 1728 cubic inches.
Gallon = 231 cubic inches.   Mile = 1760 yards.   Pound = 7000 grains.   Yard = 36 inches.

NAME.	LOCALITY.	CHARACTER.	VALUE.	
Uncia.....................	*Ancient Romans.*	superficial	0,0519	acres.
Untz ; *viktualie-wigt.*	*Sweden*..........	weight.........	0,058500	pounds.
Unze.....................	*Aix-la-Chapelle..*	....,,..........	0,064356	"
" *for gold and silver*......	*Antwerp*	....,,..........	0,064786	"
"	*Appenzell*.......	....,,..........	0,064449	"
" *for spices*.............	....,,........	....,,..........	0,064097	"
"	*Austria, generally*	....,,..........	0,077170	"
"	*Basel*	....,,..........	0,067452	"
"	*Berne*	....,,..........	0,071670	"
"	*Bremen*........	....,,..........	0,068691	"
" *old measure*	*Breslau*........	....,,..........	0,056379	"
"	*Brunswic*......	....,,..........	0,064413	"
"	*Cologne*........	....,,..........	0,064413	"
"	*Denmark*........	....,,..........	0,068803	"
" *for gold and silver*......	....,,........	....,,..........	0,064875	"
"	*Hamburg*	....,,..........	0,066743	"
"	*Hanover*	....,,..........	0,067465	"
"	*Hesse Cassel*.....	....,,..........	0,066721	"
"	*Königsberg*......	....,,..........	0,064559	"
"	*Leipsic*.........	....,,..........	0,064413	"
"	*Nürnberg*	....,,..........	0,070270	"
" *for gold and silver ; o. m.*	....,,........	....,,..........	0,065536	"
"	*Prague*......	....,,..........	0,070875	"
"	*S. Gall*......	....,,..........	0,064571	"
"	*Zurich*........	....,,..........	0,064730	"
" *apothecaries'*..........	*Antwerp*	....,,..........	0,051820	"
" ....,,.............	*Bavaria*........	....,,..........	0,066142	"
" ....,,.............	*Berlin*	....,,..........	0,065694	"
" ....,,.............	*Berne*........	....,,..........	0,065506	"
" ....,,.............	*Frankfort*	....,,..........	0,065741	"
" ....,,.............	*Hanover*........	....,,..........	0,065471	"
" ....,,.............	*Nürnberg*........	....,,..........	0,065750	"
" ....,,.............	*Würtemberg*.....	....,,..........	0,065710	"
Uper ; *mean*..............	*Belgium*	dry capacity...	0,09747	bushels.
" "	....,,..........	liquid capacity	0,90745	gallons.
Upërken.................	*Brussels*........	....,,..........	0,89450	"
Ur	*Clausenburg*.....	....,,..........	2,99049	"
Urna...................	*Ancient Romans.*	....,,..........	3,42050	"
Uzan *or* Usano	*Algiers*..........	weight.........	0,028218	pounds.
"	*Guinea*	....,,..........	0,017669	"
"	*Tripoli in Africa*	....,,..........	0,069506	"
"	*Tunis*.........	....,,..........	0,068222	"

Acre = 4840 square yards.   Bushel = 2150,42 cubic inches.   Cubic foot = 1728 cubic inches.
Gallon = 231 cubic inches.   Mile = 1760 yards.   Pound = 7000 grains.   Yard = 36 inches.

NAME.	LOCALITY.	CHARACTER.	VALUE.	
Vaam *or* Vadem............	*Holland*........	length.........	2,05944	yards.
Vaem....................	*Belgium*........	....,,..........	2.———	"
Vakia...................	*Bassora*........	weight........	4,833333	pounds.
" *for spices, etc.*........	....,,..........	....,,.........	1,166667	"
Val ; *for gold and silver*....	*Delhi*...........	....,,.........	5,63	grains.
" "	*Surat*..........	....,,.........	5,86	"
" *for pearls, etc.*........	....,,..........	....,,.........	8,54	"
Vanĕza..................	*Verona*	superficial	0,0314	acres.
Vara	*Alicant*........	length.........	0,98974	yards.
"	*Aragon*.........	....,,.........	0,84318	"
"	*Asturias*	....,,.........	0,91319	"
"	*Brazil*	....,,.........	1,18878	"
"	*Buenos Ayres*....	....,,.........	0,92741	"
" *standard*.............	*Burgos*.........	....,,.........	0,91319	"
"	*Canary I.*.......	....,,.........	0,92058	"
"	*Castille*........	....,,.........	0,91319	"
"	*Curaçao*........	....,,.........	0,92708	"
" *mercers'*	*Gallicia*........	....,,.........	1,19715	"
" *of Lisbon*.............	*Goa*	....,,.........	1,20300	"
" *old measure*	*Granada*........	....,,.........	0,75811	"
"	*Havana*.........	....,,.........	0,92741	"
"	*Lima*...........	....,,.........	0,92687	"
"	*Lisbon*.........	....,,.........	1,20300	"
"	*Mexico*.........	....,,.........	0,92741	"
"	*Valencia*	....,,.........	0,99193	"
"	*Valparaiso*	....,,...	0,92687	"
Vara ; *cubic*.............	*Spain*...........	solid	20,561	cub. feet.
Varähun................	*Madras*.........	weight.........	54,68	grains.
Vari ; *for gold and silver*....	*Madagascar*	....,,.........	30.———	"
Vassa ; *for pearls, etc.*..	*Surat*...........	....,,.........	0,142	"
Vat ; *legal*	*Belgium* and *Hol.*	liquid capacity	26,41780	gallons.
" *for grain ; old measure.*	... ,,...*mean of* 23	dry capacity...	0,76215	bushels.
" *shipping*	*Belgium* and *Hol.*	weight.........	2204,74	pounds.
" "	....,,.........,,...	dry capacity...	42,567	bushels.
" " *for wine, etc .*.	*Amsterdam*......	liquid capacity	241,57	gallons.
" " *for olive oil* ...	....,,..........	....,,.........	225,45	"
" " *measurement*...	....,,..........	solid..........	40.———	cub. feet.
" *for ashes*	*Brussels*.........	dry capacity ...	1,44415	bushels.
" *for coal ; old measure.*.	*London*	....,,.........	9.———	"
Vedro...................	*S. Petersburg*....	liquid capacity	3,24648	gallons.
Veerker.................	*Oldenburg*.......	dry capacity ...	1,29420	bushels.
Vehrt	*Stralsund*	....,,.........	0,27640	"

Acre = 4840 square yards.   Bushel = 2150,42 cubic inches.   Cubic foot = 1728 cubic inches.   Gallon = 231 cubic inches.   Mile = 1760 yards.   Pound = 7000 grains.   Yard = 36 inches.

NAME.	LOCALITY.	CHARACTER.	VALUE.	
Velte *or* Verge.............	*Antwerp*	liquid capacity	2,01040	gallons.
"	*Bord'x & Cognac*	.....,,.........	1,99191	"
"	*Ceylon*..........	.....,,.........	2.——	"
"	*Nantes*..........	.....,,.........	1,58507	"
" *legal*	*Paris*...........	.....,,.........	1,96827	"
" *usual*.................	..,,...........	.....,,.........	2,01040	"
Verge ; *surveyors'; maximum*	*Belgium ; Chimay*	length.........	7,02069	yards.
" " *minimum*	....,,....*Yprès* .	.....,,.........	4,21365	"
" " *mean of* 218	...,,............	.....,,.........	5,50404	"
" "	*Breda*...........	...,,...........	6,21469	"
" " *maximum*	*France ; Laon*...	.....,,.........	7,81562	"
" " *minimum*	...,,....*Rheims*.	...,,...........	6,15777	"
" " *mean of* 9	...,,............	.....,,.........	6,70645	"
" "	*Venloo*..........	...,,...........	5,03771	"
" *mean*	*Belgium*	superficial......	0,00626	acres.
" "	*France*..........	.....,,.........	0,00929	"
" "	*Holland*.........	.....,,.........	0,00654	"
Vergée..................	*Normandy*	.....,,.........	0,5046	"
Verre..................	*France;* 1800—'40	liquid capacity	0,02642	gallons.
"	*Lausanne*	.....,,.........	0,03567	"
Verschōk..................	*S. Petersburg*....	length.........	1,7506	inches.
Verst..................	.....,,.........	itinerary.......	0,6631	miles.
Versūra..................	*Apulia*..........	superficial	0,4985	acres.
Versus.	*Ancient Romans*.	.....,,.........	0,2163	"
Vesno	*Aleppo*..........	weight.........	25,3274	pounds.
Viādra *or* Wiader..........	*Wallachia*.......	liquid capacity	3,73812	gallons.
Vicēssis..................	*Ancient Romans* .	weight.........	14,473943	pounds.
Vierdevat ; *old measure*......	*Amsterdam*......	dry capacity....	0,19733	bushels.
Vierding..................	*Vienna*..........	weight.........	0,308699	pounds.
Vierēndeel ; *old measure*	*Amsterdam*......	.....,,.........	0,259270	"
Vierfass..................	*Bruns. & Hanover*	dry capacity ...	0,22112	bushels.
"	*Hildesheim*......	.....,,.........	0,18754	"
Viering ; *old measure*......	*Nürnberg*........	weight.........	0,231080	pounds.
Vierkäntěbūnder..........	*Brussels*.........	superficial......	0,0247	acres.
Vierling..................	*Amsterdam*......	weight.........	5,932	grains.
"	*Bremen*..........	liquid capacity	0,21276	gallons.
"	*Aarau*..........	dry capacity....	0,15976	bushels.
" *old measure*	*Augsburg*........	.....,,.........	0,18227	"
"	*Glaris*	.....,,.........	0,14669	"
"	*Mannheim*	.....,,.........	0,19702	"
"	*Ratisbon*	.....,,.........	1,04028	"
"	*Rotterdam*.......	.....,,.........	0,23774	"

Acre = 4840 square yards. Bushel = 2150,42 cubic inches. Cubic foot = 1728 cubic inches.
Gallon = 231 cubic inches. Mile = 1760 yards. Pound = 7000 grains. Yard = 36 inches.

NAME.	LOCALITY.	CHARACTER.	VALUE.	
Vierling..................	S. Gall..........	dry capacity...	0,14649	bushels.
"	Schaffhausen	.....,,.........	0,16036	"
"	Schweitz and Uri	.....,,.........	0,14565	"
"	Strasburg	.....,,.........	0,13058	"
"	Würtemberg.....	.....,,.........	0,15722	"
"	Zurich..........	.....,,.........	0,14565	"
"	Hanover..........	superficial......	0,3236	acres.
" tillage.............	Zurich..........	.....,,.........	0,2020	"
" vineyard..........	....,,...........	.....,,.........	0,1796	"
" woodland..........	....,,...........	.....,,.........	0,2245	"
Viermass.................	Brunswic	dry capacity...	0,22112	bushels.
Viermässchen ; mean.......	Wurzburg	liquid capacity	0,07296	gallons.
Viernling.................	Rhenish Bavaria.	dry capacity...	0,08868	bushels.
Viernzel.................	....,,...........	.....,,.........	0,70945	"
"	Heidelberg.......	.....,,.........	0,79033	"
"	Mannheim.......	.....,,.........	0,78806	"
"	Mentz & Nassau	.....,,.........	0,77614	"
Viertel..................	Altona..........	liquid capacity	1,91288	gallons.
"	Amsterdam......	.....,,.........	1,95240	"
"	Appenzell	.....,,.........	2,76689	"
" old measure..........	Augsburg	.....,,.........	0,07754	"
"	Basel...........	.....,,.........	1,50275	"
"	Bremen	.....,,.........	1,91483	"
"	Brunswic	.....,,.........	0,247	"
"	Coblentz	.....,,.........	1,48892	"
"	Cologne.........	.....,,.........	1,40442	"
"	Courland	.....,,.........	2,08278	"
"	Denmark........	.....,,.........	2,04160	"
" for beer............	Dresden	.....,,.........	51,94268	"
"	Frankfort.......	.....,,.........	1,89455	"
"	Glaris	.....,,.........	7,05086	"
"	Graubündten	.....,,.........	2,80792	"
"	Hamburg.......	.....,,.........	1,90737	"
"	Hanover........	.....,,.........	2,07198	"
"	Heidelberg......	.....,,.........	2,08920	"
" for wine	Hesse Cassel.....	.....,,.........	2,09692	"
" for beer............	....,,...........	.....,,.........	2,30667	"
" for wine; old measure	Hesse Darmstadt.	.....,,.........	1,83728	"
" for beer "	....,,...........	.....,,.........	2,06693	"
" legal...............	....,,...........	.....,,.........	2,11342	"
"	Leipsic.........	.....,,.........	47,70262	"
"	Lippe..........	.....,,.........	1,96325	"

Acre = 4840 square yards.   Bushel = 2150,42 cubic inches.   Cubic foot = 1728 cubic inches.   Gallon = 231 cubic inches.   Mile = 1760 yards.   Pound = 7000 grains.   Yard = 36 inches.

NAME.	LOCALITY.	CHARACTER.	VALUE.	
Viertel..................	*Lübec*..........	liquid capacity	1,97869	gallons.
" *eichmass*............	*Mannheim*......	.....,,.........	2,10708	"
" *wirthsmass*.........	.....,,.........	.....,,.........	1,79008	"
" *for wine and brandy*..	*Mentz*..........	.....,,.........	1,79112	"
" *for beer and oil*......	...,,...........	.....,,.........	1,99296	"
" *schenkmass*..........	*Nürnberg*......	.....,,.........	0,57010	"
" *visirmass*............	.....,,.........	.....,,.........	0,60604	"
"	*Rostock*........	.....,,.........	1,91371	"
" *for beer*.............	...,,...........	.....,,.........	7,65480	"
"	*S. Gall*........	.....,,.........	2,77319	"
'	*Schaffhausen*....	.....,,.........	2,77820	"
"	*Uri*............	.....,,.........	7,19235	"
"	*Vienna*	.....,,.........	3,73812	"
" *lauter-mass*..........	*Zurich*.........	.....,,.........	7,23187	"
"	*Aarau*	dry capacity....	0,63904	bushels.
"	*Altona*..........	.....,,.........	0,12336	"
"	*Appenzell*.......	.....,,.........	0,64820	"
" *legal*.............	*Bavaria*.........	.....,,.........	0,52583	"
" *old measure*..........	*Berlin*.........	.....,,.........	0,38839	"
"	*Bohemia*........	.....,,.........	0,66401	"
"	*Bremen*........	.....,,.........	0,52549	"
" *old measure*..........	*Breslau*	.....,,.........	0,52512	"
" *for wheat, etc.*	*Coburg*.........	.....,,.........	0,63104	"
" *for oats*.............	...,,........	.....,,.........	0,78320	"
" *old measure*..........	*Cologne*........	.....,,.........	0,12729	"
" "	*Dantzic*........	.....,,.........	0,36552	"
"	*Dresden*........	.....,,.........	0,73713	"
"	*Glaris*	.....,,.........	0,58260	"
"	*Gotha*..........	.....,,.........	1,23905	"
"	*Graubündten*	.....,,.........	0,85114	"
"	*Hesse Cassel*....	.....,,.........	4,56146	"
"	*Leipsic*.........	.....,,.........	0,73713	"
"	*Lucerne*........	.....,,.........	0,98624	"
" *legal*.............	*Prussia*.........	.....,,.........	0,38992	"
" *for oats*	*Rostock*........	.....,,.........	0,31088	"
"	*S. Gall*........	.....,,.........	0,58596	"
"	*Schaffhausen*	.....,,.........	0,64143	"
"	*Schweitz* and *Uri*	.....,,.........	0,58260	"
"	*Solothurn*.......	.....,,.........	3,00673	"
"	*Unterwalden*.....	.....,,.........	0,98624	"
"	*Vienna*.........	.....,,.........	0,43628	"
"	*Weimar*........	.....,,.........	0,546	"

Acre = 4840 square yards. Bushel = 2150,42 cubic inches. Cubic foot = 1728 cubic inches. Gallon = 231 cubic inches. Mile = 1760 yards. Pound = 7000 grains. Yard = 36 inches.

NAME.	LOCALITY.	CHARACTER.	VALUE.	
Viertel; *for wheat, etc.*	*Zurich*	dry capacity....	0,58260	bushels.
" *for oats.*	....,,....	....,,....	0,59344	"
" *for salt*	....,,....	....,,....	0,65332	"
" *for lime.*	....,,....	....,,....	0,59875	"
"	*Baden*	superficial	0,2224	acres.
"	*Hesse Darmstadt.*	....,,....	0,1544	"
"	*Würtemberg*	....,,....	0,1947	"
" *for firewood*	....,,....	solid	29,896	cub. feet.
Viertelein	....,,....	dry capacity ...	0,00491	bushels.
"	*Friburg*	liquid capacity	0,10316	gallons.
Vierteli	*Berne*	....,,....	0,11037	"
Viertheil; *old measure*	*Augsburg*	dry capacity....	0,04557	bushels.
"	*Ulm*	....,,....	0,06792	"
Vierzel	*Basel*	....,,....	7,75611	"
" *for wheat*	*Trèves or Trier*	....,,....	0,75656	"
" *for barley*	....,,....	....,,....	0,84059	"
" *for oats*	....,,....	....,,....	1,16952	"
Vingerhoed; *legal*	*Holland*	liquid capacity	0,00264	gallons.
Vis; *commercial*	*Masulipatan*	weight	3,515452	pounds.
"	*Pegu*	....,,....	3,392856	"
"	*Pondichery*	....,,....	3,237657	"
"	*Trichinopoly*	....,,....	3.——	"
Visay	*Madras*	....,,....	3,124821	"
Voet	*Amsterdam*	length	0,30956	yards.
" *Rhenish*	....,,....	....,,....	0,34324	"
"	*Breda*	....,,....	0,31073	"
"	*Harlaem*	....,,....	0,31258	"
"	*Leyden*	....,,....	0,34324	"
Voie; *for charcoal; old meas.*	*Paris*	dry capacity....	5,90642	bushels.
" *for coal*	....,,....	....,,....	33,22212	"
" *for plaster*	....,,....	....,,....	8,85962	"
" *for firewood*	....,,....	solid	67,692	cub. feet.
" *for stone, ashlar*	....,,....	....,,....	18,156	"
" " *rubble*	....,,....	....,,....	30,1	"
Vorling	*Calenberg; Han'r*	superficial	0,3234	acres.
Vouah	*Siam.*	length	2,10193	yards.
Waag	*Denmark & Norw*	weight	39,631	pounds.
" *for tin*	*Sweden*	....,,....	123,2668	"
Waeg; *for lump coal*	*Antwerp*	....,,....	149,9121	"
Wage ; *for iron*	*Bremen*	....,,....	131,8874	"
"	*Leipsic*	....,,....	45,3462	"

Acre = 4840 square yards. Bushel = 2150,42 cubic inches. Cubic foot = 1728 cubic inches.
Gallon = 231 cubic inches. Mile = 1760 yards. Pound = 7000 grains. Yard = 36 inches.

NAME.	LOCALITY.	CHARACTER.	VALUE.	
Wage......................	Nürnberg........	weight........	134,9185	pounds.
Wakēa...................	Abyssinia......	....,,.......	0,057323	"
" ....,.......	Algiers..........	....,,.	0,752470	"
"	Bet-el-faki.....	....,,.......	0,067969	"
"	Jidda....,.....	....,,.......	0,024401	"
Wakēga ; commercial.......	Mocha...........	....,,.......	0,1	"
" for gold and silver	...,,...........	....,,.......	0,068571	"
Wanne ; for hay...........	Würtemberg.....	solid..........	425,187	cub. feet.
Wehr ; miners'...........	Prussia.........	superficial......	0,1062	acres.
" "	Saxony...........	....,,.......	0,0948	"
Werp ; mean of 11.........	Hanover........	dry capacity...	1,50757	bushels.
Wey ; for malt ; old measure.	England.......	....,,.......	40.——	"
" of wool...............	...,,...........	weight........	182.——	pounds.
Wigtje..................	Holland.........	....,,.......	15,433	grains.
Winspel ; for lime.........	Berlin..........	dry capacity...	6,14128	bushels.
Wispel ; for grain.........	...,,...........	....,,.......	37,42126	"
" for wheat.........	Brunswic.......	....,,.......	34,66880	"
" for oats..........	...,,...........	....,,.......	41,60256	"
" for wheat and rye..	Hamburg........	....,,.......	29,88110	"
" for barley and oats.	...,,........	....,,.......	44,82340	"
"	Hanover........	....,,.......	42,36836	"
" legal.............	Mecklenburg....	....,,.......	35,31520	"
" old measure.......	Rostock.........	....,,.......	39,79135	"
"	Saxony.........	....,,.......	70,7640	"
Wiswūsa................	Malwah.........	length........	4,4802	inches.
"	Surat..........	....,,.......	4,8766	"
Wloka ; since 1819.........	Poland..........	superficial......	41,4866	acres.
Wusa or Wussa...........	Malwah.........	length........	2,48889	yards.
"	Surat........	....,,.......	2,71111	"
" timber............	..,,..........	....,,.......	1,3583	inches.
Xestas..................	Ancient Greeks..	liquid capacity	0,14252	gallons.
"	....,,.......	dry capacity....	0,015310	"
Xylon..................	....,,.......	length........	1,51715	yards.
Yabbŏlam...............	Masulipatan....	weight........	0,75	pounds.
Yan....................	China..........	length........	36,45833	yards.
Yard..................	Great Britain,etc.	....,,.......	1.——	"
"	United States....	....,,.......	1.——	"
" or Yardland ; mean...	England........	superficial.....	30.——	acres.
Yen.....-.............	An-nam........	weight........	13,7752	pounds.
Yeuk shi................	China..........	dry capacity...	0,00109	bushels.

Acre = 4840 square yards. Bushel = 2150,42 cubic inches. Cubic foot = 1728 cubic inches.
Gallon = 231 cubic inches. Mile = 1760 yards. Pound = 7000 grains. Yard = 36 inches.

NAME.	LOCALITY.	CHARACTER.	VALUE.
Yin......................	China..........	weight.........	2,666667 pounds.
Yu......................	...,,...........	dry capacity ...	3,48373 bushels.
Yugāda..................	Madrid.........	superficial	35,0724 acres.
" legal since 1801.....	Spain...........	.....,,..........	79,3550 "
"	Valencia........	.....,,..........	6,1566 "
Yusdrom.................	Constantinople...	weight.........	0,701504 pounds.
Zah....................	Tunis..........	dry capacity....	0,07812 bushels.
Zak ; old measure.........	Amsterdam......	.....,,..........	2,30034 "
"	Dordrecht.......	.....,,..........	3,44739 "
"	...,,..........	.....,,..........	2,58554 "
" legal..............	Holland........	.....,,..........	2,83782 "
"	Leyden........	.....,,..........	1,88006 "
Zappāda.................	Ionian Isles......	superficial	0,9956 acres.
Zavah..................	Masulipatan.....	dry capacity....	0,03357 bushels.
Zehnling ; legal..........	Baden	weight.........	0,110237 pounds.
Zereth.................	Ancient Hebrews.	length	8,6039 inches.
Zerla ; for wine...........	Brescia.........	liquid capacity	13,20890 gallons.
Zimment................	Bolzano	.....,,..........	0,09170 "
Zober................	Graubündten	.....,,..........	28,08873 "
" for brine............	Halle...........	.....,,..........	145,17104 "
" legal..............	Baden	dry capacity ...	42,56734 bushels.
" for charcoal or lime....	Würtemberg.....	.....,,..........	2,08523 "
Zoll...................	Aarau	length	0,9622 inches.
" builders' ; old measure...	Aix-la-Chapelle..	..,,..........	0,9472 "
" surveyors' " ...	...,,..........	.....,,..........	0,9251 "
"	Altona.........	.....,,..........	0,9399 "
" Rhenish............	Anhalt.........	.....,,..........	1,0297 "
"	Appenzell.......	.....,,..........	1,0325 "
"	Augsburg........	.....,,..........	0,9717 "
" since 1810.............	Baden	..,,..........	1,1811 "
"	Basel..........	.....,,..........	0,9992 "
" since 1809.............	Bavaria........	.....,,..........	0,9576 "
"	Rhenish Bavaria.	.....,,..........	1,0937 "
" since 1816 ; Rhenish	Berlin	.....,,..........	1,0297 "
" surveyors'............	...,,..........	.....,,..........	1,4828 "
" for all measures........	Berne.........	.....,,..........	0,9602 "
"	Bohemia	.....,,..........	0,9724 "
"	Bremen	.....,,..........	0,9488 "
" surveyors'............	...,,..........	.....,,..........	1,1386 "
"	Brunswic	..,,..........	0,9362 "
"	Coblentz	.....,,..........	0,9535 "

Acre = 4840 square yards. Bushel = 2150,42 cubic inches. Cubic foot = 1728 cubic inches.
Gallon = 231 cubic inches. Mile = 1760 yards. Pound = 7000 grains. Yard = 36 inches.

NAME.	LOCALITY.	CHARACTER.	VALUE.	
Zoll; *old measure*	*Cologne*	length	0,9437	inches.
" "	*Dantzic*	...,,...	0,9413	"
"	*Dresden*	...,,...	0,9293	"
"	*Frankfort*	...,,...	0,9338	"
" *surveyors'*	...,,...	...,,...	1,4010	"
"	*Friburg*	...,,...	0,9622	"
"	*Glaris*	...,,...	0,9843	"
"	*Göttingen*	...,,...	0,9547	"
"	*Gotha*	...,,...	0,9437	"
"	*Hamburg*	...,,...	0,9399	"
" *builders and surveyors'*	...,,...	...,,...	1,0297	"
"	*Hanover*	...,,...	0,9580	"
"	*Hesse Cassel*	...,,...	0,9437	"
" *surveyors'*	...,,...	...,,...	1,1317	"
" *since* 1818	*Hesse Darmstadt*	...,,...	0,8643	"
" *of Austria*	*Hungary*	...,,...	1,0371	"
"	*Leipsic*	...,,...	0,9259	"
" *builders'*	...,,...	...,,...	1,1111	"
"	*Lübec*	...,,...	0,9446	"
"	*Mecklenburg*	...,,...	0,9548	"
"	*Neufchâtel*	...,,...	0,9622	"
" *old measure*	*Nürnberg*	...,,...	0,9967	"
"	*Oldenburg*	...,,...	0,9707	"
"	*Schweitz*	...,,...	0,9843	"
"	*Vaud*	...,,...	1,1811	"
"	*Vienna*	...,,...	1,0371	"
"	*Weimar*	...,,...	0,9251	"
" *surveyors'*	...,,...	...,,...	1,7763	"
" *since* 1806	*Würtemberg*	...,,...	1,1280	"
"	*Zurich*	...,,...	0,9843	"
" *surveyors'*	...,,...	...,,...	1,1812	"
Zolôtnik	*S. Petersburg*	weight	0,009393	pounds.
Zucca	*Corsica*	liquid capacity	3,08208	gallons.
Zuŏja; *grande*	*Udino*	superficial	1,2892	acres.
" *piccola*	...,,...	...,,...	0,8663	"

Acre = 4840 square yards. Bushel = 2150,42 cubic inches. Cubic foot = 1728 cubic inches.
Gallon = 231 cubic inches. Mile = 1760 yards. Pound = 7000 grains. Yard = 36 inches.

WEIGHT AND MEASURE

SYSTEMS

IN THE

PRINCIPAL COUNTRIES OF THE WORLD.

THE following Classification has been added to the Dictionary, both as serving to indicate more fully its scope, as giving information of a character which its form did not allow of being introduced there, and as contributing to what has been an aim throughout and what both mutually support—an intelligent brevity. In this last regard, several Countries have been omitted from the Classification, which, in a more magnificent plan, might have had just claim to enumeration; and sometimes, denominations, and even classes of measures, have been left out whenever the term itself was significant of the relations of the measure, or whenever, in the absence of a legal determination, the usages of the particular country allow the partial or indifferent employment of foreign terms or values. The reader will hardly fail to observe and justify the application of these principles; and in other respects the text itself seems of such simplicity as to bear with it its own explanation.

WEIGHT AND MEASURE SYSTEMS.

I. AFRICA.

ABYSSINIA.

WEIGHTS.—1 rotl or rottolo = 12 wakea = 120 dirhems.
DRY CAPACITY.—At Gondar in the interior; 1 ardeb = 10 madega.
At Masuah on the Red Sea; 1 ardeb = 24 madega.
The other measures are those of Cairo and Alexandria. There is no knowledge of any local system.

ALGERIA.

Since the acquisition of this territory by France, the French metrical system is legalized and may be expected gradually to come into use. As yet, however, the old usances are retained.

WEIGHTS.—The theory appears to be as follows:

24 carob seed = 1 mitkal or metical, the weight for gold, etc.
8 mitkal   = 1 wakea or ounce.
27 wakea   = 1 rotl khebir or market pound.
18 wakea   = 1 do. gheddari, for fruits.
16 wakea   = 1 do. attari, for spices.
14½ wakea   = 1 do. feuddi, for silver.
100 of each of these rotl = 1 quontar or cantaro corresponding.

The values of these denominations in the Dictionary are from reported observations, and fall below what would be derived otherwise by ascending from the actual Mitkal.

LIQUID CAPACITY; is measured by the Khoullé and its fractions, ½, ¼, ⅛, etc.; as DRY CAPACITY; by the Saa.

LENGTH; is measured by two different Pic, the Turkish and Arab; the latter of which is used for cloth. Each is subdivided by its Rob, or *eighth* part.

There are no itinerary or agrarian measures, indigenous.

CAPE OF GOOD HOPE (COLONY.)

English standards are legalized and used here.

The same may be said, it is supposed, of the British Colonies in Senegambia and at Sierra Leone and the smaller establishments on the Gold Coast; as well as of S. Helena and their other Islands in the Atlantic. As for Mauritius on the other side of the Continent, that retains still a considerable admixture of its former French usances.

T

CANARY ISLANDS.

In these Islands, the originals of the Weights and Measures are from Spain ; and the variations of the actual standards, which (except in the case of the Vara) seem to be in the sense of degradation, are not more than occur in continental Spain itself.

CAPE VERD ISLANDS.

This archipelago, as well as the continental territory under the same Governor-Generalship, uses the Weights and Measures of Portugal. The same may be said of the Madeira Groupe under the same domination ; of the Portuguese possessions in Angola and Benguela ; and of the colonies which dwell on the other Ocean, along the Coasts of Sofalā and Mozambique.

EGYPT.

The difference between the Weights and Measures actually used in Cairo and Alexandria, the principal markets of Egypt, is so small as to indicate a common original. The great variety which has been stated to exist among the Cantaros (or Quintals,) according to the various articles intended to be weighed, is probably the result of carelessness or fraud : nor is it clear, as yet, whether this variety affects the hundred-weight or the unitary pound. It may be supposed that the weights by which the articles of greatest consumption—the necessaries of life—are determined, was the standard from which accident or negligence has deviated.

WEIGHT.—1 cantaro = 36 oke = 100 rotl = 14400 drachma.

The Rotl does not appear to be systematically subdivided.

The Harsela, applied to weighing silk, is evidently the Oke, under a special name.

DRY CAPACITY.—1 ardeb = 24 rob.

LENGTH.—1 gasab = 4 derah.

The Turkish Pic is generally used for cloths ; it is very little longer than the Derah, but not correlative.

AGRARIAN.—400 square gasab = 1 feddan al risach, or unitary acre.

GUINEA.

WEIGHT.—1 benda = 2 benda-offa = 3 eggeba = $5\frac{1}{3}$ seron = 8 piso or uzan = $10\frac{2}{3}$ quinto = 16 aguirages = 32 media-tabla = 48 akey.

The last denomination, which is the special weight for gold-dust, is only theoretically connected here ; its actual value as reported is nearly a half-grain less than the $\frac{1}{48}$ of the Benda.

LIBERIA.

This Anglo-American negro Colony at Cape Mesurado, as well as the independent one of Maryland at Cape Palmas, uses, it may be supposed, standards from the United States.

MOROCCO.

All the dependencies of this Empire, along the Western Coast of Barbary, use the Weights and Capacity-measures of Spain. There are several indigenous measures of length given in the Dictionary ; but they are without uniformity.

TRIPOLI.

In this appanage of the Turkish Empire, as well as in the dependencies of Fezzan and Barca, the Weights and Measures appear to be of European derivation.

WEIGHTS.—1 cantaro = 100 rotl = 1600 uzan = 12800 termini.

The Metical, a special weight for gold and silver, has no connection with the others ; unless it be derived in theory from an ancient Rotl or pound of 12 Uzan or ounces. The actual weight is reported as being exactly $\frac{1}{100}$ of the Venetian pound ; from which it may have originated.

LIQUID CAPACITY.—The Mataro for oil is given by gallons in the Dictionary ; from its reported weight compared with the average specific gravity, at ordinary temperatures, of that substance.

DRY CAPACITY.—1 cafiso = 20 tiberi.

TUNIS.

WEIGHT.—1 cantaro = 100 rotl = 1600 uzan = 12800 metical or termini.

In this system, where the same denominations appear to be lighter than the Tripolitan, the Metical and Uzan are specific weights.

LIQUID CAPACITY is determined by weight.

DRY CAPACITY.—1 cafiso = 16 quiba = 192 saha or zah.

LENGTH.—1 pic (woollen) = $1\frac{1}{15}$ pic (silk) = $1\frac{19}{45}$ pic (linen.)

But these last proportions appear altogether accidental.

In this enumeration, the remaining European settlements, viz., those of France on opposite sides of the Continent in Senegambia and the Isle of Bourbon, and those of Denmark and Holland in Guinea and Ashanti, have been omitted ; partly because the Weights and Measures of the mother-countries would be naturally accepted among the settlers, but chiefly because of the insignificance in population and trade of the actual establishments. The insular appanages of the Imam of Muscat, (viz., Quiloa, Zanzibar, Socotra, etc.,) on the eastern side of the Continent, are passed over for similar reasons ; while the native Powers, from Morocco through and around to Madagascar, are too uncivilized or too inaccessible, to have or to yield any thing of interest in respect to Weights and Measures.

II. AMERICA.

This Continent, for the present purpose, is best divided (instead of the usual distinctions of North, Central and South,) into Independent and Colonial America.

BRAZIL.

In this Empire, the originals of Weights and Measures are from Portugal ; and the actual standards are in general identical : though there are a few variations, both in value and denomination, shewn in the Dictionary.

HAYTI or SAN DOMINGO.

This Island, which in the numerous revolutions of policy that it has undergone has been recently modified from a Republic into a form more absolute and nominally an Empire, retains the impress of its double colonization from Spain and France, as well in the names of localities — on the western side French, on the eastern, Spanish — as in the Weights and Measures used there.

MEXICO.

Under this Republic, as well as under the numerous governments which are continually shifting or springing up in the territories of Central and South America and which it would require a special and co-temporaneous research to signalize and verify, the Weights and Measures of Spain have been throughout and are still recognized; with only such local variations as other causes, besides the cessation of European control and intercourse with a parent power, might be expected naturally to produce. Of course, this comprehensive field for the influence of the Spanish system does not include vast territories (such as Patagonia, for instance,) which, although claimed by foreign or domestic powers, are yet in fact domineered over by various indigenous tribes, more or less nomadic and uncivilized. Of systematic Weights and Measures in those territories, there are none in modern times; and ancient ones (such as in Mexico and Peru) which comparatively recent researches have partially systematized, are designedly omitted, as neither certain nor of practical application, as yet.

UNITED STATES OF AMERICA.

Weight.—1 Mint or troy pound = 12 ounces = 240 pennyweight = 5760 grains.

1 apothecary pound = 12 ounces = 96 drachms = 288 scruples = 5760 grains.

1 commercial pound = 16 ounces = 256 drams = 7000 grains.

1 long ton = 20 cwt. = 80 quarters = 2240 commercial pounds.

1 short ton = 20 hundred-weight = 2000 commercial pounds.

In the actual Government-standards the ounce troy is divided decimally, down to the $\frac{1}{10000}$ part.

These weights are identical with those of England. In both countries, they repose in fact upon actually existing masses of metal (brass) which have been individually declared by law to be the units of the system. In scientific theory, they are supposed to rest upon a permanent and universal law of Nature — the gravitation of distilled water at a certain temperature and under a certain atmospheric pressure. And in this aspect, the origination is with the grains; which must be such that 252,458 of these units, in brass, will be in just equilibrium with a cubic inch of distilled water, when the mercury stands at 30 inches in a barometer, and in a thermometer of Fahrenheit at 62 degrees both for the air and for the water. Unfortunately, the expounders of this theory in England, used only the generic term *brass*, and failed to define the specific gravity of the metal to be employed: the consequence of this omission is to leave room for an error of $\frac{1}{100000}$ in every attempt to reproduce or compare the results. This is the *minimum* possible error: the *maximum* would be a function of the difference in specific gravity between the heaviest and lightest brass that can be cast.

Liquid Capacity.—1 gallon = 2 half gallons = 4 quarts = 8 pints = 16 gills.

The Gill is not among existing standards of public authority ; though it is used in commerce. There are other denominations higher than the Gallon, such as barrels, hogsheads, pipes, etc.; but these are only *vessels* not *measures*, and are always gauged and sold by their actual capacity in gallons. The Gallon, in fact, is almost exactly equivalent to a cylinder, 7 inches in diameter and 6 inches high. In theory, it must contain just 231 cubic inches ; and, filled with distilled water at the temperature of maximum density (say 39°,8 Fah.,) weighs, according to the official report, at that temperature and at 30 inches of the barometer, 8,339 commercial or avoirdupois pounds ; or more nearly 58372,1754 grains. It is in the temperature only that this unit differs from the former wine-gallon of Great Britain.

The Apothecaries use the same gallon but divide it differently, as follows:

1 gallon = 8 pints = 128 fluid ounces = 1024 fluid drachms = 61440 minims (or drops) = 231 cubic inches.

These are graduated measures ; they also use sometimes the following approximate ones from vessels in domestic use:

1 tea-cup = 2 wine glasses = 8 table-spoons = 32 tea-spoons = 4 fluid ounces.

Dry Capacity.—1 bushel = 2 half-bushels = 4 pecks = 8 gallons.

There are also in this, as in the former measure, higher denominations (barrels, sacks, etc.) known in commerce ; whose capacity is intended to be constant. They are, however, always gauged by the Bushel. This Bushel is the old Winchester bushel of England. In fact, it is a cylinder 18,5 inches in diameter and 8 inches deep. In theory, it must contain 2150,42 cubic inches ; and holds of distilled water at the temperature of maximum density and at 30 inches of the barometer, 77,6274 commercial or avoirdupois pounds ; or more nearly 543391,89 grains.

Length.—1 yard = 3 feet = 36 inches = 432 lines = 5184 seconds = 62208 thirds.

In the actual Government-standards, at the Custom-houses, the Yard is divided decimally into tenths and hundredths.

In the measurement of cloths, muslins, linens, cotton, silk and in general of what are termed dry goods, the Yard only is used ; subdivided into halves, quarters, eighths, sixteenths and half-sixteenths. This lowest denomination = 1,125 inch.

Surveyors and Engineers employ neither the yard nor the inch ; but use the Foot and its decimal divisions.

Architects and Artificers reckon by the Foot and subdivisions as given above. Nevertheless, the most usual and most recent workman's scales bear the foot divided into inches, and eighths and sixteenths of an inch.

Mariners measure by Cable-lengths and Fathoms :

1 cable-length = 120 fathoms = 240 yards = 720 feet.

The unit of length—the Yard, upon whose subdivisions all the weights and capacity measures repose for verification—is, in fact, derived from ancient arbitrary standards of England. In theory, the Inch—the $\frac{1}{36}$ of the Yard—is presumed to be contained 39,13929 times in the length of a pendulum that, in a vacuum and at the level of mid-tide, under the latitude of London, vibrates seconds of mean time.

Itinerary.—1 statute mile = 2 half miles = 4 quarter miles = $7\frac{1}{3}$ cable-lengths = 8 furlongs = 80 chains = 320 perches or poles = 880 fathoms = 1760 yards = 5280 feet = 8000 links = 63360 inches.

1 nautical league = 3 equatorial mile = 3,457875 statute mile.

Chains and Links are denominations employed by Land-surveyors, thus :

1 Chain = 4 Poles = 66 feet = 100 links.

AGRARIAN AND SUPERFICIAL.—1 square mile = 640 acres.

1 acre = 4 roods = 10 square chains = 160 square perches = 4840 square yards = 43560 square feet.

1 square yard = 9 square feet = 1296 square inches.

Architects and Builders reckon 1 square = 100 square feet.

SOLID.—1 cubic yard = 27 cubic feet = 46656 cubic inches.

1 cubic foot = 12 reduced feet (plank measure) = 1728 cubic inches.

1 reduced foot (plank measure) = 1 square foot $\times$ 1 inch thick = 144 cubic inches.

In practice, all planks and scantlings, less than an Inch in thickness, are reckoned at an Inch.

1 perch of masonry = 1 perch (16½ feet) long $\times$ 1 foot high $\times$ 1½ foot thick = 25 cubic feet.

In fact, the dimensions given for the Perch do not result in 25 cubic Feet ; but this last number has been adopted for convenience.

1 cord of fire-wood = 8 feet long $\times$ 4 feet high $\times$ 4 feet deep = 128 cubic feet.

DANISH POSSESSIONS.

These include Greenland, Iceland, and three of the Leeward Islands in the West Indies ; viz., Santa Cruz or S. Croix, S. Thomas and S. John. In all these, the Weights and Measures of Denmark prevail ; though in the Islands, the English length-measures are also used.

DUTCH POSSESSIONS.

Holland holds on the Continent of America, the government of Surinam, which includes nominally a territory of something less than 40,000 square miles, under the name of Dutch Guiana ; on the coast of Venezuela, the Islands of Curaçao and Bonaire, with some lesser islets ; and among the Leeward Antilles, S. Eustatius, the south part of S. Martin, and Saba. In all these, the Weights and Measures of Holland prevail ; except in Curaçao, where the weights are, in fact, and the length-measures, both in fact and name, those of Spain.

ENGLISH POSSESSIONS.

Over the immense territories of British North America, the Weights and Measures of England are legalized ; but in Lower Canada, the French settlers still use their former denominations to a great extent.

In the southern peninsula, where the general name of English Guiana covers the former Dutch Colonies of Berbice, Demerara and Essequibo, the reckoning is by the Weights and Measures of Holland.

The settlements in Patagonia and the adjoining Archipelago, made chiefly with a view to the whale-fishery, recognize the English standards. And as much may be said for the Falkland Isles.

Of the numerous Islands and islets in the West Indies, among the Antilles and Lucayas, only the chief ones need be mentioned. The Weights and Measures of a few are still traceable to the source of their earlier colonization.

NAMES.	WEIGHTS AND MEASURES.
Antigua, ...	English.
The Bahamas, ...	English.
Barbadoes, ...	English.
Barbuda, ...	English.
S. Christopher's or S. Kitts', . . .	English.
Dominica, ...	English.
Grenada, ...	English.
Jamaica, ...	English.
S. Lucia, ...	French.
Montserrat, ...	English.
Nevis, ...	English.
Tobago, ...	English.
Tortola, ...	English.
Trinidad, ...	Spanish.
S. Vincent, ...	English.

In the Bermuda Groupe, English Weights and Measures are employed. All these English measures are those before the change in 1825. It would be, therefore, more literal to say, Weights and Measures of the United States.

FRENCH POSSESSIONS.

France holds on the Continent, only what used in part to be Cayenne and is now on the maps as French Guiana ; and among the West India Islands, Martinique, Guadeloupe with its dependancies, Deseada or Desirade, Marie-galante, and the groupe of Les Saintes, together with about two-thirds (on the northern side) of S. Martin.

In Guiana, the new metrical system is legalized ; but the older one continues to be used.

S. Martin reckons by the Weights and Measures of Holland ; and Les Saintes by those of England.

The others employ the old French system, with some modifications. Thus, the former English wine gallon seems to be the standard for liquids ; divided as follows :

1 gallon = 2 pots = 4 pintes = 8 chopines = 16 roquilles = 32 muces.

Of Agrarian measure, 1 carré = 10,000 pas carrés.

Besides these, France owns the isles of S. Pierre and Miquelon to the south of Newfoundland ; where the old system prevails.

RUSSIAN POSSESSIONS.

The extensive territories which Russia holds in the north-west corner of America across Bhering's Straits, are, it may be supposed, under the domain of Russian customary measures.

The establishment which that Empire had for nearly forty years in Upper California, at Bodega, has been since some time abandoned.

SPANISH POSSESSIONS.

The magnificent appanage, continental and insular, which Spain formerly held in America has now dwindled to the Islands of Cuba and Porto Rico ; where the Weights and Measures are still those of Spain.

The only territory of Sweden is the small Island of S. Bartholomew or S. Bart's ; which, though originally colonized from France, has been so long ceded (now nearly seventy years) as to have adopted Swedish Weights and Measures.

III. ASIA.

AN-NAM.

WEIGHTS.—1 quăn = 5 ta = 10 binh = 50 yen = 500 cân.

1 cân (or pound) = 1,6 nen = 16 luong = 160 dong = 1600 ly.

From the Ly, the subdivisions are regularly decimal ; viz., the Hao, Hot, Châu, Huy, Trăn and Ai, which last is the atom or millionth part of the Ly. The most of these are purely theoretical, for the Hao is itself only 0,06 of a grain, very nearly.

CAPACITY.—In these there is no uniformity nor authenticity ; each province using different measures. In Huế there appears to be the following theoretical system :

1 hoc = 10 dau = 100 thang = 1000 hap = 10,000 thuoc.

1 thuoc = 1200 grains of millet = 10 sao.

1 sao (or a handful) = 120 grains of millet ; and

1 toat = 250 grains of millet.

The division of the Thuoc into 10 Sao and 4,6875 Toat would seem to indicate two different systems ; but as the Tonquin millet and our own are not of the same size, we have no standard of comparison or determination.

LENGTH.—There are two Thuoc or cubits ; one for general use, the other which is ⅓ longer than the former, exclusively for cloths, silks and other woven fabrics.

1. Mercers'.—1 gon = 10 that = 30 truong = 300 thuoc

1 thuoc (or ell) = 10 tac = 100 phan = 1000 ly.

2. Builders', etc.—1 mau = 10 sao = 30 ngu = 150 thuoc

1 thuoc (or cubit) = 10 tac = 100 phan = 1000 ly.

AGRARIAN.—This last series is also used by Land-measurers in giving the square content of Land. They sometimes use another series, (called *Ruong luc*, in contra-distinction to the *Ruong ngu*, just given,) in which the Sao is equal to 16½ Thuoc. The Mau is, therefore, 10 per cent. longer in this last series ; and its superficial content, when squared, 21 per cent. greater.

The Dictionary gives only the values in the first and most usual series.

ITINERARY.—These are very vague and only approximate :

1 dam = 2 ly = rather less than a half mile.

BIRMAH.

WEIGHT.—1 vis = 3 catty = 100 tical.

LENGTH.—1 bambou = 28 taim = 504 palgat.

ITINERARY.—1 taing = 250 bambou = 7000 taim.

But these are by no means certain.

CHINA.

WEIGHT.—Almost every thing in China, (timber, liquids, live-stock, etc.,) is sold by weight, actual or nominal.

1 shik = 1½ tam = 4 kwan = 60 yin = 120 kan, or catty.

1 kan = 16 leung, or tael = 364 chu = 3840 lui = 38400 shu, or kernels of grain.

The weights above the Yin are only nominal and for account : and those below the tael are generally denoted by the adjuncts *li, ho, tsin, fat,* etc., i. e. one tenth, one hundredth, one thousandth, etc.

CAPACITY.—This is regulated, as before said, by weight ; the existing dry *measures,* which have been adopted for the convenience of commerce for grain and seeds, vary considerably in consequence of the irregularity of the material (bamboo) of which they are made. The theory is supposed to be as follows :

1 ping = 5 yu = 16 hok = 32 shik = 80 tau.

1 tau = 10 shing = 100 kop = 200 yeuk = 1000 cheuk = 10000 chau = 100000 tsut = 1000000 kwai = 6000000 suk, or grains of maize.

Of all these, there are only four actual measures ; viz., the Tau, the Shing, the half-Shing and the Kop. These are also upon two different modules, distinguished by the adjuncts *shi* and *tsong ;* and in proportionate capacity as 100 to 65 respectively. It may be supposed that the latter were intended for *liquid* measures ; and their average contents are so reduced accordingly, in the Dictionary.

LENGTH.—1 yan = 10 cheung = 100 chik = 1000 tsun = 10000 fan.

The chik, fixed by the Mathematical Board at Pekin = 13,125 inches ; used by tradesmen in Canton = 14,625 to 14,81 inches ; employed by Engineers of Public Works = 12,7 inches ; and that by which distances are usually measured = 12,1 inches.

ITINERARY.—1 to = 25 fan = 125 tsun = 250 li, or miles.

1 li = 1826 English feet.

This is the count since the intervention of European mathematicians at Pekin. The former used to be

1 to = 192½ li = 79300 po = 396500 chik

1 li = 1897½ English feet.

Some ambiguity arises from the use of the same word, Li, (probably from European ignorance of the language in not discriminating between similar but not identical terms) as a lower measure, the $\frac{1}{10}$ of the Fan. The same ambiguity extends itself also to the following series.

AGRARIAN.—1 king = 100 mau = 400 kok = 1000 fan = 24 000 po.

But these are so uncertain that they have not been given in the Dictionary.

SOLID MEASURES are products of the Cheung ; which is generally in this series 14,6 English Feet.

HINDOSTAN.

The Weights and Measures of the indigenous governments of this vast country, (such as, for instance, Sindh, Nepaul, and the confederated Sikhs, etc..) are either too little known or too uncertain to admit of any system. All that will be done is to give the relations of the principal measures in common use, where European domination prevails or European commerce has established itself.

U

BRITISH POSSESSIONS.
Bombay.

WEIGHT.—1 candy = 20 maunds, or maons = 800 seer = 24000 pice.
DRY CAPACITY.—1 candy = 8 para = 128 adoulie.

Calcutta.

WEIGHT.—1 maon, or maund = 40 seer = 640 chattac = 3200 sicca.
DRY CAPACITY.—1 pallie = 4 raik = 64 khoonkĕ = 320 chattac.
LENGTH.—1 haut, or covid = 8 gheria = 72 jaob.
ITINERARY.—1 coss = 4000 haut.
AGRARIAN.—1 biggah = 20 cottah = 320 chattack = 6400 square covid.
The Chattack is, in fact, a surface 5 Covid in length by 4 Covid in width.

Madras.

WEIGHT.—1 garcé =20 candy, or baruay =400 maund, or maon = 3200 visay.
      1 visay = 40 pollam = 400 varahun.
DRY CAPACITY.—1 garcé = 80 para = 400 marcal = 3200 puddy = 25600 ollock
LIQUID CAPACITY, like the dry, is determined by weight ; and the denominations
are the same as in the latter.
AGRARIAN.—1 casseney = 24 maony = 240 square covid.

DANISH POSSESSIONS.
Serampore and Tranquebar.

The Weights and Measures here are legally those of Denmark ; and by custom
those of Calcutta and Madras respectively.

FRENCH POSSESSIONS.
Pondichéry.

The colonial denominations and divisions are identical with those of Madras ;
although the values are different.

PORTUGUESE POSSESSIONS.
Goa.

Here Portuguese Weights and Measures are employed.

JAPAN.

WEIGHT.—1 pecul = 100 catty = 1600 tael = 16000 mas = 160000 condorine.
The connection of the other measures is not known.

OTTOMAN ASIA.
Aleppo, Smyrna, etc.

The Weights and Measures here are so variant, or are rather so mixed up with the
units and values of foreign commerce, as not to admit of satisfactory classification.

PERSIA.

WEIGHT.—1 batman = 6 ratel = 300 dirhem = 600 mascais.

This is the Batman of Tauris; that of Shiraz, which is twice the value, appears properly to be part of the same system.

The other measures are unsystematic.

SIAM.

WEIGHT.—1 pecul = 100 catty = 2000 tael = 8000 tical.

DRY CAPACITY.—1 cohi = 40 sesti = 1600 sat.

LENGTH.—1 vouah = 2 ken = sok.

ITINERARY.—1 roëneng = 2000 vouah.

IV. EUROPE.

AUSTRIAN EMPIRE.

AUSTRIA PROPER : Vienna.

WEIGHT.—1 pfund = 2 mark = 4 vierling, or vierding = 16 unze = 32 loth = 128 quent = 512 pfennig.

Apothecaries' : 1 pfund = 1½ mark = 12 unze = 96 drachma=288 scrupel = 5760 gran.

The Mark is identical in both series ; and is the unit of gold and silver weight.

1 centner = 5 stein = 100 pfund.

LIQUID CAPACITY.—1 fuder = 32 eimer = 128 viertel = 1312 (imperial) mass.

1 mass = 2 kanne = 4 seidel = 8 pfiff.

DRY CAPACITY.—1 muth = 30 metze = 120 viertel = 240 achtel

1 achtel = 2 mühlmassel = 8 futtermassel = 16 becher = 128 probmetze.

LENGTH.—1 klafter = 6 fuss = 72 zoll = 864 linie = 10368 punkt.

ITINERARY.—1 meile = 4000 klafter = 24000 fuss.

AGRARIAN.—1 joch, or jochart = 3 metze = 576 square ruthe = 1600 square klafter = 57600 square fuss.

BOHEMIA : Prague.

WEIGHT.—1 centner = 6 stein = 120 pfund.

The lower subdivisions are as in Vienna ; but their values, as well as of the terms just given, correspond with a lighter pound than the imperial standard.

LIQUID CAPACITY.—1 fass = 4 eimer = 128 pinte = 512 seidel.

DRY CAPACITY.—1 strich = 4 viertel = 16 massel = 192 seidel

AGRARIAN.—1 joch of Vienna = 2 strich.

VENITIAN LOMBARDY.

Milan.

Weight.—Peso grosso: 1 libbra = 4 quarto = 28 oncia.

Peso sottile: 1 libbra = 12 oncia = 288 denaro = 6912 grano.

Gold and silver are by the Marco; subdivided as follows:

1 marco = 8 oncia = 192 denaro = 4608 grano.

Apothecary: 1 libbra peso sottile = 12 oncia = 96 drachma = 288 scrupolo = 6912 grano.

In 1803 the French kilogramme with decimal subdivisions was introduced; which is the *new Italian pound* or *metrical pound* of the Dictionary.

1 rubbio = 10 libbra metrica = 100 oncia = 1000 grosso = 10000 denaro = 100000 grano.

Liquid Capacity.—1 brenta = 3 staja = 6 mina = 12 quartaro = 16 bassa = 48 pinta = 96 boccale.

Dry Capacity.—1 moggio = 8 stajo = 16 starello = 32 quartaro = 128 meta = 512 quartino.

In the new metrical system, Capacity is reckoned as follows:

1 soma = 10 mina = 100 pinta = 1000 coppo.

Length.—1 braccio = 12 oncia = 144 punto = 1728 atomo.

New measure in 1803: 1 metro or braccio = 10 palmo = 100 dito = 1000 atomo.

Itinerary, since 1803.—1 miglio = 1000 metro.

The old mile of Milan is not correlative; but appears, in theory, to be equivalent to 3000 braccio.

Agrarian.—1 pertica = 24 tavola = 96 square cavezzo = 3456 square piede.

The *piede*, or foot, used here, is not employed in any other part of the system. It seems to have been originally $\frac{3}{4}$ of the Braccio.

Since 1823: 1 tornatura = 100 square palmo.

The Tornatura is identical with the French *Are*.

Venice.

Weight.—Peso grosso: 1 libbra = 2 marco = 12 oncia = 72 saggio = 2304 carato = 9216 grano.

Peso sottile: 1 libbra = 12 oncia = 72 saggio = 1728 carato = 6912 grano.

The *Peso grosso* is used in general commerce; the *Marco* and its subdivisions are for gold and silver and precious stones: the *Peso Sottile* for drugs, colors, coffee, tea, sugar, silk, rice and butter. This last is estimated at $1\frac{2}{9}$ of the former. When used for medicines, it is subdivided as the Austrian apothecary-pound.

Liquid Capacity.—1 anfora = 4 bigonzio = 8 concia, or mastello = 48 secchio = 192 bozza = 512 boccale = 768 quartuccio.

1 botta = 5 bigonzio.

Dry Capacity.— 1 moggio = 4 stajo, or staro = 16 quarto = 64 quartarolo.

Length.—1 braccio = 2 piede.

This Braccio is for woollens, etc.; that for silk is shorter.

Itinerary.—1 miglio = 1000 passo = 5000 piede.

Agrarian.—1 campo = 640 tavola, or square pertica, or square cavezzo = 25920 square piede.

New measure: 1 migliajo = 1000 square passo = 25000 square piede.

The metrical Weights and Measures, described under Milan, are also employed here as there in all governmental transactions. Otherwise, the local measures are still in use.

In the other parts of the Austrian dominions, such as Dalmatia, Hungary, Moravia, etc., local systems, if they ever existed, are now only discernible in the names and values of a few disconnected and apparently arbitrary measures.

BADEN.

WEIGHT.—Old measure : 1 pfund = 32 loth = 128 quentchen.
New measure : 1 pfund = 10 zehnling = 100 centass = 1000 pfennig = 10000 ass.

The new measure was established in 1810 ; when the value of the *pfund* was taken at $\frac{1}{2}$ Kilogramme, and a decimal division adopted ; but the old division is still retained and is applied both to the old unit and to the new.

The mark of Cologne is employed for gold and silver ; and the value and subdivisions of the Nürnberg apothecary-pound for drugs and medicines.

LIQUID CAPACITY.—1 fuder = 10 ohm = 100 stütze = 1000 mass = 10000 glas.
1 ohm = 15 decalitres of France.

DRY CAPACITY.—1 zuber = 10 malter = 100 sester = 1000 mässlein = 10000 becher.
1 sester = 15 decalitres of France.

LENGTH.—1 ruthe = 10 fuss = 100 zoll = 1000 linie = 10000 punkt.
1 ruthe = 3 mètres of France.

The old Fuss was 3 per cent. shorter ; but has been merged into the new one.

ITINERARY.—1 meile = 2 stunden = 8$\frac{8}{9}$ kilomètres of France.

AGRARIAN.—1 morgen = 4 viertel, or quart = 400 square ruthe = 40000 square fuss.

SOLID.—1 klafter, for fire wood = 6 F. long $\times$ 6 F. high $\times$ 6 F. deep = 128 cubic fuss.

What is here called *deep*, signifies in every case the length of the billet or log.

BAVARIA.

WEIGHT.—I pfund = 16 unze = 32 loth = 128 quentchen.

A uniform value was established for the unit in 1811 ; corresponding with the new French weight. The apothecary-pound was at the same time defined at $\frac{3}{4}\frac{6}{8}$ of the unit ; and is divided liked the Nürnberg apothecary-pound. Gold and silver are by the mark Cologne.

LIQUID CAPACITY.—1 eimer = 60 masskanne = 240 quartel.

DRY CAPACITY.—1 scheffel = 6 metze = 12 viertel = 48 massel, or achtel = 96 mässlein = 192 dreissiger.
1 scheffel = 208 liquid masskanne, in actual content.

LENGTH.—1 fuss = 12 zoll = 144 linie = 1728 punkt.

This unit was established in 1809, and defined in terms of the old French measure, at 129,58 *lignes de Paris*. The near approach of this value to 3 decimètres in the new French system, allows the *Fuss*, as is frequently done, to be decimally divided. Thus the *Elle* of Rhenish Bavaria is 4 Fuss of this count, or 12 decimètres of France. The legal Elle is 2 Fuss 10$\frac{1}{4}$ Zoll of the legal value, above.

ITINERARY.—1 meile = 2400 ruthe = 24000 fuss.
1 meile of Anspach = 2 stunde = 2880 ruthe = 28800 fuss.

AGRARIAN.—1 juchart, morgen or tagwerk = 400 square ruthe = 40000 square fuss.

SOLID.—1 klafter for fire wood = 6 F. long $\times$ 6 F. high $\times$ 3½ F. deep = 126 cubic fuss.

In Rhenish Bavaria, generally, the billets are 4 F. long ; which makes the klafter = 144 cubic fuss.

Augsburg : Nürnberg.

The denominations and values of local measures retained in both of these places, and elsewhere in Bavaria, are given in the Dictionary. The apothecary-weight of Nürnberg, which is general over all Germany for medicines, (as the Mark of Cologne is for specie,) is ¾ of the old Nürnberg money-pound ; which last is divided as follows :

1 pfund = 2 mark = 16 unze = 16 loth = 128 quart = 512 pfennig = 8220 asducat.

The apothecary-pound, as under :

1 pfund = 12 unze = 96 drachma = 228 scrupel = 576 obolus, or heller = 5760 gran.

BELGIUM.

WEIGHT.—Old measure of Brussels.

Commercial : 1 livre, or pond = 4 quarteron = 16 once = 64 satin = 128 gros = 9216 grains.

Specie : 1 livre, or pond = 2 mark = 16 once = 320 esterlin = 1280 felins = 10240 as = 1 pond troy of Holland.

The new weight is the kilogramme and its decimal subdivisions ; established since 1816.

The apothecaries' unitary pound, subdivided like that of Nürnberg, is, since 1817, ⅔ of the kilogramme of France ; but in this respect there is not entire uniformity.

The other measures are all in value corresponding with the metrical system of France, and decimally subdivided. Thus, the unit for liquids (the *vat*) and that for dry (the *mudde*) are each = 100 litres of France. The unitary *El* or *aune* = 1 mètre ; the agrarian unit (the *vierkantebunder*) = 1 are of France ; or nearly 4 square perches English ; the metrical *miil* or mile = 1 kilomètre. Other terms remaining from the old systems, but now disconnected, are given in the Dictionary.

BREMEN.

WEIGHT.—1 pfund = 2 mark = 16 unze = 32 loth = 128 quentchen = 512 ort = 498,59 grammes of France ; since 1818.

There is another Pfund used in retail commerce ; which is 6 per cent. lighter than the standard.

Gold and silver are weighed by the Mark of Cologne ; and medicines by the apothecary-pound of Nürnberg.

1 schiffpfund = 20 liespfund = 290 pfund.

1 frachtpfund or pfundschwer = 300 pfund.

1 centner = 116 pfund.

LIQUID CAPACITY.—1 fuder = 4 oxhoft = 6 ohm = 24 anker = 120 viertel = 270 stübchen = 1080 quartier = 4320 mingel.

DRY CAPACITY.—1 scheffel = 4 viertel = 16 spint.

LENGTH.—1 elle = 2 fuss = 24 zoll = 240 linie.

Surveyors divide the Fuss decimally.

ITINERARY.—1 ruthe = $2\frac{2}{3}$ klafter = 8 elle = 16 fuss.

The usual Meile contains 20000 Rhenish feet.

AGRARIAN.—1 morgen = 120 square ruthe = 30720 square fuss.

SOLID.—1 faden = 6 F. long $\times$ 6 F. high $\times$ 2 F. deep = 72 cubic fuss.

Firewood is also sometimes measured by the *Reep* or *Reif*; a circular pile $17\frac{1}{2}$ fuss in circumference, the billets varying from $4\frac{1}{2}$ to 6 Fuss in length. The Reif yields from 1 to 2 Faden, accordingly.

BRUNSWIC.

WEIGHT.—1 pfund = 2 mark = 32 loth = 128 quentchen = 512 pfennig = 1024 heller.

1 schiffpfund = 20 liespfund = 280 pfund.

Gold and silver by the Mark of Cologne ; medicines by the apothecary-pound of Nürnberg.

1 fuder = 4 oxhoft = 6 ohm = 240 stübchen = 960 quarteer = 1920 nössel.

1 fass of beer =4 tonne = 108 stübchen = 432 quartier = 864 nössel.

1 fass of mum = 100 stübchen = 400 quartier = 900 nössel.

DRY CAPACITY.—1 scheffel = 10 himt = 40 vierfass = 160 becher, or löcher

LENGTH.—1 elle = 2 .schuh = 24 zoll.

ITINERARY.—1 ruthe = 8 elle = 16 schuh.

The usual Meile contains 34424 Rhenish Feet.

AGRARIAN.—1 morgen = 120 square ruthe = 30720 square schuh.

CRACOW.

WEIGHT.—1 funt = 2 mark = 48 skoyciec.

Apothecary-weight is that of Nurnberg.

LIQUID CAPACITY.—1 stangiew = 2 beczka = 72 garniec = 288 kwart.

DRY CAPACITY.—1 korzec = 2 polkorzow = 4 cwierc = 32 garcy, or garniec.

LENGTH.—1 stopa = 12 calow = 144 liniow = 1728 punkt.

The other measures are those of Poland.

DENMARK.

WEIGHT.—1 pund = 2 mark = 16 unze = 32 lod = 128 quintin = 512 ort.

62 pund = weight of 1 cubic fod of rain water at $16\frac{2}{3}°$ centigrade.

Gold and silver is weighed by a Pund, nearly 6 per cent. lighter than, but not aliquot with the commercial pound ; and subdivided like this last, only more minutely, into 8192 as = 65536 gran. The Royal Mint uses, however, the Mark of Cologne.

Apothecaries' weight is that of Nürnberg.

1 last = $16\frac{1}{4}$ skippund = $144\frac{4}{9}$ waag = 325 lispund = $433\frac{1}{3}$ bismerpund = 5200 pund.

1 skippund = 20 lispund = 320 pund.

LIQUID CAPACITY.—1 aam = 4 anker = 20 viertel = 40 stübchen = $77\frac{1}{2}$ kande = 155 pot = 620 pägel.

DRY CAPACITY.—1 toende = 4 fjerding = 8 skieppe = 32 fjerdingkar = 144 pot.

LENGTH.—1 aln = 2 fod = 24 tomme = 288 linie.

The Fod represents $\frac{2}{3}\frac{2}{3}$ of the pendulum beating seconds, in a vacuum, at the level of the sea, under the mean parallel of 45° north latitude.

ITINERARY.—1 miil = 2400 rode = 4000 favn= 12000 aln = 24000 fod.

AGRARIAN.—1 pflug = 8 toende (hartkorn) = 32 toende (sädeland) = 64 skieppe = 256 fjerdingkar = 768 album = 3072 penge = 17920 square rode = 1792000 square fod.

The measures of Holstein are chiefly those of Hamburg ; and those of Norway differ only locally, not systematically, from the Danish.

FRANCE.

WEIGHT.—1 kilogramme = 100 hectogramme = 100 decagramme = 1000 gramme = 10000 decigramme = 100000 centigramme = 1000000 milligramme.

The unit, or Kilogramme, is the weight of a cubic decimètre of distilled water at the temperature of maximum density ; taken at 4° Centigrade, or 39°,2 Fahrenheit.

1 tonneau = 10 quintal = 100 myriagrammes = 1000 kilogrammes.

Apothecary-weight has not been so symmetrically and uniformly constructed. In the French pharmaceutical Codex, the *gramme* has been adopted as the key of the system, and is considered as equivalent to $\frac{1}{4}$ of the old *drachme*. The *once*, habitually of 8 drachmes, is then 32 grammes. But as this number is irrational with a decimal division, a compromise has been made as follows :

1. 1 double-livre (kilogramme) = 2 livre = 4 demi-livre = 8 quarterons (of 4 onces) = 1000 grammes.

2. 1 once = 8 gros, or drachme = 640 grain = 1280 demi-grain = 32 gramme ; instead of $31\frac{1}{4}$ gramme, as it must have been, if the same binary division had been carried through.

LIQUID AND DRY CAPACITY.—1 kilolitre = 10 hectolitre = 100 decalitre = 1000 litre = 10000 decilitre = 100000 centilitre = 1000000 millilitre.

The unit, or Litre, is the cubic decimètre ; the Kilolitre is therefore a cubic metre. The myrialitre = 10 kilolitre.

LENGTH AND DISTANCE.—1 myriamètre = 10 kilomètre = 100 hectomètre = 1000 decamètre = 10000 mètre = 100000 decimètre = 1000000 centimètre = 10000000 millimètre.

The Mètre, or unit, is assumed to be the ten-millionth of the quadrant, or the forty-millionth of the whole circumference of the Globe, measured over the poles. The actual value assigned to it, in spite of the pains taken in the geodetical and artistical operations, is, after all, owing to the nature of the very operations, to be considered as only a near approximation. The provisional mètre of 1795, is, in fact, (as more recent investigations show,) nearer the most probable value aimed at, than the one adopted in the law of 1799. But the utmost error is only about $\frac{1}{3000}$ of the length ; or, absolutely, less than $\frac{1}{8000}$ of an inch.

AGRARIAN.—1 hectare = 100 are = 10000 centiare or square mètres.

This part of the system admits the same decimal multiplication and subdivision as the others, in theory ; but in point of fact, the intermediate terms have been rejected.

SOLID.—1 decastère = 10 stère = 100 decistère.

The Stère is the cubic mètre ; and its content, therefore, is the same as the capacity of the Kilolitre. The terms given are all that are retained in the nomenclature.

The names even of the old measures of France having been interdicted since 1840 by law, their relations and combinations are of no remaining practical interest. The terms and values will be found in the Dictionary.

FRANKFORT.

WEIGHT.—1 pfund = 2 mark = 16 unze = 32 loth = 128 quentchen = 512 pfennig = 1024 heller.

There is also a commercial pound for retail, called *silber-pfund*, about 8 per cent. lighter than the former ; but similarly divided. Flour and Malt are weighed by a pound of 32 $\frac{9}{10}$ Loth silber-pfund ; meat and butter by 33 Loth of the same system, and fish by one of 35 Loth.

Gold and silver are reckoned by Cologne weight ; and drugs and medicines by the apothecary-pound of Nürnberg.

LIQUID CAPACITY.—1 fuder = 6 ohm = 120 viertel = 480 eich-mass = 540 neu-mass.

1 mass = 4 schoppen.

DRY CAPACITY.—1 malter, or achtel = 4 simmer = 8 metze = 16 sechter = 64 gescheid = 256 mässchen, or viertel = 1024 schrott.

A Malter of Wheat weighs from 175 to 190 lb. flour-weight.

Rye . . . . . 165 to 480	"	"
Barley . . . . 150 to 165	"	"
Oats . . . . . 95 to 110	"	"
Flour 143	"	"

This includes the tare of the sack, which is reckoned at 3 flour-pounds.

LENGTH.—1 werkschuh = 12 zoll = 144 linie.

1 ruthe = 12$\frac{1}{2}$ werkschuh = 10 feldfuss = 100 zoll = 1000 linie.

AGRARIAN.—1 hufe = 30 morgen = 4800 square ruthe = 480000 square feldfuss.

SOLID, for firewood : 1 klafter = 6 W. long $\times$ 7 W. high $\times$ 3 W. deep = 126 cubic werkschuh.

1 stecken = 3$\frac{1}{2}$ werkschuh, cubed = 43$\frac{3}{4}$ cubic werkschuh.

GREAT BRITAIN.

The Imperial standards adopted since 1825, altered only the value of the capacity-measures.

The Weights and the Long, Agrarian and Solid measures are identical with those of the United States.

Capacity-measures are the same, both for liquids and things dry. The origination of these, is with the *gallon ;* which contains 10 pounds avoirdupois of distilled water at 30 inches of the barometer and 62° Fahr. both for the air and the water. Eight of such gallons make the bushel. The old subdivisions and nomenclature, as far as applicable, are retained.

WEIGHT.—Troy and apothecary have been given under the head, United States.

Avoirdupois : 1 ton = 20 hundred-weight = 80 quarter = 2240 pound = 35840 ounce = 573440 dram.

Wool : 1 last = 12 sack = 24 wey = 156 tod = 312 stone = 624 clove = 4368 pound.

x

LIQUID CAPACITY.—Old Wine measure: 1 tun = 2 pipe = 3 puncheon = 4 hogshead = 6 tierce = 8 quarter-casks = 252 gallon = 1008 quart = 2016 pint.

Old Beer measure: 1 butt = $1\frac{1}{2}$ puncheon = 2 hogshead = 3 barrel = 6 kilderkin = 12 firkin = 108 gallon.

Ale measure was the same as to the Gallon and its subdivisions; but the Firkin of Ale was only 8 Gallons, and the Hogshead of Ale, 48 Gallons, instead of 9 and 54 Gallons respectively.

DRY CAPACITY.—Old measure: 1 last = 2 wey = 10 quarter = 20 coom = 80 bushel = 320 peck = 640 gallons = 5120 pint.

LENGTH.—1 yard = 3 foot = 36 inches = 108 barley-corn = 432 line.

Cloth-measure: 1 French ell = $1\frac{1}{5}$ English ell = $1\frac{1}{2}$ yard = 2 Flemish ell = 6 quarters = 27 nail = 54 inch.

HAMBURG.

WEIGHT.—1 pfund = 2 mark = 16 unze = 32 loth = 128 quentchen = 512 pfennig.

Gold and silver are weighed by the Mark of Cologne; and medicine, by Nürnberg apothecary-weight.

1 schiffpfund = $2\frac{1}{2}$ centner = 20 liespfund = 280 pfund.

This is sea-freight; waggon-weight is also called Schiffpfund, but = 320 pfund.

LIQUID CAPACITY.—1 fuder = 4 oxhoft = 5 tonne = 6 ahm = 24 anker = 30 eimer = 120 viertel = 240 stübchen = 480 kanne = 960 quartier = 1920 össel.

1 fass, for whale-oil = $1\frac{1}{4}$ tonne = $7\frac{1}{2}$ stechkanne = 120 margel = 160 quartier.

DRY CAPACITY.—1 last, for wheat and grain generally, and seeds = 3 wispel = 30 scheffel = 60 fass = 120 himt = 480 spint.

1 stock, for oats and barley = $1\frac{1}{2}$ last; and similarly subdivided.

The Scheffel is hardly used; the Fass is the principal measure.

The indications of the steel-yard used for weighing grain, and quoted in the Price-current, is upon $1\frac{1}{2}$ fass of such grain respectively. The established weight of the Fass is, of

Barley,	68 pfund.	Peas,	100 pfund.
Beans,	108 "	Rye,	81 "
Oats,	52 "	Wheat,	86 "

LENGTH.—1 elle = 2 fuss = 24 zoll = 192 achtel.

Ship-builders, for the measurement of spars, etc., divide the Fuss into 3 Palm.

Engineers and surveyors use the Rhenish foot and inch, decimally divided.

ITINERARY.—1 meile = 200 ruthe = 24000 Rhenish fuss.

AGRARIAN.—There are two Ruthe, or perches, in land-measure; the Marschruthe equal to 7 Ell, and the Geestruthe to 8 Ell. Of course, 1 square geestruthe = $1\frac{30}{98}$ marschruthe = 256 square fuss.

1 morgen = 600 square marschruthe = 117600 square fuss.

SOLID.—1 klafter, or faden = $6\frac{2}{3}$ F. long $\times$ $6\frac{2}{3}$ F. high $\times$ 2 F. deep = $88\frac{8}{9}$ cubic fuss.

1 messbergerfaden = $6\frac{2}{3}$ F. long $\times$ 8 F. high $\times$ 2 F. deep = $106\frac{2}{3}$ cubic fuss.

HANOVER.

WEIGHT.—1 pfund = 2 mark = 16 unze = 32 loth = 128 quentchen = 512 örtchen.

Gold and silver are weighed by the Mark of Cologne. The apothecary-pound is ¾ of the commercial pfund ; subdivided like that of Nürnberg ; which last is, itself, frequently used.

LIQUID CAPACITY.—1 fuder = 4 oxhoft = 6 ahm = 15 eimer = 24 anker = 120 viertel = 240 stübchen = 480 kanne = 960 quartier = 1920 nössel.

1 fass for beer = 4 tonne = 104 stübchen = 208 kanne = 416 quartier.

DRY CAPACITY.—1 last = 2 wispel = 16 malter = 96 himt = 288 drittel = 384 vierfass.

LENGTH.—1 elle = 2 fuss = 24 zoll = 192 achtel = 288 linie.

ITINERARY.—1 meile (since 1818) = 1462½ ruthe = 11700 elle = 25400 fuss.

The old, or Polizei-meile, was 2274 ruthe.

AGRARIAN.—1 morgen of Calenberg = 1⅓ drohn = 2 vorling = 120 square ruthe = 30720 square fuss.

HESSE-CASSEL.

WEIGHT.—1 pfund = 16 unze = 32 loth = 128 quentchen.

In retail, the pfund of Berlin (which is about 3 per cent. lighter) is employed ; subdivided as above.

Gold and silver are by the Cologne—medicine etc., by the Nürnberg weight.

LIQUID CAPACITY.—1 fuder = 6 ohm = 120 viertel = 480 mass = 1920 schoppen.

DRY CAPACITY.—1 scheffel = 2 himt = 8 metze = 32 mässchen.

LENGTH.—1 waldfuss, or standard = 12 zoll = 144 linie.

ITINERARY.—1 ruthe = 7 elle = 14 land-fuss, or surveyors' foot.

The Ruthe is sometimes divided decimally into 10 Fuss, etc.

AGRARIAN.—1 acker = 150 square ruthe = 29400 square land-fuss.

SOLID.—1 klafter = 5 F. long × 5 F. high × 6 F. deep = 150 cubic waidfuss.

HESSE-DARMSTADT.

The old Weights and Measures were those of Frankfort. Those established in 1821, are as follows :

WEIGHT.—1 pfund = 32 loth = 128 quentchen = 512 richtpfennig = ½ kilogramme of France.

Gold and silver are still reckoned by the Mark of Cologne ; and Nürnberg furnishes the apothecary-weight.

LIQUID CAPACITY.—1 fuder = 6 ohm = 120 viertel = 480 mass = 1920 schoppen.

The Schoppen = ½ litre of France.

DRY CAPACITY.—1 malter = 4 simmer = 16 kümpf = 64 gescheid = 256 mässchen = 128 litre of France.

LENGTH.—1 klafter = 10 fuss = 100 zoll = 1000 linie.

The Fuss is ¼ metre of France ; the Elle is ⅔ metre.

AGRARIAN.—1 morgen = 4 viertel = 400 square klafter = 40000 square fuss.

SOLID.—1 stecken = 5 F. long × 5 F. high × 4 F. deep = 100 cubic fuss.

The old Stecken was 6 × 6 × 4 = 144 cubic feet, old measure.

HOLLAND.

Since 1817, the values and divisions of the Weights and Measures have been according to the metrical system of France ; retaining more or less of the old nomenclature, as will be found in the Dictionary.

IONIAN ISLES.

Since 1817, when the new Constitution of these Isles was ratified by the English Parliament, the standard Weights and Measures have been those of Great Britain. There still remain, however, several detached usances of Turkish and Venitian origin , which will be found in the Dictionary.

LÜBEC.

WEIGHT.—1 pfund = 2 mark = 16 unze = 32 loth = 128 quentchen = 512 pfennig.

Gold and silver weight is that of Cologne ; apothecary-weight, of Nürnberg.

The Schiffpfund and Tonne are divided as at Hamburg.

LIQUID CAPACITY.—1 fuder = 4 oxhoft = 6 ahm = 24 anker = 30 eimer = 120 viertel = 240 stübchen = 480 kanne = 960 quartier = 1920 plank = 3840 ort.

DRY CAPACITY.—1 last = 8 drömt = 24 tonne = 96 scheffel = 384 fass.

LENGTH.—1 elle = 2 fuss = 24 zoll = 144 linie = 1728 punkt.

Other usances here are the same as at Hamburg.

LUCCA.

The Weights and Measures of this Territory are, in system, the same as those of Tuscany ; of which it will hereafter form a part. Its local values and denominations will be found in the Dictionary.

MECKLENBURG-SCHWERIN.

What is under this, will also apply to the other Grand Duchy of Mecklenburg-Strelitz ; both of whose systems of Weights and Length-measures are those of Hamberg ; while the Capacity-measures are, in fact, those of Lübec.

MODENA.

WEIGHT.—1 libbra, or lira = 12 oncia = 192 ferlino.

1 libbra, for gold and silver = 12 oncia = 96 ottava = 192 ferlino = 1920 carato = 7680 grano.

Apothecary: 1 libbra = 12 oncia = 96 drachma = 288 scrupolo = 6912 grano.

LIQUID CAPACITY.—1 barile = 20 fiasco = 40 boccale.

DRY CAPACITY.— 1 sacco = 2 stajo.

AGRARIAN.—1 biolca = 72 tavola = 288 square cavezzo = 10368 square piede.

The Piede of Reggio has the same relations, but a different value, with that of Modena, the city.

The other measures appear arbitrary.

OTTOMAN EMPIRE or TURKEY IN EUROPE.

Neither our knowledge nor perhaps the actual state of Weights and Measures in this Empire allow of their being arranged in any satisfactory, systematic exhibition; and the same may be said of the modern Kingdom of Greece. The value and denominations of isolated units have been given in the Dictionary.

PARMA.

WEIGHT.—1 libbra = 12 oncia = 288 denaro = 6912 grano.

Gold and silver are weighed by the Marco of Milan, or by the new Italian pound. The apothecary-pound is identical with the commercial Libbra. The Rubbio is 25 Libbra.

LIQUID CAPACITY is measured as at Milan.

DRY CAPACITY.—1 stajo = 2 mina = 16 quartarole.

LENGTH.—1 pertica = 6 braccio di legno = 72 oncia = 864 punto = 10368 atomo.

AGRARIAN.—1 biolca = 6 staro = 72 tavola = 288 square pertica = 10368 square braccio.

PORTUGAL.

WEIGHT.—1 arratel = 2 marco or meio-arratel = 4 quarta = 16 onça = 128 outava = 384 escropulo = 9216 grao.

This weight, from the Onça down, answers for all purposes.

Gold and silver are reckoned by the Marco of 8 Onças; and medicines are weighed by a Libra of 12 Onças, which is therefore $\frac{3}{4}$ Arratel.

1 tonelada = $13\frac{1}{2}$ quintal = 54 arroba = 1728 arratel.

LIQUID CAPACITY.—1 almude = 2 alqueire, or cantaro = 12 canada = 24 meia-canada = 48 quartilho = 96 meio-quartilho.

1 tonelada = 2 pipa, or bota = 52 almude = 104 alqueire.

DRY CAPACITY.—1 moio = 15 fanga = 60 alqueire = 120 meio-alqueire = 240 quarto = 480 outava = 960 maquia, or meia-outava.

LENGTH.—1 covado = 3 palmo da craveira = 24 pollegada = 36 dedo = 144 grao = 288 linha = 3456 ponto.

The commercial Covado, called *covado avantejado*, has $24\frac{3}{4}$ pollegadas.

ITINERARY.—1 braça = $1\frac{1}{3}$ passo = 2 vara = $6\frac{2}{3}$ pe = 10 palmo da craveira.

1 legoa = 3 milha = 24 estadio.

AGRARIAN.—1 geira = 4840 square vara.

PRUSSIA.

The Weights and Measures were reformed here in 1816.

WEIGHT.—1 pfund = 2 mark = 16 unze = 32 loth = 128 quentchen.

The unitary Pfund is $\frac{1}{66}$ of a cubic foot of distilled water, weighed, and reduced to a vacuum, at the temperature of 15° Reaumur ($65\frac{3}{4}$° Fahrenheit.)

Gold and silver are still reckoned by the Mark of Cologne, to which the Prussian Mark is considered as equivalent; and the apothecary-pound, divided like that of Nürnberg, is $\frac{3}{4}$ Pfund.

1 schiffpfund = 3 centner = 15 stein = 20 liespfund = 330 pfund.

Liquid Capacity.—1 fuder = 6 ohm = 12 eimer = 24 anker = 720 quart = 1440 össel.

The Eimer contains 3840 cubic Zolle or inches.

Dry Capacity.—1 last, for wheat and rye = 4 wispel = 6 malter = 72 scheffel = 288 viertel = 1152 metze = 4508 mässchen.

1 last, for barley and oats = 48 scheffel.

The Scheffel is $\frac{4}{5}$ of the Eimer in absolute capacity, or 3072 cubic Zolle.

Length.—1 fuss (Rhein-fuss) = 12 zoll = 144 linie = 1728 scrupel.

This unit has been established at 139, 13 lignes de Paris.

The Elle is $25\frac{1}{2}$ Zolle.

Itinerary.—1 ruthe = 10 land-fuss = 12 Rhein-fuss.

The Land-fuss is also sub-divided decimally into 10 zoll = 100 linie = 1000 scrupel.

1 post-meile = 2000 ruthe = 24000 Rheinfuss.

Agrarian.—1 morgen = 180 square ruthe = 25920 square Rheinfuss.

Solid.—1 klafter = 6 F. long × 6 F. high × 3 F. deep = 108 cubic Rheinfuss.

1 haufen = $4\frac{1}{2}$ klafter = 18 F. long × 9 F. high × 3 F. deep = 486 cubic Rheinfuss.

The old values and denominations which are still retained, as well in the Capital as in several principal Cities, are given in the Dictionary.

ROMAN STATES.

Under this name is intended what has, until recently, been known as the State of the Church. Late events have shewn this last title to be uncertain. Two principal Cities comprehend all that is systematic in Weights and Measures.

Bologna.

Weight.—1 libbra = 12 oncia = 96 ottava = 192 ferlino = 1920 carato = 7680 grano.

This weight serves also for gold and silver: though the new Italian metrical pound (the kilogramme) is also employed, as well as the Libbra of Rome. In Ferrara, use is still had of the Marco of Milan.

Apothecary: 1 libbra = 12 oncia = 96 drachma = 288 scrupolo = 6912 grano.

This Libbra weighs $11\frac{1}{4}$ commercial Oncie.

Liquid Capacity.—1 corba = 2 mezza-corba = 4 quarterone, or quarterole = 60 boccale = 240 foglietta.

Dry Capacity.—1 corba = 2 stajo, or staro = 8 quarterone = 32 quarticino, or quartuccione.

These two Corbe are of the same capacity.

Agrarian.—1 tornatura = 140 square pertica = 14000 square pié.

Rome.

Weight.—1 libbra = 12 oncia = 288 denaro = 6912 grano.

The same weight serves for gold and silver, and for medicine.

Liquid Capacity.—1 botta = 16 barile = 512 boccale = 2048 foglietta = 8192 quartuccio.

The Barile for oil contains only $\frac{7}{8}$ of the above, or 28 Boccale. But oil has a proper measure, viz:

1 soma = 2 mastello, or pelle = 20 cugnatello = 80 boccale.

DRY CAPACITY.—1 rubbio = 2 rubbiatella = 4 quarta = 8 quartarella = 12 staja = 16 starello = 22 scorzo = 88 quartuccio.

LENGTH AND DISTANCE.—1 canna (ordinary) = 2 braccio = 6 pié = 8 palmo = 24 linea.

1 canna (architects, etc.,) = 7½ pié = 10 palmo = 120 oncia = 600 minuto = 1200 decimo.

1 canna di ara = 1½ braccio di ara = 9 palmo di ara.

1 catena = 10 stajolo = 57½ palmo (architects').

AGRARIAN.—1 rubbio = 4 quarta = 7 pezza = 16 scorzo = 32 quartuccio = 112 square catena = 11200 square stajolo = 370300 square palmo (architects').

RUSSIA IN EUROPE.

S. Petersburg.

WEIGHT.—1 funt = 12 lana = 32 loth = 96 zolotnic = 9216 doli.

This is used for gold and silver, also ; and the Nürnberg weight, by apothecaries.

1 packen = 3 berkowitz = 30 pud = 1200 funt.

LIQUID CAPACITY.—1 vedro = 4 tschetwerk = 8 osmuschka = 88 tscharkey.

Since 1819, the vedro = 100 tscharkey.

1 sarokowaja = 13⅓ anker = 40 vedro.

DRY CAPACITY.—1 tschetwert = 2 osmin = 4 pajak = 8 tschetwerik = 32 tschetwerka = 64 garnetz.

LENGTH AND DISTANCE.—1 archine = 2 stopa = 24 verschok = 32 paletz.

This was the old measure. Within the last twenty years, both the English Foot and the Rhine Foot have come into use ; and since 1831, the former has furnished, it is believed, the normal standard of value. At present, the Archine is divided into 16 Verschok.

1 verst = 500 sachine = 1500 archine = 24000 verschok.

The Sachine is 7 feet exactly.

Besides the Verst, the Meile of Lithuania is also used, equivalent to 28530 Rheinfuss.

Warsaw.

The legal Weights and Measures of Poland are supposed to be, since 1831, subordinate to those of the Russian Empire, of which it forms a part. The establishment, in 1819, while Poland had still its own legislature, and which rested upon the French metrical system, is nearly as follows :

WEIGHT.—1 funt = 16 lana = 32 loth = 48 skoyciec = 128 drachme = 384 skrupulow = 9216 granow = 50688 granikow = 405504 milligrammow.

The Milligrammow is exactly the Milligramme of France.

The apothecary-pound is 358½ Grammes of France, and divided like Nürnberg weight.

The old Funt of Warsaw proper was ⅟₁₅ lighter ; and the old Quintal was of 5 Kaminieck, or 160 Funt. The new Kaminieck is of 25 Funt.

LIQUID CAPACITY.—1 stangiew = 2 beczka = 50 garniec = 200 kwarti = 800 kwaterki.

The Kwarti is the Litre of France ; and the Beczka, therefore, the hectolitre.

Formerly the Beczka was divided into 36 Garniec, and 144 Kwarti.

DRY CAPACITY.—1 korzec = 4 cwierc = 32 garniec, or garcy = 128 kwarti = 512 kwaterki.

The Kwarti is the same for all capacity ; and the Korzec is, therefore, 128 Litres of France.

LENGTH.—1 lokiec = 2 stopa = 4 cwierc = 24 calow = 288 liniow = 576 milli-metrow = 576 millimètre of France.

1 sznurow = 10 pretow = 100 precikow = 150 stopa = 1000 lawek = 1800 calow. The Precikow is the geometrical foot, used by surveyors.

Itinerary distances are measured by the Verst of Russia ; 8 of which (= 29633 stopa) make the unitary league.

AGRARIAN.—1 wloka = 30 morgow = 90 square sznurow = 9000 square pretow = 900000 square precikow.

SARDINIA.

The Weights and Measures of the Island of Sardinia, which cannot be called sys-tematic, will be found in the Dictionary.

DUCHY OF GENOA.

WEIGHT.—1 libbra (peso scarso) = 12 oncia = 288 denaro = 6912 grano.

This is the ordinary weight of commerce ; which is used also by apothecaries. The Rottolo is 1½ Libbra. The Peso-grosso is 10 per cent. heavier than the Peso-scarso ; and has sometimes its Rottolo. Gold and silver are weighed by the Marco of Turin. The Rubbio, or quarter of the Centinajo, has 25 Libbra in either weight.

LIQUID CAPACITY.—1 mezzaruola = 2 barile = 100 pinta = 180 amola.

DRY CAPACITY.—1 mina = 8 quarto = 96 gombetta.

LENGTH.—1 piede liprando = 12 oncia = 144 punto = 1728 atomo.

1 piede manuale = 8 oncia.

1 canna = 4²⁄₇ braccio = 10 palmo = 6²⁄₃ piede manuale.

But this last is hypothetical. The land-surveyors use a Canna of 12 Palmo ; which is properly a Canella. But Canne are found of all lengths from 8 to 12 palmi.

PIEDMONT: Turin.

WEIGHT.—1 libbra = 1½ marco = 12 oncia = 96 ottavo = 288 denaro = 6912 grano = 165888 granottino.

For gold and silver, the Marco is divided as under :

1 marco = 8 oncia = 192 denaro = 1152 carato = 4608 grano = 110592 granottino.

The apothecary-pound is 1¼ Marco; and is divided like the same weight at Bologna.

LIQUID CAPACITY.—1 carro = 10 brenta = 360 pinta = 720 boccale = 1440 quartino.

DRY CAPACITY.—1 sacco = 3 stajo = 6 mina = 12 quartiere = 48 copello = 960 cucchiaro.

LENGTH.—The smaller measures are divided as at Genoa.

1 pertica = 2 trabucco = 10²⁄₇ raso = 12 piede liprando.

ITINERARY.—1 miglio = 1300 tesa = 4333⅓ piede liprando = 6500 piede manuale.

AGRARIAN.—1 giornata = 100 tavola, or square pertica = 400 square trabucco = 14400 square piede liprando.

SAXONY.

For the Weights and Measures of this Kingdom, where there has been no recent establishment, will be taken what prevails at Leipsic.

WEIGHT.—1 pfund = 2 mark = 16 unze = 32 loth = 128 quentlein = 512 pfennig = 7680 gran.

Gold and silver are by the Mark of Cologne. Apothecary-weight is that of Nürnberg.

The Centner, or hundred-weight consists generally of 110 Pfund ; but for live-stock it is only 102 Pfund ; that called *berg-gewicht*, at the mines, is 114 Pfund ; and *stahlgewicht*, for iron and steel, is 118 Pfund.

LIQUID CAPACITY.—1 fuder = $2\frac{2}{5}$ fass = 4 tonne = 6 ahm = 12 eimer = 14 anker = 756 kanne = 1512 nössel = 6048 quartier.

The Fuder of Dresden is similarly divided, but is smaller ; containing only 672 kanne of Leipsic.

DRY CAPACITY.—1 wispel = 2 malter = 24 scheffel = 96 viertel = 384 metze = 1536 mässchen.

LENGTH.—1 elle = 2 fuss = 24 zoll = 240 linie.

The Fuss is also decimally divided.

1 ruthe = 10 elle = 16 fuss.

ITINERARY.—1 polizei-meile = 2000 ruthe = 16000 elle = 32000 fuss.

1 post-meile = 1500 ruthe = 12000 elle = 24000 fuss.

AGRARIAN.—1 morgen = 300 square ruthe = 76800 square fuss.

THE TWO SICILIES.

The Weights and Measures of the Island of Sicily are given in the Dictionary, corresponding to the localities of Messina, Palermo and Syracuse; they are too unsystematic to be detailed here. What follows, belongs properly to the City and District of Naples.

WEIGHT.—1 libbra = 12 oncia = 360 trapeso = 7200 accino.

This weight is for gold and silver, for silk, for spices, for drugs and colors. All other articles are weighed by the Rotolo of $2\frac{7}{9}$ Libbre, or $33\frac{1}{3}$ Oncie.

The apothecary-unit is the same Libbra, but divided as follows :

1 libbra = 12 oncia = 120 drachma = 360 scrupolo = 7200 accino.

LIQUID CAPACITY.—1 carro = 2 botta = 24 barile = 1440 caraffa.

1 salma, for oil = 16 staja = 256 quarto = 320 pignata = 1536 misurella.

DRY CAPACITY.—1 carro = 36 tomolo = 864 misura.

LENGTH AND DISTANCE.—1 canna = 8 palmo = 96 oncia = 480 minuto.

1 pertica, or passo = $7\frac{1}{2}$ palmo.

1 miglio = $933\frac{1}{3}$ passo = 7000 palmo.

AGRARIAN.—1 moggia = 900 square passo = 50625 square palmo.

SPAIN.

The Weights and Measures given for this Kingdom apply especially to Castille, and are recognized at Madrid. Considerable differences in value, and some also in nomenclature, will be found in the Dictionary as existing in several of the great pro-

v

vinces of Spain ; as for example, in Valencia, where long comparative independence naturally led to a result of this kind, which is further contributed to elsewhere by the remarkable number of distinct races by which Spain is peopled. But these variations are not sufficiently material to be detailed here.

WEIGHT.—1 libra = 2 marco = 16 onza = 128 ochava = 256 adarme = 768 tomine = 9216 grano.

Gold and silver are by the same weight ; but the Marco is the unit, and is divided for *gold* only, as follows :

1 marco = 50 castellano = 400 tomine = 4800 grano.

This division has been, to be sure, interdicted by law ; but it still remains, and is especially exemplified in the former South-American dependencies of Spain.

In apothecary-weight: 1 libra = 1½ marco = 12 onza = 96 dracma = 288 escrupulo = 576 obolo = 1728 caracter, or quilate = 6912 grano.

1 tonelada = 20 quintal = 80 arroba = 2000 libra.

1 quintal macho = 6 arroba = 150 libra.

LIQUID CAPACITY.—1 arroba mayor, or cantara = 4 quartilla = 8 azumbre = 32 quartillo = 128 copa.

This Arroba, in theory, should contain 35 Libras of distilled water, at the ordinary pressure and temperature. The Arroba menor for oil, is divided in the same manner ; but weighs only 27¼ Libras, as before.

DRY CAPACITY.—1 cahiz = 12 fanega = 144 almude, or celemine = 288 medio = 576 quartillo = 2304 racion = 9216 ochavillo.

LENGTH.—1 vara = 3 pie, or tercia = 4 palmo, or quarta = 6 sesma = 36 pulgada = 48 dedo = 432 linea = 5184 punto.

DISTANCE.—1 estadal = 2 estado, toesa, or braza = 2⅔ paso = 4 vara = 8 codo = 12 pie.

There is also a former estadal, (before 1801,) which still serves as a basis for an agrarian measure and = 11 pie.

1 cuerda = 8¼ vara = 24¾ pie = 33 palmo mayor.

But in Valencia : 1 cuerda = 20 braza = 40 vara.

1 legua (till 1568) = 3 milla = 24 estadio = 3000 paso = 5000 vara = 15000 pie.

1 legua (of Philip V.) = 7605 vara = 22815 pie.

This was a League of which 17½ were supposed to make a degree, and was directed to be used on all maps.

1 legua (since 1766) = 4800 paso = 8000 vara = 24000 pie.

It is by this, that the distances along the great roads are marked. But there is also a Legua frequently used, estimated at 800 cuerda = 6600 vara = 19800 pie.

AGRARIAN.—1 yugada = 50 fanegada = 600 celemin = 2400 quartillo = 28800 square estadale = 460800 square vara.

But in Valencia ; 1 yugada = 6 cahizada = 36 fanegada = 7200 square braza ; and is but the $\frac{1}{15}$ nearly of the legal yugada.

1 arançada (for vineyards and crops of oats) = 400 square estadale = 48400 square pie : the estadale being here but 11 pie.

SWEDEN.

WEIGHT.—1 skälpund (viktualiewigt) = 16 untz = 32 lod = 128 qwintin = 8848 as.

There are several commercial pounds in this Kingdom, applicable under different circumstances and to different articles. But none are commensurable with the Skäl-pund, except that called *jernwigt*, or the iron-pound, which is $\frac{4}{5}$ of the other. They are all to be found in the Dictionary under the word Skeppund ; by which multiple, indeed, they are usually counted.

Gold and silver is weighed by the Mark of Stockholm, which is incommensurable with the Skälpund, but very nearly half of it. It is divided as follows :

$$1 \text{ mark} = 8 \text{ untz} = 16 \text{ lod} = 64 \text{ qwintin} = 4384 \text{ as.}$$

The apothecary-pound, or libra = 7416 as ; and is subdivided like the Nürnberg pound.

$$1 \text{ skeppund} = 20 \text{ lispund} = 400 \text{ pund.}$$

LIQUID CAPACITY.—1 tunna = 48 kanna = 96 stop = 384 qwarter = 1536 ort, or jungfru.

DRY CAPACITY.—1 tunna = 2 spann = 4 half-spann = 8 fjerding = 32 kappe = 56 kanna = 112 stop = 448 qwarter = 1792 ort.

LENGTH.—1 famn = 3 aln = 6 fot = 72 tum = 864 linie.

But in late times the Foot is divided decimally for all purposes.

$$1 \text{ stäng} = 8 \text{ aln} = 16 \text{ fot.}$$

$$1 \text{ mil} = 2250 \text{ stäng} = 6000 \text{ famn} = 18000 \text{ aln} = 36000 \text{ fot.}$$

AGRARIAN.—1 tunna = 2 spannland = 4 half-spannland = 8 fjerding = 32 kapp-land = 56 kannland = 218$\frac{3}{4}$ square stäng = 14000 square aln = 56000 square fot.

SOLID.—1 vedfamn = 6 F. long $\times$ 6 F. high $\times$ 3 F. deep = 108 cubic fot.

SWITZERLAND.

Nearly every one of the twenty-two Cantons of which this confederation is com-posed, appears to present some variety in the values, subdivisions and nomenclature of its Weights and Measures. To explain them summarily is impossible ; to expose them in detail, would occupy a space manifestly disproportionate to their practical in-terest. What prevails at Berne, Lucerne and Zurich, (the three Legislative Capitals, biennially in rotation, of the Swiss confederacy,) is all that need be given here.

Berne.

WEIGHT.—1 pfund = 16 unze = 32 loth = 128 quent = 512 pfennig.

This is the ordinary commercial weight ; that for gold and silver, etc., is divided into 2 Marks, and then like the preceding. The Mark in this weight is the old Marc of France ; the ordinary pfund = 17 onces poids de marc of France.

The apothecary-weight is, in fact, about $\frac{1}{3}$ of one per cent. lighter than the Nürn-berg ; it is, no doubt, in theory the same, and is divided similarly.

LIQUID CAPACITY.—1 landfass = 6 saum = 24 eimer, or brenter = 600 mass = 2400 vierteli = 4800 becher.

DRY CAPACITY.—1 mütt = 12 mäss = 24 mässli = 48 immi = 96 achterli = 192 sechszehnerli.

LENGTH.—1 fuss = 12 zoll = 144 linie = 1728 secunde.

The *steinbrecher fuss*, used for quarrying and building-stone = 13 zoll. The Elle happens to be exactly $1\frac{58}{100}$ of the Fuss ; but this is an accidental coincidence, as they are not used commensurably.

ITINERARY.—1 ruthe = 1$\frac{1}{4}$ klafter = 3$\frac{1}{3}$ wald-schritt = 4 feld-schritt = 10 fuss.

The ordinary Swiss Meile is no longer commensurable with any Swiss foot. It seems to have been originally $26666\frac{2}{3}$ Fuss ; for its length would not differ materially from that multiple of the Fuss.

AGRARIAN.—1 juchart, or feld acker = 400 square ruthe = 40000 square fuss.

For woodland, the Juchart is 450 ; for gardens 360 ; for meadow-land, 350 and 320 ; and finally for suburban mensuration, $312\frac{1}{2}$ square Ruthe.

SOLID.—1 klafter = 6 F. long × 5 F. high × $3\frac{1}{2}$ F. deep = 108 solid fuss.

Lucerne.

WEIGHT.—1 pfund = 36 loth = 144 quentchen.

This is the division of Lucerne, proper ; but the weights of Zurich are also in use. Gold and silver are weighed by the Mark of Zurich ; but the apothecary-pound is the old medicinal weight of France.

LIQUID CAPACITY.—1 saum = $3\frac{1}{3}$ ohm = 100 mass = 400 schoppen = 4000 prima.

DRY CAPACITY.—1 malter = 4 mütt = 16 viertel = 32 halb-viertel = 160 immi = 256 becher = 2560 prima.

LENGTH.—1 elle = 2 schuh, or Rhein-fuss.

The carpenters' foot (tischler-schuh) is nearly 3 per cent. shorter ; and the builders' and surveyors' foot (feld-schuh) 10 per cent. shorter than the Rhein-fuss. Other measures are those of Zurich.

Zurich.

WEIGHT.—1 pfund = 18 unze = 36 loth = 144 quenten.

1 pfund (of Antorf, for gold and silver, etc.) = 2 mark = 16 unze = 32 loth = 128 quent = 512 pfennig.

This weight is $\frac{3}{8}$ of the commercial weight. The apothecary-pound is that of Lucerne.

LIQUID CAPACITY.—1 eimer (lauter-mass) = 4 viertel = 30 kopf = 60 mass = 120 quärtli = 240 stotzen.

The Eimer (stadt-mass) for wine in retail, is subdivided in the same manner, but is 10 per cent. smaller.

1 eimer (trübes mass) = 4 viertel = 32 kopf = 64 mass = 128 quärtli = 256 stotzen.

This Eimer (which, as its name implies, is for wine unrefined, as the lauter-mass is for fined wine) is $\frac{1}{15}$ larger than the latter.

DRY CAPACITY.—1 malter = 4 mütt = 16 viertel = 64 vierling = 256 mässli = 576 immi.

The Malter for grain generally, and all *dry* seeds and fruits (*glatte frucht*) contains $12\frac{1}{4}$ cubic feet; that for oats and for *green* articles (leguminous growth, *rauhe frucht*) contains $12\frac{7}{18}$ cubic feet.

LENGTH.—1 fuss = 12 zoll = 144 linie = 133 *lignes de Paris*.

The same Fuss is divided decimally by surveyors. The architectural foot, since 1820, is $\frac{6}{1330}$ longer, but divided like the ordinary Fuss.

1 ruthe = 2 elle = 10 fuss.

AGRARIAN.—The ordinary juchart = 400 square ruthe = 4000 square fuss.

There are also Juchart in the same variety (except the very smallest) and similarly applicable as at Berne.

Solid.—1 klafter, for fire-wood = 6 F. long ✕ 6 F. high ✕ 4 F. deep = 144 cubic fuss.

There are also Klafter of 72 and 108 cubic fuss; the billets being 2 and 3 feet long respectively.

The Klafter for turf (torb-klafter) contains 12 korb of 6 cubic fuss, each = 72 cubic fuss.

In 1828, a new system of Weights and Measures was proposed and adopted for the Cantons of Aarau, Basel, Berne, Friburg, Lucerne, Solothurn and Vaud; which rested upon the metrical system of France : but, except in the Canton of Vaud, it has not been generally carried out.

TUSCANY.

Weight.—1 libbra = 12 oncia = 96 drachma = 288 denaro = 6912 grano.

The same weight answers for gold and silver, and for apothecary use. The legal Centinajo or Cantaro (as in all the cases hitherto not specially mentioned) is 100 Libbre ; but the Cantaro for wool, meat and salt-fish is yet 160 Libbre.

Liquid Capacity.—1 barile = 20 fiasco = 40 boccale = 80 mezzetta = 160 quartuccio : weighing 133⅓ libbra.

1 barile for oil, or orcio = 16 fiasco = 32 boccale = 64 mezzetta = 128 quartuccio ; weighing 120 libbre.

The Soma for oil is 2 Barile.

The Barile of alcohol, brandy and rum weighs 120 libbre.

Dry Capacity.—1 moggio = 8 sacco = 24 stajo = 48 mina = 96 quarto = 384 metadella = 768 mezzetta = 1536 quartuccio = 3072 bussole.

Length.—1 canna = 4 braccio = 8 palmo = 80 soldo = 960 denaro.

1 canna (architects and surveyors') or pertica = 2½ passetto = 5 braccio = 10 palmo = 60 crazia = 100 soldo = 300 quattrino = 1200 denaro.

Itinerary.—1 cavezzo = 2 passo = 6 braccio.

1 miglio = 566⅔ canna (architects') = 2833⅓ braccio = 5666⅔ palmo.

Agrarian.—1 saccato = 10 stajolo = 13¾ stioro = 165 panoro = 660 square pertica = 16500 square braccio.

WÜRTEMBERG.

Weight.—Divided as the Prussian ; from which it differs but slightly in value. Gold and silver are weighed by the Mark of Cologne ; and medicine, by the apothecary-weight of Nürnberg.

Liquid Capacity.—1 fuder = 6 eimer = 96 immi = 960 mass = 3840 schoppen.

The Eimer is of a different capacity, according as it is for clear or unrefined wine. The latter is nearly 4½ per cent. larger than the former.

Dry Capacity.—1 scheffel = 8 simri = 32 vierling, or viertel = 64 achtel = 128 mässlein = 256 ecklein = 1024 viertelein.

Length.—1 fuss = 10 zoll = 100 linie =1000 punkt.

This measure was established in 1806 ; when the Fuss was fixed at 127 *lignes de Paris*. The Elle is not aliquot with the Fuss ; being 214⅓ *lignes de Paris*.

1 ruthe = 1⅔ klafter = 10 fuss.

This is the modern division.   In the older habits there was 1°. a Ruthe of 16 Fuss ;
2°. one of 12 Rheinfuss ; and 3°. one of 15 Rheinfuss. These different lengths
affected, of course, the value of the acre.

AGRARIAN.—1 morgen = 4 viertelmorgen = 384 square ruthe = 38400 square fuss.

This is the legal measure ; which corresponds in value with the old count of 150
square Ruthe (of 16 Fuss in length) to the Morgen.   There is, also, the little Morgen
(old measure) of 150 square Ruthe (No. 3) = 33750 square Rheinfuss ; and the great
Morgen (old measure) containing 400 square Ruthe (No. 2) = 57600 square Rhein-
fuss.

1 juchart, or jauchert = 1½ morgen.

Printed in Great Britain
by Amazon